INSTITUTE OF INTERNATIONAL STUDIES
YALE UNIVERSITY

Freedom and Welfare in the Caribbean

A COLONIAL DILEMMA

The Yale Institute of International Studies was organized in 1935 for the purpose of promoting research and training in the field of international relations. Although concerned with all aspects of international affairs, its studies have been primarily devoted to clarifying contemporary problems in the foreign policy of the United States. The present publication, "Freedom and Welfare in the Caribbean: A Colonial Dilemma," analyzes the conflict between social and economic development and political growth in the Caribbean dependencies of Great Britain and the United States.

Earlier publications of the Institute are: A. Whitney Griswold's "Far Eastern Policy of the United States," George T. Davis' "A Navy Second to None," Arnold Wolfers' "Britain and France between Two Wars," Nicholas John Spykman's "America's Strategy in World Politics" and "The Geography of the Peace," and Samuel Flagg Bemis' "The Latin-American Policy of the United States."

More recent publications have been William T. R. Fox's "The Super-Powers," David Nelson Rowe's "China among the Powers," and Percy E. Corbett's "Britain: Partner for Peace." "The Absolute Weapon," written by members of the Institute and edited by Bernard Brodie, was a collaborative analysis of atomic power. The most recent volume was William Reitzel's "The Mediterranean: Its Role in America's Foreign Policy."

Frederick S. Dunn, Director

Freedom and Welfare in the Caribbean

A COLONIAL DILEMMA

Annette Baker Fox

New York

HARCOURT, BRACE AND COMPANY

Table of Contents

Acknowledgments

Among the members of the Institute of International Studies to whom I am particularly indebted for aid in completing this study are the Director, Professor Frederick S. Dunn, and Professors Klaus Knorr and Percy Corbett. They read the manuscript and offered innumerable valuable suggestions. It is impossible to express adequately my gratitude to my husband, William T. R. Fox, for his indispensable assistance at every stage. Two of the many others inside and outside the government service who aided me to understand colonial problems in the Caribbean were Charles W. Taussig, first chairman of the United States Section of the Caribbean Commission, and his assistant, Mrs. Frances McReynolds Smith. I deeply regret that the sudden and untimely death of Mr. Taussig prevents me from thanking him personally for his kindness in reading the manuscript. I was very fortunate to have the benefit of Mrs. Smith's knowledge of the Caribbean Commission and its work in the area. Any errors in fact and interpretation appearing in this study are of course my own responsibility.

To Miss Veronica O'Neill for typing and clerical aid and to Mrs. Suzanne Petersson for editing the manuscript I am much obliged.

Thanks are due also to the following publishing companies and authors for permission to quote extensively from their publications: George Allen & Unwin Ltd. for excerpts from *Fabian Colonial Essays* by H. N. Brailsford and others; Duell, Sloan & Pearce, Inc. for excerpts from *Netherlands America* by P. H. Hiss; Arthur Calder-Marshall for excerpts from his *Glory Dead,* published by Michael Joseph Ltd., and the Social Science Research Center, University of Puerto Rico, for excerpts from *The Net Income of the Puerto Rican Economy* by Daniel Creamer.

ANNETTE BAKER FOX

*Freedom and Welfare in
the Caribbean*

A COLONIAL DILEMMA

I. The Twin Problems:
Poverty and Dependence

SELF-GOVERNMENT and freedom from want: these two demands came urgently from the Caribbean dependencies of America and Britain as the mother countries faced World War II. Like colonial peoples elsewhere, those in the Caribbean wanted to share in the material progress of the rest of the world, not continue as outcasts from prosperity. They also wanted to control their own affairs. This placed the United States and Great Britain in a dilemma, for satisfaction of one demand was very likely to prejudice fulfillment of the other. Reinforcing these strong requests were complaints from influential groups within the mother countries, about both their own colonies and those of other imperial powers. Added to all this was an abundance of criticism from the outside, directed at British and American colonial policies.

To win praise instead of disapproval, the United States must find an answer to a most difficult question: What policy compatible with our democratic values can we adopt toward our own colonies and those of other powers which will reconcile these two demands and thus diminish conflicts within dependent areas and concerning them? *

Conditions in most tropical colonies challenge the demo-

* The Caribbean colonies discussed in this study are Puerto Rico and the American Virgin Islands; and the British colonies of Jamaica, Barbados, Trinidad, the Leeward Islands, the Windward Islands, the Bahamas (which do not regard themselves as part of the West Indies), and British Guiana and British Honduras (mainland colonies). When the British dependencies are considered, emphasis is on the first three.

cratic belief in individual liberty, equality, and fraternity, and invite the spread of competing ideologies. Like urban slum dwellers, the colonial people are not the only ones to bear the ill effects of past mistakes; the results are felt far beyond their boundaries. Substandard colonial conditions tend to pull down living standards elsewhere; their cost is too great; and they provide a breeding ground for violence in the outside world. Such has been the case in America's most vulnerable area, the Caribbean, whose once-rich islands are now suffering from the tragic consequences of conquest, slavery, and thoughtless exploitation.

The misery in the Caribbean is not lessened by independence. In fact, aid from the mother country makes life better in many of the colonies than it is in the republics. Still, there is no great difference in material matters. The chief difference is that the dependencies continue to suffer an extreme low in living standards *without* the self-government so strongly coveted by many inhabitants of both British and American possessions. Yet this independence from outside authority which the Caribbean republics enjoy has not been matched by the extension of individual liberties within their borders. A grossly unequal distribution of income and political power generally prevails. Furthermore, their peoples live under constant threat of civil violence. Until recent times, the resulting instability has made these countries easy subjects for international bickering.

Conditions in the independent countries of the Caribbean point up the dilemma facing the United States and Great Britain in their own colonies. Since their goal is to promote democracy in their Caribbean possessions, how can they develop a widely distributed higher standard of living for their dependent peoples and accede to demands for greater autonomy at the same time?

To answer this question, one must understand both the

conditions which underlie the demands for autonomy and economic improvement, and the difficulties to be overcome in changing them. The Caribbean colonies are not all alike in their troubles. And there are several important variations from other colonial regions of the world.[1] Still, singly and collectively, they exhibit many of the distinguishing characteristics which make up the "colonial problem."

Dependence and Backwardness in the Caribbean Colonies

What constitutes dependence? As a status, it implies a subordinate constitutional relationship to a ruling state. In practice, it means that all important decisions on the affairs of the dependent area are made elsewhere. Its chief administrators are chosen by the metropolitan government and are responsible to that government. The manner in which public funds are expended is determined in the last analysis by the metropolitan government.

To market its products, the colony is dependent on the mother country and the outside world. It cannot supply itself with manufactured goods and even many simply processed necessities, with capital, with technical and managerial personnel, or with transport. For security against external attack, for the conduct of its foreign relations, and often even for the maintenance of internal law and order, it must depend on the mother country. To a greater or lesser degree this description fits all the British and American colonies in the Caribbean. Fortunately, it is gradually becoming less applicable, as a result of fundamental changes in British and American colonial policy.

Dependence and backwardness are not synonymous, but they frequently go hand in hand. The Caribbean colonies are typically "backward areas." * The per capita wealth is very low. The inhabitants are hounded by disease, malnutrition, high mortality rates, and ignorance. The countries have been periodically depressed by fluctuations in world market conditions, with consequent unemployment and underemployment. Most of the region is not only densely settled but has exhibited an increase in population wholly out of proportion to the resources available for sustaining the increase in numbers, even at their present low standard of living.[2]

The colonies are for the most part nonindustrial, and their economies have depended upon one or a very few export products. They are technologically primitive, and the workers' productivity is low compared to that in more advanced countries. Large-scale production is controlled by Europeans (or Americans), and the subsistence farming or small-scale native agriculture still to be found in many other backward areas has never been common in most of this region. Agricultural workers therefore lack the security of the small landholder. The surplus rural population has drifted to the towns in numbers far too great to be absorbed, losing even the security of those who retain some contact with the land.†

Insecurity is only one of the social problems affecting the colonies, and poverty is not the only source of their troubles. Many of the colonial people are illiterate. In some colonies a multiplicity of languages has prevented the social integration created by a common tongue. Communication is primitive except for a very few newspapers. The press often tends to warp the scant news it presents, and there is little or no

* The following characterization of these dependencies is not intended to illustrate the consequences of colonialism. It is simply a description of conditions in these colonies—conditions which are only gradually being modified with changes in colonial policy.

† Many West Indian plantations continued to provide partial employment to unneeded but dependent workers at the expense of modernization and more efficient methods.

organized public opinion outside local communities. Reformers often deplore the absence of a social will to better living conditions. Group conflicts are more likely to erupt into direct action than to be adjusted through legal or political means.

There frequently is no "constitutional consensus," that is, no general acceptance of common understandings regarding fair and peaceful procedures for determining public policy. Leaders have often been demagogues, and there has been only a limited pool from which to draw civil servants who would put the public good above conflicting private interests.

The Caribbean dependencies, like other underdeveloped areas, lack a substantial middle class. The base of the social pyramid is very broad, while the members of the elite are few and usually of European (or American) origin. Social mobility is limited, and educational and economic handicaps dangerously restrict opportunities for the youth in the population. The maldistribution of income and social status is far too great to be compatible with any conception of a democratic society. In the British West Indies and the American Virgin Islands, further insecurities and instabilities arise from the conflict between European civilization and the remnants of the cultural practices forming the African heritage of the majority of the inhabitants. Evidence of the resulting social disorganization is the weakness of any form of family life and the prevalence of praedial larceny.*

Each of these traits could be duplicated to some degree in almost all other colonial areas, the chief modifying factors being geographical endowment and extent of contact with European civilization. These characteristics also apply in varying degree to many independent but poverty-stricken

---

* Theft of growing crops and small animals commonly occurring in the British West Indies.

Cultural conflict in Puerto Rico assumes more refined forms because it takes place against a more completely European background.

and "backward" countries. In the latter case, however, the legal status of the countries has already been determined; the conflict between greater autonomy and higher living standards does not have to be faced directly.

In the Caribbean, the problem of promoting better living conditions together with self-government is complicated by the consequences of slavery, which existed until just about a century ago. These consequences not only affected the social structure but have had other far-reaching economic and polit-ical effects. They left a residue of attitudes which included a reluctance to be employed for manual labor, especially field labor, and a disposition to project responsibility upon others.[3] A long history of slavery also meant that race reinforced economic status, to accentuate the class distinctions so clearly marked in the Caribbean. Recently, there has been some in-crease in race consciousness, but color is not an insuperable obstacle to economic and political advancement. There is none of the extreme color prejudice common in the United States.

Neither religion nor culture sharply divides the popula-tion within most of the colonies.* The problem of the plural community is thus not so serious in the Caribbean as it is in the East, except perhaps for Trinidad and British Guiana, which have large unassimilated East Indian populations. Within the framework of Western European civilization, however, there is a strong conflict in Puerto Rico between the old Spanish conventions and the new American ways. Some of the latter were in the past imposed on an unwilling

---

* With an important exception, no church has been a powerful instru-ment of social control in the Caribbean colonies, despite the firm hold which various denominations have on the British West Indies educational systems. The church organizations are as foreign to the mass of West Indians as is their government, and the moral conventions of the Christian churches have not succeeded in completely displacing their ancestral ways, particularly those relating to family life. The exception is overwhelmingly Catholic Puerto Rico, but even here the church is not very active politically.

population. The conflict was most acute over the question of language in the schools.* Unlike the other Caribbean dependencies, Puerto Rico has developed some national character of its own in which there is considerable pride.[4]

In general, group conflicts are not so serious in the Caribbean colonies as to prevent the development of a constitutional consensus; it is rather the differences in economic status and the oppressive poverty which are too great to permit a healthily functioning democratic regime.[5]

Although there are few irreconcilable social cleavages within the Caribbean dependencies, group cohesion for positive purposes is little in evidence. Puerto Ricans, like many other Latin Americans, have been well known for their exaggerated individualism. The strong sense of local community which characterizes many Eastern dependencies is lacking in the Caribbean colonies. Voluntary civic and economic associations are rare, with the exception of primarily European groups like the chambers of commerce. Co-operatives have not yet taken a strong hold in these dependencies, although advances are being made, especially in Puerto Rico and Jamaica. Labor unions have a short history, and for the most part are still somewhat inchoate groups, following magnetic leaders. In the same fashion political parties, where they exist, depend largely on personalities.†

Insularity of outlook has been one of the most marked characteristics of the Caribbean colonies. In the past the British West Indies have strongly resisted a variety of efforts to unite them for particular purposes. The British Empire is

* This conflict did not arise in the Virgin Islands of the United States, whose inhabitants speak English in spite of their history as a Danish possession.

† These evidences of the lack of concerted group action may also be found in some formally independent countries. The degree in which they exist partially defines whether or not the country is "backward" or "advanced."

still the strongest unifying symbol for them. In Puerto Rico, on the other hand, an inhabitant thinks of himself primarily as a Puerto Rican, not an American subject. Very little community feeling bridges the individual Virgin Islands, and that is often based on resentment against the United States Government, which Virgin Islanders tend to blame for all their troubles.*

Blaming "the government" for all kinds of difficulties is by no means confined to the Caribbean colonies. What distinguishes the colonies from independent countries is that "the government" is not their own, or at least not wholly their own. The almost universal desire in the Caribbean for greater autonomy, in some form, constitutes a major colonial problem. It is based on a psychological need for respect, as urgent as the economic needs mentioned above.

Although Puerto Rico is much the furthest advanced toward complete self-government, it is still subject to the will of Congress, in which it has no voting representative; it also must submit to a limited degree of administrative supervision. Greater control is exercised over the Virgin Islands; they are to some extent directly governed by metropolitan officials. The British West Indies exhibit many variations on "representative government" (the British distinguish this from "responsible government," in which the administrative officials are responsible to the local legislature, not to the British Colonial Office). The chief characteristics are restricted power of the colonial legislature, a limited franchise in most cases, and appointment of metropolitan officials to the most important administrative posts (and sometimes to the legislature). As in the American dependencies, ultimate power over the colonial governments resides in the

* The term "Virgin Islands" as used in this study refers to the American dependencies. The British Virgin Islands are part of the Leeward Islands and are too minuscular for separate reference.

metropolitan legislature, in which there is no colonial representation.*

In fiscal matters, the traditional emphasis in colonial constitutions has been on some metropolitan control to prevent extravagant expenditures, but not to force colonial legislatures to make expenditures against their will. This allocation of powers was consistent with the economic regime under which colonies were meant to be more or less self-sufficient although politically dependent.

Until the 1930's, British and American colonies were theoretically expected to keep their expenditures within the income they could realize on their own resources. It finally became clear that extensive outside aid would be essential if the social and economic disabilities afflicting the colonies were to be solved. However, the simultaneous rise in metropolitan subsidies and colonial sentiment for self-government complicated the problem of autonomy and fiscal control. Increased financial aid would seem to demand more rather than less metropolitan authority. Without such aid, however, the economic and social basis for greater autonomy might never be laid. This problem constitutes the chief one among many apparently vicious circles which plague the Caribbean colonies.

Vicious Circles in the Colonial Problem of the Caribbean Dependencies

The truism that poverty is its own cause is acutely relevant in the case of the Caribbean colonies. Poorly endowed by nature, their chief resources are population and a physical environment suitable for growing certain tropical products. However, the productive ability of the people is limited by

* A detailed discussion of constitutional arrangements in the colonies appears in Chapter IX.

their low living standards, which in turn cannot be greatly
raised without an increase in their colonial output. Concentration on the few crops which the colonies can most efficiently
grow has left them at the mercy of world market conditions.
These conditions have been from time to time so unfavorable
to their products as to plunge them into depressions from
which they have never fully recovered. The mother countries
have protected them to some degree from the full rigors of
world competition by tariff preferences, but these indirect
subsidies tend to intensify agricultural specialization in the
colonies.

Preferences also raise the cost of living because of the
high prices the colonies must pay in protected markets for
the majority of their needs, which specialization prevented
them from meeting at home. Poverty of resources has hindered the influx of capital from outside, but without such
capital the colonies cannot hope to develop what resources
they do possess. Where private capital has been attracted there
has been a perennial complaint that the profits from development were drained away, leaving the colonies not much
better off than before. Were the colonial governments to tax
outside investment for sufficient revenue to carry on their
own development, they would run the risk of repelling capital and drying up this revenue source.

Although under certain circumstances a large population
can be viewed as an economic resource, the density to be
found in the Caribbean island colonies has not operated to
good effect; it is, in fact, a major handicap in improving
colonial conditions.* In these dependencies the insular income
has to be divided up among so many that ill-health, disease,
and malnutrition are the common lot. High death rates have
been accompanied by high birth rates. Welfare measures to

* Except in British Guiana and British Honduras which are underpopu-
lated in terms of potential development.

lower infant mortality rates and to save lives in other ways
have aggravated the population problem—the Malthusian
law still operates in these areas.

But, in spite of their apparent futility, welfare activities
must be undertaken. If expenditures for development are
confined to economic measures to increase the insular income,
they will fail of their objective. For chronic ailments and
familiarity with death have produced attitudes of resignation
and fatalism, which in turn have discouraged the necessary
effort to remove the economic basis of ill health and high
mortality rates. Until concrete social changes improve these
attitudes, the achievements of exclusively economic development will continue to be slight.*

None of these pairs of counteracting forces has operated
independently of the others, nor are they traceable to any
single basic factor. These forces are all intricately related;
and the general tendency of their interaction is to prevent
an improvement in the economic and political situation of the
colonies and even to intensify colonial problems. According
to the principle of cumulation, however, the action of these
variables upon each other need not result in a stalemate nor
in a downward spiral.[6] Modification of a carefully chosen
combination of these variables may reverse the direction of
the "vicious circle."

The relation between social and political problems is shown
in the vicious circle of low educational standards as both cause
and effect of dependent status. There is much substance in
the assertions of some colonial administrators that because
their wards lack the necessary educational qualifications they

* Many of these problems have also confronted some independent countries, which, because such conditions existed, have sometimes been characterized as "colonial" despite their legal status. While these conditions may
describe the plight of most poverty-stricken lands, whether or not politically
dependent, the significant fact here is that they are to be found in areas
for which the great democracies are responsible.

cannot yet be trusted to govern themselves. Yet responsibility for not improving educational facilities to the point where the natives are competent to take over their government appears to rest on metropolitan shoulders.

Many outspoken critics of "imperialism" do not stop at this point. They argue further that several other deplorable characteristics of colonial areas are at least as much a consequence as a cause of political dependency. They assert, in the case of some colonies, that it is in the interest of the ruling groups in the metropolitan country to prevent industrialization and crop-diversification. They say that it pays the colonial power to keep natives ignorant, for then they will not become dangerous advocates of freedom from imperial rule. They question the sincerity of the colonial powers when their governments stress the necessity of continued outside control to prevent the conflicting local groups from preying upon each other. These critics declare that the administering governments are only following the old maxim of divide and rule, and that they themselves produce the antagonisms within the colonial societies.

The general theory that colonial powers have created the very problems in their colonies which are cited as reason for opposing greater independence distorts the appearance of the real difficulties. It is founded on insufficient knowledge, and makes solutions look simpler than they really are.[7] Most criticism of colonial powers is predicated on the assumption that colonies are still profitable to the mother countries, and that the exploitation still goes on. This is an assumption which we shall see is seriously open to question. Such criticism does not sufficiently take into account that social distress in dependent areas may often be unremedied because the governing states do not know how to deal with it or are preoccupied with other matters. Ignorance and misunderstanding may be at fault at least as much as ill will and shortsighted selfishness.

Critics of the colonial powers tend to avoid the difficult question of whether or not the colonies would have been better off if independent. Nevertheless, they do call attention to the irrefutable fact that under the jurisdiction of the colonial powers, once-rich areas have been freely mined without adequate provision for the future or wholehearted efforts to pass on to the colonies the political and economic benefits of Western European civilization. The colonial powers are now being held to account for the mistakes of the past.

Conditions in the Caribbean colonies have been an embarrassment to the mother countries because their correction is expensive and politically very difficult, and because they hinder military efforts to render the area more secure. They point up the universal colonial dilemma, that poverty-stricken countries require financial assistance and aid in social reconstruction to a degree which makes it almost impossible to grant the simultaneous demand for greater political autonomy. Social and economic reconstruction raises the question, development toward what? Despite frequent assertions that the chief problem of the Caribbean dependencies is economic, not political, their economic and social development will have important political consequences.

There will be repercussions within the colonies, between the colonies and the mother countries, and between the mother countries and other independent states. There will be international effects, if only because the American and British policies in their Caribbean colonies indicate what might be done (or avoided) in other colonies where demands for self-government and economic improvement are made. Out of their experience may come some answers to the problems posed by backward areas generally. The problems are especially acute for such countries as Great Britain, which is hard pressed to implement democratic values in an empire clamoring for political and economic reforms. They are also acute for all other colonial powers. Without exception, the colonial powers stand to lose by continued colonial disaffection and turmoil, which can be so well exploited to the advantage of the Russians.

II. Colonial Problems As a Cause of International Friction

SERIOUS differences exist between Russia and the Western world about the treatment of dependent territories and peoples. Differences also exist among the Western colonial powers themselves. They disagree about the solutions for low living standards and about the lack of self-government. These discords and others encourage troublemakers to capitalize on conditions in colonial areas, and further aggravate controversy among the great powers. Although Americans, like Russians, clamor for colonial reform, especially in British colonies, the British Empire is not regarded as a threat to American security. Indeed, if colonial liberation meant a rise in Russian influence, the United States would certainly not view the diminution of British control as conducive to future peace. However, the same fear of Russian expansion produces an American concern for the diminution of conflicts arising in colonial areas.

The problems of dependence are problems in their own right, requiring solutions acceptable alike to the believer in democracy and to the colonial peoples. But they also constitute problems in world politics. A new colonial policy must reckon with the elementary facts of life in contemporary international relations.[1] The question is not merely to find the "right" solution in the immediate interest of the dependent peoples. The solution must also be one which the great powers will permit to work.

Great-Power Conflicts over Colonies

Historically, international conflicts regarding colonies arose over the question of sovereignty, not over dependent status and living conditions. Colonies were desirable because they were believed to enhance the prosperity of the imperial power during peace and increase its strength in time of war. Furthermore, they added to the war potential of the mother country by assuring it access to resources necessary for the prosecution of war. They were also useful in furthering emigration policies adopted as the solution for periodic "overpopulation" in the mother country. Finally, certain colonial areas were strategically valuable because of their location along lines of communication. This last advantage still applies to certain colonies which have long since been without any other value.

Today conflicts over colonial areas no longer take the traditional form of "imperial rivalry." The powers do not now compete to determine which state shall exploit which colonial people. Instead they vie with each other in their protestations of friendship for submerged peoples and in their promises of a bright future for the colony which returns the friendship. Each colonial power alleges that its dependencies are being maintained for the colonists' own good. It is loyalty and friendship rather than sovereignty that each competitor wishes to see acknowledged. When the colonial power has had to choose between maintaining sovereignty and maintaining its influence, it has not hesitated to surrender sovereignty.

In a sense, colonial conflicts are now ideological rather than economic. A growing belief that colonies no longer paid followed the spread of free trade in the nineteenth century. Between World Wars I and II, theoretical deflation of the colonies' economic usefulness became marked, and the possession of colonies seemed an economic burden instead of

a benefit.[2] Now, however, colonies are likely to assume a new value if international trade fails to revive. In 1947, for instance, Great Britain took a sudden interest in her colonies as sources of material which her dollar shortage prevented her from purchasing elsewhere.*

The prestige attached to empire is still important to some countries, especially France, and several colonial areas are considered desirable, for their at least temporary strategic value. Nevertheless, the "white man's burden," even if tarnished as a phrase, has become the dominant motif in debate on colonial problems, and the imperial powers defend their colonial administration as a responsibility at least as much as a right.

Forces Favoring Colonial Reform

Several forces have been operating to bring about improvements in the colonies. For one thing, technical progress in communication has made for an increase in the knowledge of colonial conditions. As more and more people became aware of how the other half of the world lived, interest in those areas increased. Missionary activities also spread information and pricked consciences. The prestige of empire was damaged as evidence piled up regarding standards of living in the colonies. Pride thus called out for ameliorating measures. Fear of colonial revolts and especially of Communist agitation led not only to attempts at suppression but also to efforts at reform.

Shifts in the ruling groups of the metropolitan countries also account for changed policies. Thus the once-powerful sugar barons who controlled the West Indian economy have long since lost their ascendant position in the British Govern-

---

* This provides a new motive for colonial development, since the colonies will otherwise remain inefficient producers of needed materials.

ment. Other interests have become influential which are better served by loosening colonial ties. For example, American vegetable oil producers strongly supported Philippine independence, because it would push the competing coconut oil producers outside the tariff wall. In the United States, the sentiment for colonial liberation which was expressed by some Negro groups received political attention as their voting power became important.

As the opportunities for exploiting backward areas disappeared, new economic theories emerged to support a changed colonial policy.[3] One new argument, supporting the British Colonial Development and Welfare fund, was that only prosperous and thriving colonial peoples would make good customers for British goods.

Of fundamental significance for colonial policy was the spread of democratic teachings. The ruling countries could not stop it if they wished, and two world wars greatly facilitated the diffusion of democratic theories regarding self-government and popular participation in government. Simultaneously, the colonial peoples became acutely aware of the difference between their living standards and those of the governing countries.

Along with the increased emphasis on human rights and the dignity of the individual came another change. Whereas colonies were formerly regarded as the strictly private affair of their respective metropolitan countries, there has gradually developed an "international interest" in dependent areas.[4] Evidence of this is the International Labor Organization's code of minimum standards of social policy in dependent areas, which was incorporated in a convention in 1947, in addition to four other conventions applying to the colonies.[5] States had entered into agreements about certain dependencies and certain colonial problems before the United Nations came into being. With the framing of the United Nations

Charter, however, came the most comprehensive expression of international interest in colonies. In the chapters dealing with trusteeships and non-self-governing territories, most of the civilized world registered agreement on the general outlines of a desirable colonial policy.

The United Nations Agreement on Ultimate Colonial Goals

The discussions leading to the framing of the Charter provisions on the colonies and the subsequent negotiations in carrying them out revealed several points of controversy among the powers. One of the principal issues was the definition of the ultimate goals toward which to work.[6]

The Russians demanded at San Francisco that the political aim be "independence," while the British, with United States support, urged "self-government" as the desirable end. The Charter provision was a compromise embodying both aims. The difference between the two terms was ideological, rather than a matter of substance, since there are several examples to prove that a self-governing area may have more real freedom in making its own decisions than some nominally independent areas. Nevertheless, the term "independence" to Western nations meant a greater degree of autonomy than it meant to the Soviet Union, accustomed to tight Communist party control over constitutionally independent states. The conflict permitted Russia to speak of its "moral superiority" over the other two powers in appealing to colonial and semicolonial countries. The dual vocabulary which the Russians could employ to refer to legal and political status and which in practice meant a distinction between sovereignty and supremacy, enabled them to take an "advanced" position on the issue.

The powers seemed to be in closer agreement about eco-

nomic and social development. But when it came to actual
procedures, differences naturally developed.[7] Thus the great
powers can scarcely disagree over the theoretical desirability
of raising standards of living in dependent areas. But difficulties arise when they try to concert their policy to correct
real or alleged maladministration of particular colonies.

Assuming a general will to peaceful adjustment, two conditions would seem to be necessary to prevent serious conflicts
between the great powers over dependent areas. There must
be an implementation of the general principles regarding
colonial welfare and self-government which is mutually
agreeable to these states. This means a reconciliation of differ-
ing views on ways of achieving increased autonomy and improved social and economic conditions in the colonies. But
this is not sufficient. There must also be a reasonable state of
harmony and contentment within dependent areas. Otherwise
internal struggles between different groups in the colonies or
between colonial inhabitants and the metropolitan governments will add fuel to conflicts between the great powers, or
even ignite new ones.

Interrelations of Social, Economic, and Political Development

At San Francisco the members of the United Nations responsible for the administration of non-self-governing territories promised, among other things,

> to ensure, with due respect for the culture of the peoples
> concerned, their political, economic, social, and educa-
> tional advancement, their just treatment, and their pro-
> tection against abuses. . . .[8]

The United States, Great Britain, France, and the Netherlands have already inaugurated projects for social and economic development in some of their colonies and have laid

plans for more extensive programs in the future.[9] But "just treatment" is not the only standard by which colonial policy is to be tested. There are two other standards which the Charter obligates colonial powers to apply. They are:

> . . . to develop self-government, to take due account of the political aspirations of the peoples, and to assist them in the progressive development of their free political institutions, according to the particular circumstances of each territory and its peoples and their varying stages of advancement. . . .

and "to further international peace and security." [10]

The goals of self-government and international peace and security being fixed in mind, the main questions raised in the first chapter can now be amplified. What kinds of economic and social measures will be essential in furthering the agreed-upon goals? What kinds would tend to defeat these political purposes? What kinds would make the transition to autonomous, responsible local government with the least disturbance and conflict? What methods of organization and administration to implement the selected social and economic policies would promote the political ends already determined? [11]

A similar set of questions should be raised in the choosing of appropriate measures for greater autonomy. What constitutional changes will be required to produce popularly controlled self-governing territories? What steps towards self-government might promote social and economic development? What constitutional policies might obstruct these ends, or favor rather than hinder the growth of violence?

Finding mutually compatible answers to the dual problem of self-government and improved living standards should contribute significantly to harmonious relations between the great powers by removing as a source of conflict unsatisfactory colonial conditions.

The Caribbean Demonstration

From recent experience in the Caribbean dependencies of the United States and Great Britain, the policy-maker can obtain some guidance in meeting the dilemma presented by poverty and dependence. Colonial problems in this region resemble those of many other dependent areas. The economic and social development which has been under way here since the thirties should suggest some answers to similar problems elsewhere. The experience is doubly valuable because in this recent period some steps have also been taken toward greater autonomy for several of the colonies. Thus there may be found in the Caribbean a demonstration of the interrelationships of social and economic policies with the political development of colonial areas.

The Caribbean Commission provides a further reason for examining the recent history of the region. Through this agency, the mother countries are co-operating to solve social and economic problems, thus testing the possibilities of constructive international, or multinational, colonial policy. These colonies are too obviously within the acknowledged sphere of influence of the United States to be a direct cause of serious conflict between the American and Soviet governments. Nevertheless, they are strategically important to the United States. Therefore programs for improving economic, social and political conditions in this region are adopted for the sake of security as well as humanitarianism.

Experience drawn from this area may well be applicable to other colonial areas that are more likely to be a direct cause of conflict between the United States and other countries. When the Indonesian case came before the Security Council, the United States found itself under the necessity of defining the goals of colonial policy even for the colonies of other states halfway around the world. In this and other areas its political influence and its investment policies are likely to be of first importance. Success in the Caribbean is worth achieving for its own sake. It is also excellent preparation for the responsibilities of world power. "Success," to repeat, means meeting the twin demands for better living conditions and self-government.

III. Colonial Reform in the Caribbean Dependencies

THE onset of World War II brought again to domestic and international attention the British and American colonies in the Caribbean, which had conveniently disappeared into the background in the interwar period.* Those who were still aware of their existence bestowed upon them such epithets as "America's poorhouse," "white elephants," "England's West Indian slums," "economic sore spot," "stepchild," or, in the more dignified words of the United States Section of the Caribbean Commission, "a social and economic anachronism in a progressing Western Hemisphere." [1] Approaching hostilities brought renewed consideration of their strategic locations, just off the mainland of the United States and guarding the approaches to the Panama Canal. Civil commotion had already indicated to the outside world the deep-lying discontent existing in this area. The United States and Great Britain became seriously concerned over their past neglect and failure to solve the economic, social, and political problems of their Caribbean dependencies. Not only did these weaknesses in a vital area threaten British and American security; they belied the democratic ideology which was the moral defense of the mother countries.

* The French and Dutch colonies also emerged from obscurity, but primarily for reasons of American military security.

The Caribbean Colonies in History

The oblivion into which the Caribbean dependencies had fallen in the early decades of the twentieth century was in striking contrast to their earlier role in world politics. In the three centuries following Columbus, the Caribbean was a cockpit of imperial rivalry. Hardly one of the dependencies failed to change hands at least once, and the sovereignty of many had been altered several times. Great Britain, France, Spain, and the Netherlands all fought for their possession. The most recent change was of course the assumption of American sovereignty over the former Spanish possession of Puerto Rico and the purchase of Denmark's Virgin Islands. Except for the advent of independence in some former Spanish and French possessions, there have been no other changes since 1814.

Why was the Caribbean the scene of international conflict for centuries? The search for precious metals, the riches of the East, and new markets led Spain to the discovery and conquest of many parts of the Caribbean. Other ambitious nations could not stand idly by during this process, for they believed that one state's gain was necessarily a loss for all the others. If Spain were finding what she regarded as valuable in the Caribbean, then her rivals must either try to overcome her lead or seize what she already possessed.

The islands of the Caribbean did not yield up a significant measure of gold, but they did produce very large quantities of sugar, once slaves from Africa had been introduced to replace the original inhabitants. They could also profitably produce other tropical resources of less strategic significance than sugar, such as tobacco and coffee. The area had additional advantages, but in the first period of imperialistic expansion possession of Caribbean colonies was most valued as a brake on the territorial expansion of other states and on their acquisition of revenues from trade with these colonies. Thus, the general balance of power could either be tipped in favor of the possessor, or at least be prevented from changing to benefit an opponent.

During the nineteenth century the value of the Caribbean area to imperial powers began its long decline. There were several external reasons for the lessening interest in this area, such as the opening up of more lucrative territory elsewhere and the development of free trade. The subsidizing of beet sugar in Europe gave a body blow to the Caribbean sugar industry. Internal conditions also contributed to the devaluation of the Caribbean colonies. The sugar industry depended upon slavery to remain profitable, but the advance of democratic humanitarianism gradually abolished the slave trade and slavery itself. Furthermore, colonies which had been employing soil-depleting methods of production over a very long period eventually were faced with the disappearance of the soil conditions which had once made them so productive. Nature seemed set against them. Recurrent hurricanes and droughts, as well as the spread of plant diseases, further diminished their productivity.

Some Caribbean colonies have remained efficient sugar producers, but even the most efficient have suffered from a disability which afflicted tropical agricultural areas everywhere. Under pre-World War II conditions, the supply of their products far outran the effective world demand. The terms of trade under which they exchanged their sugar and other products for goods from the outside world grew progressively less favorable. Because their purchasing power was so low, they were poor customers. Of declining strategic and commercial importance to the states of Europe, the Caribbean colonies were no longer highly prized.

For the United States, however, the Caribbean territories

were strategically important despite their dwindling economic value; they were situated on main lines of communication. The United States established itself athwart these lines by acquiring Puerto Rico and the Virgin Islands. German submarines penetrating the Caribbean in World War II emphasized the military importance of the area. American security would be threatened if any part of it were in unfriendly hands.

The United States' interest is therefore not confined to its own insular possessions. A measure of this interest was its lease of military bases in the British West Indies in 1940. Directly and indirectly the United States has sought influence in the independent countries of this region and in the remaining dependencies of European states. While the British possessions have exhibited noteworthy loyalty to their mother country, Great Britain's control over its Caribbean colonies is now based more on American than on British military strength. American concern with the conditions prevailing in the British colonies grew as the United States assumed more and more responsibility for their security. The United States Government became deeply involved in the affairs of both the republics and the colonies of others in the Caribbean. Its interest seemed nearly as great as in America's own Puerto Rico and Virgin Islands.

Unrest in the Caribbean

The long-suffering people in the Caribbean colonies found themselves in an increasingly miserable state in the years just before the outbreak of World War II.

The world-wide depression of the early thirties had aggravated the already depressed condition of this area. As the United States and Great Britain took cognizance of domestic social distress, they also became aware of the greater poverty of their colonial peoples. The principle of state intervention to improve economic conditions was extended to the colonies after it had become established in the mother countries. This process was greatly stimulated by social unrest and violence in many of the dependencies. In Puerto Rico, for example, independence demonstrations by extremists culminated in the assassination of the American Chief of Police in 1936. More serious disturbances in the British West Indies began as strikes in 1935, which spread rapidly from island to island. The riots and demonstrations dramatized the plight of the Caribbean dependencies. They called attention to conditions which not only appalled humanitarian consciences but did serious injury to the prestige of the great democracies.

Neither the United States nor its British ally could afford disaffection in the Caribbean which might give the enemy a foothold in this region. Prevailing conditions in the British and American colonies were providing an antagonistic environment for American military installations. To add to their troubles, the breakdown in transport due to the war brought intensified suffering to the people in these isolated communities. There is no doubt that the reforms instituted in the Caribbean colonies in this period were partly motivated by security considerations. Nevertheless, through the American New Deal and the British Colonial Development and Welfare program the mother countries acknowledged that democratic respect for human rights and aspirations demanded the acceptance of responsibilities toward dependent peoples. For both power and welfare reasons the metropolitan governments took a new interest in the social and economic development of their Caribbean colonies and in the demands these made for greater self-government.*

* President Roosevelt's strong sentiments favoring greater political and social progress in the colonies were an important personal factor in the new official interest in this field.

In the British West Indies a systematic attack on social and economic problems grew out of a series of investigations which began with reports on the disturbances in Trinidad and Barbados in 1937. These produced extremely disquieting information. Then came a Colonial Office Labor Adviser's intensive study of the epidemic of labor violence in the West Indies.[2] The accelerating deterioration in living conditions and unrest in the West Indies finally led to the appointment of the West India Royal Commission headed by Lord Moyne. As a result of its recommendations the Colonial Development and Welfare Act was passed in 1940.[3] Although the terms of the act and the funds made available applied to the British colonies as a whole, special provision was made for financial aid to the West Indies. To supervise the execution of the act as it pertained to the West Indies and to co-ordinate their social and economic development, the British Government set up a local organization under a Comptroller for Development and Welfare in the West Indies.

The West India Royal Commission laid only minor emphasis on political problems, and its recommendations for constitutional change were very modest. Nevertheless, the British Government has sanctioned modifications for some West Indian constitutions in the direction of self-government, especially in Jamaica. In 1945 this colony obtained an all-elective legislature, universal suffrage, and an embryonic system of ministerial responsibility for administration.

Since the early 1930's the United States has spent much more money in its Caribbean dependencies than have the British. Nevertheless, the attack on colonial problems has been less co-ordinated than the planned development in the British West Indies. True, a systematic rehabilitation of Puerto Rico was sought in 1934 by the Puerto Rico Policy Commission, a federally appointed committee of Puerto

Ricans which prepared the Chardón Plan (named after the commission chairman).*

A result of its recommendations was the creation of the Puerto Rico Reconstruction Administration. This Federal agency was intended to promote diversification of agricultural and industrial enterprises and to aid in repairing the economic and cultural basis of Puerto Rican life. It administered a variety of projects to improve rural living standards; but within a few years the refusal of Congress to vote it further funds greatly diminished its usefulness. During the same period Puerto Rico enjoyed the services of many new Federal agencies: The Public Works Administration, Works Progress Administration, Farm Security Administration, Agricultural Adjustment Administration, and the United States Housing Authority all extended their operations to Puerto Rico.

In 1941 began a noteworthy local program of social and economic development under the rule of the *Populares*, a new Puerto Rican political party headed by Luis Muñoz Marín. Governor Rexford G. Tugwell supplied vigorous leadership during his term of office. Taking advantage of a sharp increase in the internal revenue on the sale of Puerto Rican rum in the United States, which by Federal law reverted to Puerto Rico, the Insular Government undertook a variety of economic and social measures through a system of public corporations.

During the 1940's there were continuous efforts to obtain more self-government for Puerto Rico. Progress in clarifying the future constitutional status of Puerto Rico was blocked in Congress in 1945, but the executive branch used its power to put as much of the government as possible into Puerto

* The plan concentrated on land reform and the reorganization of agriculture as basic to the solution of Puerto Rican social and economic problems.

Rican hands. Thus President Truman chose the Puerto Rican Resident Commissioner, who had been elected at large, to succeed Governor Tugwell. Although the ultimate status of Puerto Rico was still left untouched, in 1947 Congress finally approved an act providing for an elected governor and permitting the governor to appoint, with the consent of the Insular Senate, two of the three administrative officials formerly appointed by the President.*

Many New Deal agencies operated also in the Virgin Islands; both the PWA and the WPA contributed to the improvement of living conditions there. The most significant measure was, however, the establishment of a Federal corporation, the Virgin Islands Company, for a many-sided attack on the problem of their faltering economy. In 1944 Congress finally provided a substantial sum for sorely needed public works, especially for the improvement of public health. The Virgin Islands Organic Act of 1936 made drastic constitutional changes to democratize its government and provide for more self-rule.

The Caribbean Commission

When World War II greatly accentuated the difficulties with which the colonial governments were faced, the United States and Great Britain joined forces in the Anglo-American Caribbean Commission. The joint communiqué of March 9, 1942, which was the legal basis for the commission, stated in part:

> For the purpose of encouraging and strengthening social and economic co-operation between the United States of America and its possessions and bases in the

* The attorney general and the commissioner of education. The auditor remained a Federal official. In January, 1949, Muñoz Marín became Puerto Rico's first elective governor.

area known geographically and politically as the Caribbean, and the United Kingdom and the British colonies in the same area, and to avoid unnecessary duplication of research in these fields, a commission, to be known as the Anglo-American Caribbean Commission, has been jointly created by the two Governments.

During the war years the commission, as a consultative, advisory, and expediting body, helped to solve several short-run, war-induced problems and laid the groundwork for many permanent reforms.

Upon the establishment in 1944 of the West Indian Conference, an auxiliary forum composed of representatives from the dependencies, the people of the colonies could participate more directly in the discussion of common economic and social problems. The commission's membership was broadened to include the French and Dutch governments in 1945 and the Anglo-American prefix was therefore dropped. An international secretariat was established in Trinidad in 1946. For certain activities the independent republics in the Caribbean have also been invited to participate in the work of the commission. The formal agreement for the establishment of the reorganized body, signed October 30, 1946, declared the functions of the commission to be:

(1) To concern itself with economic and social matters of common interest to the Caribbean area, particularly agriculture, communications, education, fisheries, health, housing, industry, labor, social welfare and trade.

(2) To study, formulate and recommend on its own initiative, or as may be proposed by any of the Member or Territorial Governments, by the Research Council or the Conference, measures, programs and policies with respect to social and economic problems designed to contribute to the well-being of the Caribbean area. It shall advise the Member and territorial Governments on all such matters, and make recommendations for the carry-

ing into effect of all action necessary or desirable in this connection.

(3) To assist in co-ordinating local projects which have regional significance and to provide technical guidance from a wide field not otherwise available.

(4) To direct and review the activities of the Research Council and to formulate its rules of procedure.

(5) To provide for the convening of the sessions of the Conference, to formulate its rules of procedure, and to report to the Member Governments on Conference resolutions and recommendations.[4]

Joining in the Caribbean Commission's development activities was a new departure for France and the Netherlands. In their Caribbean colonies there had been no general counterpart to the British and American programs. The Netherlands had concentrated its colonial reforms in the Netherlands East Indies, and the French had shown greater interest in their African possessions than in their Caribbean colonies. Cuba, Haiti, and the Dominican Republic, suffering from many of the same economic and social ills as the neighboring colonies, had taken some governmental action to alleviate distress. Since these countries were formally independent, however, their problems differed qualitatively from those of the Caribbean dependencies.* For these reasons it is the British and American colonies in this region which furnish the most significant guidance for colonial development in general.

The Caribbean Commission's terms of reference are limited to social and economic fields, and do not authorize treatment of governmental questions.[5] But had the United States and Great Britain confined their colonial reforms to economic and social development, they would have offered only a one-sided

---

* For example, in their relations with the United States they were treated with a deference not accorded to dependent areas. On the other hand, they had to finance social and economic development chiefly from their own treasuries.

solution of the colonial problems to be found in the Caribbean. Although the metropolitan governments have thus restricted their joint activities through the Caribbean Commission to "non-political" affairs, they cannot avoid considering constitutional subjects in treating their own colonies separately. In fact, their policies have been many-sided if not comprehensive or always consistent with both ultimate objectives, a decent standard of living and self-government.

The following chapters will describe and analyze the interactions of particular policies which the United States and Great Britain have adopted for the economic, social, and governmental development of their Caribbean colonies. From this examination should emerge some conclusions regarding the kinds of measures which do not counteract the effects of other equally desirable measures or which may even tend to reinforce each other in progressing toward final objectives. Although the United States and Great Britain have not solved the dilemma of low living standards and governmental dependence, they have at least taken significant steps in that direction which have lessons for the future.

IV. Development and Welfare in the Caribbean: Economic Measures

IN the discussion of the recent British and American colonial development activities, a rough separation can be made between economic measures (those designed to increase productivity) and social measures (those designed to extend benefits to hitherto deprived elements of the population). Economic measures include such activities as agricultural rehabilitation, industrialization, and improvements in transportation and communications, which can lay the economic foundation for improved living standards by augmenting production. They likewise can provide the economic basis for greater political autonomy.

The economic difficulties which faced the American and British colonies in the Caribbean were essentially the same. Even more than most tropical countries, they depended on agriculture for their economic existence. There have been practically no valuable minerals found in these countries, except for bauxite in British Guiana and oil in Trinidad. Sugar cane has been by far the most important agricultural product in the area. As the colonies increased their efficiency in this field, the main problem became one of finding profitable markets.* Wartime isolation intensified the economic inse-

---

* The British and American Caribbean colonies are high-cost producers compared to other sugar-producing countries in the Caribbean and elsewhere. Furthermore the major sugar importing countries have long regulated the production and purchase of sugar to favor narrow national interests.

curity of these colonies, which were unable to feed themselves after the disruption of normal trade patterns.

The terrific pressure of population on the land demanded much more intensive exploitation of the colonies' admittedly meager but underdeveloped natural resources. To develop them, improved facilities for transportation and communication and better marketing methods are imperative. And since the soil can no longer support the increasing population in many of the Caribbean colonies at even the existing living standards, other income-producing activities required exploration.

Similar economic problems have brought forth somewhat similar responses in the British and American dependencies. Because of political and sociological differences, however, their economic programs have differed in emphasis and financing as well as in administrative detail. Puerto Rico, in a class by itself with its huge population, Latin culture, and high degree of home rule, has been the scene of the most extensive and controversial measures for economic development.

Puerto Rican Economic Development

Two million people (who may expand to three million by 1960) are trying to find a living on a small and mountainous island thirty-five miles wide and a hundred long. Many observers declare their economic problem insoluble. Nevertheless, since the early 1930's, both the Federal and Insular governments have made repeated attacks upon it. The most comprehensive was the program begun during Governor Tugwell's administration and supported by the Popular Democratic Party (the *Populares*).

After the transfer of Puerto Rico to the United States in 1898 there was a period of rapid development, chiefly under private American auspices; the production of sugar cane came to dominate the economy. Although living standards improved under American rule, so that Puerto Ricans were better situated than inhabitants of most other Latin American countries, the startling increase in population tended to offset most of the potential advantages of economic development. Misery and discontent continued to prevail.[1] Disastrous hurricanes and the world-wide depression added to Puerto Rico's distress.

Earlier governmental efforts to develop the island economically were directed primarily toward improving the returns from sugar cane. From the beginning of the American regime Puerto Rico's inclusion within United States tariff walls raised the price obtained for Puerto Rican sugar above the world price and stimulated the growth of this product at the expense of most others.*

When the price of agricultural products declined sharply in the thirties, Puerto Rico was included in the various domestic and international quota schemes which were intended to raise prices through restricted production. Benefit payments gave an extra and sizable subsidy to the sugar producers under the Sugar Act of 1937 as well as to producers of other commodities coming under the Agricultural Adjustment Act, in the same fashion as if they had been continental producers.†￼ The wartime bulk purchase and price support programs of the Federal Government were an additional aid to Puerto Rican producers.[2]

However efficient the sugar economy may be, the dangers inherent in too great dependence on a single crop have led to repeated Federal and Insular government encouragement

* Tariff protection also benefited the tobacco industry (which produced tobacco for cigar making), but helped to ruin the coffee industry, since there has been no United States tariff on coffee.

† The 1947 Sugar Act set new quotas and continued incentive payments as well as continuing the Secretary of Agriculture's power to establish sugar prices paid to growers.

of mixed farming, both on small holdings and on the larger commercial farms. Cane sugar producers are now particularly vulnerable because of revolutionary developments in the competing American beet sugar industry. New and improved crops of commercial importance, including some for industrial use, are being tried out on a pilot plant basis by the Insular Agricultural Development Company. This public corporation was established in 1945 to give practical application to the experiments of research agencies and thereby to stimulate private production.

Many Federal and Insular agencies have contributed to more efficient production. In former times sugar cane received the main attention, but at present there is also great emphasis on increasing the production of other farm commodities. Agricultural research, advice and training, the provision of new seed and livestock, soil erosion control, and irrigation and drainage programs—these are all adding to Puerto Rico's agricultural productivity.[3]

Not only is the soil yielding more. Smaller producers are also getting more income per acre from their fields because they have had help in farm management and marketing, and in organizing and financing co-operatives for these purposes. Among several agencies which have improved the distribution system, the Puerto Rico Reconstruction Administration and the Agricultural Development Company have contributed especially.[4]

Two long-neglected natural resources, forests and fisheries, have recently begun to emerge as additional bases for economic development. Federal and Insular agencies are co-operatively seeking to remedy the sadly denuded state of the once luxuriously forested island. Forests are being protected and developed for soil and water conservation as well as for commercial purposes.[5] Similarly the local fishing industry is being stimulated to supplement the diet of the mass of Puerto Ricans, which consists largely of salt fish, rice, and beans.

The most important phase of recent Puerto Rican economic development has been the Insular Government's industrialization efforts. These activities have been opposed both by local conservatives attached to the sugar industry and by congressmen attached to laissez-faire ideas. The most obvious industry for Puerto Rico would be the refining of the sugar it produces. This development has been effectively barred by the terms of the Sugar Act of 1937 (continued in the 1947 act), which limited to an insignificant quantity the amount of refined sugar the United States would import from Puerto Rico.[6]

Nevertheless, a bold beginning in industrialization has been made. Government companies lead the way for private industrial enterprises. Government funds are available for capital investments, to train technicians and skilled craftsmen, and to conduct research on design, costs, and markets. Puerto Rico has begun or planned for many kinds of manufacturing. They include production of articles to serve existing industry (especially glass and paper containers for the rum industry); manufactures using the by-products of existing industry, such as bagasse (a waste product of sugar milling) for construction material; articles which use available local resources, such as clay for tile; and some made by semimechanized industries, producing such things as leather goods, furniture, and rugs.

The Puerto Rican Industrial Development Company, operating chiefly on appropriations made possible by the windfall of internal revenue receipts from rum, has made a thoroughgoing study of the island's industrial possibilities. It established new industries and took over and expanded a successful cement plant already constructed by the Puerto Rico Reconstruction Administration. Rapid industrial expansion is coming through the Development Company's program of building plants to be leased and eventually sold to private industrialists at cost. In 1948 this program involved an investment of more than $25,000,000 and was expected to provide 5,000 jobs and an annual payroll of more than $5,000,000.[7] Among the first plants thus provided were a shoe factory and flour and textile mills, to be operated by continental firms.

The Insular Government has also established a Development Bank to provide investment funds for new enterprises. Local and continental investors had concentrated on the sugar industry. They were unwilling to venture into these strange fields, at least alone. New industries have been granted a temporary exemption from property and income taxes and excise levies on machinery and raw materials. This has proved a very effective incentive for continental firms to conduct enterprises in Puerto Rico, especially those where labor costs are an important consideration.

Industrialization has been facilitated in Puerto Rico by the extensive public power system, which has been built up over a period of years with the aid of Federal public works funds. It takes advantage of the mountainous terrain and heavy periodic rainfalls and is connected with the irrigation services provided by the Insular Government. The power system proved invaluable during the war-isolated years and has had no difficulty in obtaining private credit in New York. It is administered by the Insular Water Resources Authority, which also gradually absorbed the private power companies.[8] Another element of the industrialization program was the planning of a $15,000,000 sewerage system and a $25,000,000 water supply, purification, and distribution system, to be financed with the assistance of the Development Bank and operated by the Puerto Rican Aqueduct and Sewer Service.[9]

An industrial program in Puerto Rico has the advantage

of transportation and communications facilities much less primitive than those in the rest of the Caribbean. Most of the island is easily accessible by automobile, the road system having profited since 1937 from grants-in-aid under the Federal Highway Act of 1917.

During the Tugwell regime transportation and communications authorities were created to take over, co-ordinate, and expand facilities with the object of achieving improved service at lower rates. Air service to and from the mainland has been frequent and relatively inexpensive, and it has expanded with the federally aided development of insular airports. Ocean transportation, on the other hand, has been the cause of much irritation, for Puerto Rico has been included in the coastwise shipping laws. Not only has shipping between the mainland and Puerto Rico been confined to American bottoms, but the service is costly.

The monopolistic position of the American shipping lines serving Puerto Rico has not helped the expansion of the tourist industry, a likely means of increasing Puerto Rico's income. The Insular Government's prewar efforts to stimulate tourism had to be abandoned, but a new and enlarged program is now under way. For this purpose the Industrial Development Company has begun to construct hotels, which will be managed by continental chains.

Planning a definite program for economic development has been one function of the Insular Planning, Urbanizing, and Zoning Board, which was established in 1942 with the aid of the then-existing National Resources Planning Board. The Six-Year Financial Program, revised annually, has apportioned the expected public revenues among government programs, and master plans have also been drawn up for particular types of development, such as airports and highways. This was an important step forward in weighing and co-ordinating the demands of the island for various kinds of capital expenditures. The Planning Board has emphasized activities designed to broaden the economic base, to provide new sources of income and increased purchasing power.

Without the most prudent and hard-headed planning, raising Puerto Rican living standards through economic development will prove to be what some already fear, an impossible achievement. The difficulties are illustrated by the findings of a report on the net income of Puerto Rico for the war period. Wage-earning families would have to treble their real annual income of 1941-42 to reach a figure between seven and eight hundred dollars (in prewar prices), the level at which some believe the population problem would solve itself. Yet in a period marked by an unusually sharp rise in per capita net income, the net increase from 1940 to 1944 was only 25 per cent.[10] The report continues:

> During the war period, which, on balance, was an auspicious time for the expansion of the Puerto Rican economy, the average annual gain in per capita income (in prewar prices) was $5.20. On the assumption of 5.2 persons per family reported by the *Census of Population, 1940*, this amounts to an average annual real gain per family of $26. If this average annual addition to family income could be continued without interruption, it would require about 18 years to achieve the objective. That is, the goal would be achieved in 1960 when, according to estimates based on medium assumptions, the population would be about 2,800,000. It would not be far wrong to assume further that a tripling of the real income per wage-earner family would also entail a tripling of the real per capita net income. The latter, in prewar prices . . . is estimated at $140 in 1942; tripled, it amounts to $420. This figure multiplied by the estimated population for 1960 yields a net income total of $1,200,000,000 in prewar prices. Thus, to apply the economic brake on population growth would entail in

18 years an insular net income, in prewar prices, five times larger than the prewar net income of $228,000,000. Such a rate of expansion of real income is without precedent.[11]

Economic Development in the Virgin Islands

Compared to the troubles of teeming Puerto Rico, the problems of thirty thousand Virgin Islanders seem minute. But they differ chiefly in scale. The same major question confronts them: how to support the population on the meager resources of the islands. The available means are far fewer than in Puerto Rico; there is no natural fresh water supply; and the smallness of the colony is in itself a special handicap. Of the two chief islands, St. Thomas has existed chiefly on its business as a bunkering port; St. Croix has lived by sugar cane (although present acreage is less than one-third of that devoted to cane in its heyday), and by cattle raising which is the only other noteworthy agricultural activity. The manufacture of alcoholic beverages has become a major support of both islands.*

Frequent droughts and the marginal quality of the land on St. Croix were killing off the sugar industry of this island. The world-wide decline of sugar prices in the thirties delivered the final blow. In 1934 the Federal Government took a radical step to reorganize the economy of St. Croix, which was facing complete collapse. A government corporation, the Virgin Islands Company, was created to rehabilitate the sugar industry and engage in related agricultural activities. It also had the task of physical reconstruction and housing in the rural areas. The company operated the only sugar mill

* The third inhabited island, St. John, is combined with St. Thomas for administrative purposes, and this "municipality" is governed by a council distinct from the "municipal council" of St. Croix.

and one of the two rum distilleries on the island. As the backbone of the economic life of St. Croix, it furnished wage employment for field and factory laborers and processed cane for about five hundred small farmers.*

Nevertheless, the activities of the Virgin Islands Company are on a very small scale; the sugar produced since 1934 would barely suffice to feed the United States a few days. The company showed a deficit for a number of years, but balanced out its losses in sugar by making an unusual profit on rum during the war when American whisky was not being distilled. The company, essentially a relief operation, has an uncertain future because of its special dependence on the favor of Congress. In 1948, the company's charter was renewed for only one year.

The tourist industry has been regarded as the salvation of the Virgin Islands. Its special virtue is that the local resources favoring tourism—climate and scenery—are unlikely to disappear as they are enjoyed. The Federal Government built the Bluebeard Castle Hotel (which opened in 1935), improved roads and sanitation, and stimulated the handicraft industry, which thrives on tourist trade. Recently, it allowed the military airfield and barracks at Benedict Field to be converted to accommodate tourists.

Several Federal agencies have made modest contributions to the economic development of the Virgin Islands. They have provided market facilities, aided agriculture, and revived the cattle industry, which was practically the only agricultural enterprise other than sugar cane capable of bringing money in from outside. The Federal Department of Commerce received a small appropriation in 1947 to interest local and outside capital in new industry in the islands. Except

---

* It grew 40 per cent of the sugar cane crop, processed between 60 per cent and 70 per cent of the raw sugar, and produced 80 per cent of the rum on St. Croix.

for the Virgin Islands Company, however, the only large-scale Federal assistance came late in 1944 when Congress passed a $10,000,000 public works program for the Virgin Islands. It was to be spread over five years and constructed by the Federal Works Agency. Not until 1947 did this program actually get under way.

An embryonic planning policy began to take form locally in 1945. At that time the Virgin Islands Legislative Assembly made the governor responsible for a continuing study of income, population, agricultural and industrial development, and of other factors determining economic stability and progress. The first steps have now been taken to make a rational appraisal of the possibilities for future economic development.

Economic Development in the British West Indies

Unlike the American dependencies, the British territories in the Caribbean are spread over great distances. Despite wide variations in historical background and geographical conditions, however, the economic problems of the various British West Indies were sufficiently similar to permit the West India Royal Commission to make many blanket recommendations regarding them.

There were two phases of the Royal Commission's report. The first dealt with changes which could be made only on the metropolitan level, the objectives being to raise and stabilize the monetary return from the sale of the colonies' principal products, particularly sugar. The Royal Commission's recommendations for an increased preference and higher quota for West Indian sugar in the London market were rendered irrelevant by the onslaught of World War II. However, since the middle thirties the British Government has been taking steps to achieve the same goals by guaranteeing prices and markets for the total exportable surplus of several of the major West Indian products.

The second phase concerned more intensive utilization of local resources. In this direction the Development and Welfare organization followed closely and expanded upon the Royal Commission's recommendations. Both agencies emphasized the institution of systematic agriculture to replace the common practice of shifting cultivation. They advocated diversified farming, including an expansion of animal husbandry, in place of complete dependence upon a single crop. Believing that "good farming is the key to the economic and social problems of the West Indies," the Inspector-General of Agriculture attached to Development and Welfare stressed a comprehensive approach to agricultural reform which embraced all aspects of rural life from education to provision for rural amenities.[12]

To promote more intensive use of resources, Development and Welfare also helped the colonies to protect and expand their forests and fisheries. Because orderly marketing methods were a condition of the successful development of minor products, reforms in the distribution system have been actively sought since the report of the Royal Commission. In all these endeavors Development and Welfare emphasized co-operation among the British West Indies and co-ordinated efforts to raise productivity.[13]

Development and Welfare aid in improving roads and constructing airfields has facilitated more efficient marketing in particular and co-ordination of the British West Indian economic development in general. Recent years have seen a pronounced expansion of air transportation. Intercolonial services were provided by British West Indian Airways, a British-subsidized local company which was absorbed by British South American Airways after a period of independent operation. Partly as a result of the war, shipping services were still very inadequate in 1947, when the British West Indies organized a joint commission on shipping and sought additional help from the mother country to improve transportation facilities.

Development and Welfare has also helped establish a uniform system of wireless communications throughout the British West Indies, for aeronautical and meteorological purposes. Telecommunications have expanded through the operations of Cable and Wireless Limited, now a nationalized British corporation. Radio broadcasting services have also increased, aided in part by Development and Welfare and by the British Broadcasting Corporation.

The improvement of transportation and communications facilities is removing one hindrance to industrial development. However, the West India Royal Commission and the Development and Welfare organization in its earlier years took a cautious view of industrialization, in the belief that new industries would not greatly reduce unemployment. However, war conditions caused several of the colonial governments to venture into publicly financed business enterprises, and Development and Welfare did establish an experimental cotton-spinning plant in Barbados which was later expanded by the local government.

Criticism of the conservative industrialization policy and the realization that a welfare program could not be built on a wholly agricultural economy in this densely populated region eventually brought a shift in sentiment.[14] With the passage of the Colonial Development and Welfare Act of 1945, amending and expanding the 1940 act, much greater emphasis was placed on planned economic development as opposed to piecemeal and primarily welfare activities.[15] A natural accompaniment to the advent of the Labor Government was an increased metropolitan interest in government-aided industries in the colonies. Some of the colonial governments began to encourage the establishment of privately operated industries in the West Indies, through the grant of particular privileges, including certain types of tax exemption.

The problem of economic development was finally approached in a bold fashion. In 1948 Parliament approved the Overseas Resources Development Act, which provided for a Colonial Development Corporation with power to borrow £100,000,000.* This corporation was intended to undertake on a commercial basis, or assist in the undertaking of, productive projects in individual colonies which would be likely to increase their wealth and stimulate production of goods desired by the outside world. Like the operations of the Puerto Rican Development Company, its projects will be business enterprises rather than basic public services for economic development such as water supplies. It will concentrate on the exploitation of local resources, particularly emphasizing agricultural products, but will also establish some secondary industries to process local products for local consumption. Thus a foundation is being laid which may eventually provide a local basis for a social welfare program.

Planning for Economic Development

The Overseas Resources Development Act of 1948, joined with the Colonial Development and Welfare Act, represents planning for colonial development at the very highest government level. Aiding the Colonial Secretary in the administration of this planning, a Colonial Economic and Development Council advised him on comprehensive programs for

---

* Simultaneously, the Overseas Food Corporation was organized to carry on food production activities overseas. It could operate in a colony on invitation from the Secretary of State for the Colonies.

the economic and social rehabilitation of the colonies as well as on general economic and financial policy. On the local level, Development and Welfare assisted the colonial governments in preparing ten-year plans for development which required metropolitan aid; these were then examined by the Colonial Economic and Development Council.

In contrast to British Parliamentary action, there has been no comprehensive Congressional policy for the economic development of Puerto Rico and the Virgin Islands. House and Senate committees which investigated social and economic conditions in Puerto Rico in the early forties produced chiefly negative results. They were in varying degree critical of the Federal and Insular administrative agencies.[16] A distinctive feature of the Puerto Rican planning was its local origin. To be sure, some Federal administrative agencies have undertaken planning activities in these territories. Under the auspices of the now-defunct National Resources Planning Board, continental officials prepared a development plan for the Virgin Islands in 1943, which was revised by local direction in 1947.[17] But Congress has even failed to provide adequate funds for the understaffed Division of Territories and Island Possessions, whose administrative jurisdiction over these dependencies is too handicapped by lack of money to undertake any comprehensive plans for economic development.

On the international level, however, more progress is discernible. The United States has participated in the initial stages of development planning as a member of the Caribbean Commission. The advisory decisions of the commission may ultimately impel Congress to adopt and implement a comprehensive policy for the economic development of the American dependencies. Meanwhile the Caribbean Commission has brought about agreement between Great Britain and the United States on several economic questions which look toward a general development policy.

The general lines of development proposed by the Caribbean Commission, many of them worked out through the sessions of the West Indian Conference, emphasized regional treatment of the economic problems of the Caribbean dependencies. The United States and Great Britain issued a joint statement, based on the report of the first West Indian Conference (1944), in which they agreed upon several economic policies and procedures to implement them.[18] These included agricultural diversification, both for locally consumed foodstuffs and for export; encouragement of industrial development; improvement in transportation facilities; promotion of intercolonial trade; public works programs coordinated with agricultural, industrial, and trade development; the strengthening of statistical machinery; and the further study of overpopulation problems.

The two states recognized the necessity of government assistance, direct and indirect, to carry out these policies. They favored positive methods of encouraging development, such as financial aid, and frowned upon such negative means as restriction of foreign imports by additional tariff barriers. The two governments promised to review continuously policies relating to the sugar industry; to expand the trade of their possessions in every possible direction; and to consider the problems of international dumping and countervailing duties during negotiations for the general regulation of international commercial practices.

The policies outlined in the joint declaration have subsequently been elaborated upon by the Caribbean Commission. Extension of membership to France and the Netherlands did not change their direction.

Where separate national action is required, the member states do not necessarily put into effect the proposals of the West Indian Conference. The recommendations of special conferences held by the Caribbean Commission, and even the advice of the main body need not be accepted by individual states. However, the commission itself has actively promoted projects useful to the economic development of the Caribbean colonies. It organized a very successful schooner pool for the eastern British West Indies which not only solved a war problem by improving the efficiency and safety of the schooners, but also pointed the way to a regular, co-ordinated service after the war.

The commission also sponsored an extensive fisheries survey of the British West Indies. One of its most significant development activities is the industrial survey concluded in 1948, which will provide a basis for an intensified and co-ordinated industrialization. Another contribution is an interterritorial radio information program which is broadcast by various stations throughout the area.* Also under its auspices a Caribbean Tourist Development Plan has been inaugurated, in which a large number of the colonies are participating.

As in the case of Development and Welfare for the British West Indies, the Caribbean Commission has performed two important functions necessary for the planned economic development of the Caribbean colonies. It has aided the fact-finding which must precede detailed planning, and it has furthered the pooling of information which increases the effectiveness of metropolitan assistance to the colonies.[19] In so far as it can promote the more effective exploitation of local resources, the commission is helping to lay the economic basis for better living conditions as well as for greater political autonomy. Even with international co-operation and extensive metropolitan aid, the colonies may never reach a stage of

* During the war the West Indian Radio Newsletter was broadcast from the United States under the auspices of the Caribbean Commission, and West Indian officials had an opportunity to help produce the program and to learn new radio techniques.

economic development capable of maintaining living standards comparable to those in advanced countries. Nevertheless, such co-operation and aid increase the likelihood of their achieving this goal, provided the development is systematically planned.

V. Development and Welfare in the Caribbean: Social Measures

COLONIAL economic development is not an end in itself; it is a means of attaining other goals, including a rise in mass living standards. It could hardly be otherwise for Great Britain and the United States, where there is a strong belief in the dignity of man and his right to a share in the benefits of material progress. Paradoxically, some rise in living standards is a prerequisite to extensive economic development. Malnutrition, disease, ignorance, and bad housing are not only results but causes of the low productivity of labor.

Because of their living conditions, it has been difficult for colonial people to shake off an attitude of hopeless resignation. They seem unable to exert themselves energetically in the improvement of their economic situation. Low living standards are not only an enemy to the economic progress necessary to ameliorate them; they also impede the political progress which depends upon economic development. Advance toward autonomy and a more broadly based local democracy is further hindered by the insecurities accompanying a low standard of living. Uncertainty about the most elemental needs of food and shelter has kept the mass of the people from playing any effective role in politics except as instruments for the personal aggrandizement of demagogues.

Governments can help to raise the low income of the mass of the people by such activities as extensive health services, public housing, social insurance, the reorganization of land tenure, and improvements in labor conditions. In the long run, a substantial increase in the colonial income ultimately depends upon economic development.

Social welfare measures, on the other hand, have a short-run effect on particular groups by directly adding to personal income. Such measures divide up the available colonial income in different ways; they do not, at least not immediately, expand the total. Since the early 1930's, the metropolitan and colonial governments have carried on ever-increasing social welfare activities in the Caribbean dependencies. The choice of measures was determined by the value systems of the policy-makers and by limitations in resources, personal and material. The balance struck between economic and social development and the priority given certain measures within these two categories produced important political consequences. They re-distributed power locally and between the colonies and the outside world.

Social Development in Puerto Rico

Although her living standards are low compared to those of even the most ill-favored American states, Puerto Rico is better off by far than other Caribbean territories.

Since the beginning of the American jurisdiction over Puerto Rico, notable advances have been made in health and education, but the sharp increase in population canceled out many of the gains.[1] Additional obstacles were poverty, ignorance, indifference, and superstition, which continue to baffle the health officials. To counteract them, the Puerto Rican Department of Health has pursued a comprehensive program modeled on continental practice, paying special attention to tuberculosis, malaria, and venereal disease, the chief communicable diseases of the island.

The Federal Government has made important contributions to the program. Especially helpful was the expert assistance of the United States Public Health Service, together with relief funds of the Works Progress Administration, and an extension of the public health sections of the Federal Social Security Act. The health measures taken by the military authorities during the war significantly improved conditions in the island. The School of Tropical Medicine, attached to the University of Puerto Rico and affiliated with Columbia University, has been an important center of research, consultation, and training.

Many health problems stem from the shocking housing conditions of both urban and rural Puerto Rican workers. The slums of San Juan, almost literally built over sewage, are among the worst in the world. Federal and Insular funds have built some new hurricane-proof housing, both urban and rural. Nevertheless, though Puerto Rican public housing has been commended for being especially suited to local conditions, the usual housing problem remains unsolved: how to reach the lowest income groups.[2]

Like the public health program, Puerto Rican educational efforts have been extensive rather than intensive, and for the same reason—too many people.[3] Most of the children get to school, but the school age population has increased so rapidly that hardly more than half can attend school at any time. In line with the system on the mainland, direct Federal aid has been restricted to a very few special purposes, such as vocational education and the school lunch program.

The Insular Government has been spending between a fifth and a third of its budget on education (the percentage varied inversely with the size of the revenues), a much higher proportion than in most other dependencies. Furthermore, its free education through high school has distinguished Puerto Rico (and the Virgin Islands) from the British West Indies. Puerto Rico has been commended for some ingenious innovations designed to meet its special requirements. One is the "second unit rural school," a combination academic and vocational institution which also serves as a cultural center for the adult community. Another is the School of the Air, which broadcasts educational and cultural programs for classroom use and for the public. Nevertheless, Puerto Rico has a gigantic task yet to fulfill before all the children are reached and effectively educated. This task was greatly augmented by American insistence that the teaching be in English in the upper grades.[4]

The Puerto Rican school system has the great advantage of association with the University of Puerto Rico, an Insular university which also receives a metropolitan subsidy as a Federal land grant institution. Under Governor Tugwell, the university was reorganized to free it so far as possible from political influence. Several new departments and schools have been added to increase its public usefulness, especially a School of Public Administration and a Social Science Research Center; and the university is fast developing into a cultural meeting place for North and Latin America. On its campus a large industrial arts and trades school opened in 1948. It was one of a series to be established as an integral part of the Insular industrialization program.*

Education for industrialization ultimately helps fill another social need, that for jobs. The very high unemployment rate is the chief labor problem in Puerto Rico. The temporary migration of laborers, which has occurred in minor degree, provides another partial solution of this problem. However, after an initial recruitment during the war, Congress refused to authorize further official importation of migrant Puerto Rican labor for work in essential occupations,

* Under the auspices of the Industrial Development Company and the Veterans Administration, veteran students are also being sent on scholarships to the continent to study new industrial techniques in order to qualify for technical and managerial posts in the island's new enterprises.

despite the fact that large numbers of West Indians were thus recruited. (The latter had no legal right to remain in the United States permanently.)

Some population experts believe a large-scale, officially directed, permanent migration, *if combined with other measures*, would give the necessary stimulus to improved living standards, prerequisite to a reduction in the birth rate. In view of the attitude of Congress during the war, the prospects for early Federal promotion of Puerto Rican migration do not seem good. In 1947 the Insular Government adopted a program of guiding and regulating (but not encouraging) prospective migrants, in co-operation with some mainland authorities, and it included the training of potential migrants in the island's vocational education program.[5]

Both Insular and Federal governments have developed elaborate systems to improve Puerto Rican labor conditions in the usual ways: Each has regulated minimum wages and working conditions. Both governments have promoted collective bargaining and labor education; they have also provided conciliation services. Insular law has long prohibited child labor under sixteen generally. Social security is the only field not well covered by Federal or Insular law.* The two governments are gradually co-ordinating labor services, and Puerto Rico has assumed all responsibility for some activities.

Puerto Rico has made great progress in solving problems of labor, education, and health, but the outstanding social development in recent years has been the reorganization of land tenure. The island's land program is remarkable for its variety of measures, and because its most striking innovations were insular in origin. It is none the less exceptional

---

* Despite continual pressure on Congress to extend the Social Security Act to Puerto Rico, in 1948 only the public health, maternal, and child welfare sections applied to the island. Puerto Rico has had its own workmen's compensation insurance system since the early 1930's.

for presenting some possible solutions of a situation which mere subdivision and redistribution would only aggravate.

Land reform has been a perennial issue, often associated with anti-American agitation. The demand for land reform was understandable. Holdings of five hundred acres or more (about one-third of the total land and most of the best land) were in the hands of only one per cent of the landowners; most of this land was either owned or controlled by the large sugar corporations.[6] Earlier attacks on the problem of land concentration and absentee ownership in the sugar industry emphasized one phase only—satisfying the land hunger of the agricultural workers.*

As far back as the first Organic Act for Puerto Rico in 1900, a provision was included limiting corporate landholding to five hundred acres. However, this provision, continued in the second Organic Act of 1917, went unenforced until 1941.[7] Meanwhile, a Homestead Commission, created in 1921, established a number of small-scale family farms, mostly in remote and rather unproductive regions; in 1938 the Federal Farm Security Administration began to facilitate well-managed farm ownership through supervised loans combined with special farm and social services; and the Forest Services made available small parcels of good land scattered among the forests, for subsistence farming.

The Puerto Rico Reconstruction Administration, beginning in 1935, conducted several programs. Implementing part of the Chardón Plan, in the coffee, fruit, and tobacco regions it set up subsistence farms which were grouped near its Central Service Farms, which provided supervision and guidance,

* As in the San Juan slums, many low-income rural inhabitants have been merely insecure squatters paying no rent at all and living in their packing case hovels at the uncertain sufferance of the property owners. Similarly, they secured part of their food by foraging. Even sugar cane workers, living more securely on large plantations, frequently could not maintain subsistence gardens near their homes.

fertilizer, seeds, breeding stock, and other services to the settlers. PRRA established family-size farms of varying acreage, garden home communities for agricultural laborers, and squatters' settlements. It also loaned funds to a group of individual sugar cane farmers organized as a co-operative. Combined with borrowings from a private bank, this loan enabled them to acquire a medium-sized sugar mill and the lands formerly belonging to it.

Prior to the Land Law of 1941, PRRA made an experiment designed to combine the efficiency of a large-scale sugar cane enterprise with small-scale ownership. It acquired Central Lafayette, a large estate with a sugar mill, and divided it into twelve land co-operatives eventually to be owned and managed by the laborers. It loaned the co-operatives money secured by lands and growing crops and appointed a manager to operate them as a unit. Financial difficulties led to the dissolution of the co-operatives within three years; the report of the investigating committee preceding their dissolution stated that laborers' agricultural co-operatives in the area of Central Lafayette would most likely be unsuccessful.*

After the electoral victory of the *Populares* and a Supreme Court decision affirming the illegality of the corporate landholdings exceeding five hundred acres, the Puerto Rican Legislature passed the Land Law of 1941.[8] This created a Land Authority to purchase acreage from the oversized corporate holdings and other sources, and to establish individual holdings (now limited to between ten and one hundred acres), "proportional benefit farms," and squatter (*agregado*) settlements on very small plots.

* The investigating committee attributed their financial distress to excessive mortgage debt, faulty financial organization, low yields, low operating efficiency, high indirect costs, the laborer's attitude, and lack of education. These findings were disputed by some leaders, especially by Governor Tugwell.

The proportional benefit farm idea is a novel and promising approach to the problem of maintaining the high efficiency of the large estates with a wider distribution of profits. The Land Authority leases large amounts of land to farmers, agronomists, and others experienced in agricultural management, who manage the property and obtain a fixed percentage of the net profit. The remainder of the profits are distributed among the laborers according to the number of days worked and wages received. Unlike the PRRA co-operative plan, the proportional benefit farms have succeeded financially and help to make the Puerto Rican land tenure system the most progressive in the Caribbean.* By 1948 the Land Authority owned about 11 per cent of the acreage devoted to sugar cane.[9] Of all the social changes in Puerto Rico in recent years, land reform has departed most strikingly from continental practice.

Social Development in the Virgin Islands

Compared to the extensive social measures in Puerto Rico, reform in the Virgin Islands is hardly spectacular. These islands are tiny; they lack resources; and there is no pronounced local demand for improvements.† However, progress can be reported in some fields. Malaria and typhoid, common in the tropics, are no longer a problem in these islands. Federal grants for public health have enabled the dependency to conduct an aggressive program to control

---

* The profits made by these farms are not strictly comparable to the earnings of the property before its acquisition by the Land Authority. For instance, Agricultural Adjustment Administration payments were at a higher rate than those paid when the property was classified as under simple large-scale private ownership.

† Thus for years the municipal councils refused to pass adequate sanitary ordinances to protect the food supply, even after the Federal Government had constructed a modern market.

tuberculosis and venereal disease; Federal subsidies have also promoted the public health training of medical officers and nurses.

Perhaps the most striking social progress is in education. Almost all children of school age are in school regularly, and the literacy rate in the Virgin Islands is well above 90 per cent.[10] Plant and equipment are very inadequate, but the school program includes scholarship loans and in-service teacher training (on the continent and in Puerto Rico as well as at home). Limited commercial and vocational education is available and there are evening schools for adults. A federally aided school lunch service completes the program.

Child welfare services were also federally aided under a section of the Social Security Act which was extended to the Virgin Islands in 1947. The $10,000,000 public works program mentioned earlier will include improvements in the schools, hospital facilities, recreation, water supply, and sanitation.

A modest homesteading program has been developed in the Virgin Islands. It began in 1931 when Congress provided funds for subdividing large estates no longer cultivated and for their resale to small farmers. From time to time both Federal and local agencies have participated in the program, providing financial aid, supervision, some housing, and agricultural and home demonstrations.

But none of the Virgin Islands activities has yet made more than an oblique attack on one of the colony's most fundamental needs, a social reorganization which would provide children with a stable family background.

Social Development in the British West Indies

In common with the mass of Puerto Ricans and Virgin Islanders, most West Indians are never sure how and when they will next eat. The elementary needs of food, clothing, and shelter are uppermost in their minds; other considerations seem unimportant. Nevertheless, like the Virgin Islands, the British West Indies have other kinds of social problems, such as the weakness of family life and color prejudice.[11] These may not disappear with the disappearance of poverty, and they make the conquest of poverty more difficult.

More fundamental than poverty itself, there are attitudes prevalent in these colonies which make West Indian life unsatisfying to the inhabitants and which are also obstacles to the attainment of the desired Western European standards.* As a former Social Welfare Officer of Development and Welfare stated, "The whole problem of the promotion of development and welfare in the West Indies turns on the bringing of the West Indian culture into reasonably close accord with that of the world outside, without destroying it altogether, or overstraining economic resources in the attempt." [12] Colonial policy in the West Indies is beginning to show an awareness of this basic problem, although action has been chiefly evident in more tangible fields.

British policy has tried to set a new educational standard for the West Indies. The hope was to improve greatly on existing local standards, not to imitate the English ones, which are hardly applicable.[13] Development and Welfare was willing to make grants for buildings and sanitation, free books and stationery, teachers' housing, some teacher training and vocational training.

But a general and continual subsidizing of teachers' salaries, necessary if the West India Royal Commission recommendations regarding qualitative and quantitative improve-

* Observers of West Indian peoples have frequently remarked on a widespread tendency among them to expect improvements in their condition without exertion from themselves. In view of their tragic history this is easily understood. And it is fostered by their dependent status.

ments in teaching were to be carried out, was rejected. Colonial officials decided that the proposals for teacher training and the abolition of the pupil-teacher system

> cannot be followed in some colonies without prejudicing either the extension of education to all the children or the growth in self-responsibility of the colonies; for these colonies cannot now or in the foreseeable future afford enough trained and adequately paid teachers for all their children, in classes of reasonable size.[14]

A modified program has therefore been advocated, which would provide a "diluted" education for more children, chiefly by increase in the use of pupils as teachers, accompanied by expansion of teacher-training facilities.

Development and Welfare also sought to infuse more practical and esthetic training and local orientation into the curriculum, which had been much criticized for blindly aping nineteenth century "literary" education in England. Church opposition locally and in England prevented the colonial governments from further extending their control over denominational schools, even when financial aid was increased.*

Long years of agitation have finally culminated in the establishment of a West Indian University in 1948. Following the recommendations of the Commission on Higher Education in the Colonies and its special committee on the West Indies, the disagreement on location which had impeded the organization of a university was dissolved by the creation of a unified institution in Jamaica. Transportation expenses of the resident students from other islands are to be paid by the University General Fund, to be contributed to by all the

---

* Granting that denominational schools in the West Indies may be helpful in moral instruction, they nevertheless have tended to keep educational standards low. The churches could not afford adequate facilities, and there were too many competing denominations providing separate schools in particular areas.

colonies; extramural courses are to be available in other islands.[15]

Recognizing that an effective obstacle to public health progress in the British West Indies was a lack of trained men, the new university will give priority to premedical instruction among the courses to be offered at the outset. Similarly, aid in the training of public health officials has formed an important part of Development and Welfare's approach to West Indian health problems. The organization emphasized preventive measures rather than curative facilities. The latter are politically easier to obtain but more expensive and less effective. Special attention was directed to sanitation, prenatal and maternal care, child welfare, control of endemic diseases, and health education. Development and Welfare facilitated a number of health surveys conducted by specialized British agencies such as the National Association for the Prevention of Tuberculosis. These helped to provide information basic to the development of health programs in the West Indies.

In housing, Development and Welfare also used the preventive approach. It promoted town planning, investigations to reduce housing costs, and the preparation of model housing laws. To the problem of land settlement, Development and Welfare's chief contribution was advice rather than extensive financial aid for particular projects.

As in Puerto Rico, the reform of land tenure has been a controversial issue in the British West Indies for many years. It was a problem not only because of prevalent land hunger but also because, as elsewhere, there was strong disagreement among the reformers. Prior to the West India Royal Commission inquiry, unrest among the landless proletariat was already critical. A few colonies, notably Jamaica, tried land settlement as a solution. That this activity was a "palliative to agrarian discontent," and not a cure-all for the ills of the colonies was the strongly expressed opinion of the West

India Royal Commission; Development and Welfare concurred. These bodies gave priority to improving the husbandry of existing small holders.

Where public assistance in resettlement appeared desirable, they emphasized that the government should retain sufficient controls to prevent fragmentation of the land and to provide suitable safeguards for good agricultural practices. Development and Welfare approved grants to a limited number of new land settlement projects, while continually stressing the desirability of the leasehold in preference to the freehold for resettlement programs.[16] It also urged that landlord-tenant relations be defined to provide greater security for tenant farmers and to compensate them for unexhausted improvements.

Although the West India Royal Commission and Development and Welfare did not produce radical changes in West Indian land tenure, they did attack social discontent in a related field, labor relations. In a relatively short time the nineteenth century legal status of labor was transformed by modern legislation which legalized and regulated trade-unions. Conciliation and arbitration procedures were introduced. New laws protected employed women and children and regulated working conditions and wage rates. Labor departments were established, and a beginning was made in the field of workmen's compensation.

Much of this is progress on paper only. Still, industrial relations are reported to have improved in recent years, despite a few outstanding postwar strikes. Some of these were attributable to special circumstances or to the inflation. In many stable industries, terms of employment have been regulated through joint negotiations, conciliation, and wage boards.

The number and size of trade unions have greatly increased, partly as a consequence of replacing a somewhat repressive labor policy with one of encouraging and directing labor organizations.[17] Trade-union membership has often been only nominal, for laborers were slow to learn the necessity of joint effort for a common cause. They tended to confuse "mass action" with collective bargaining, and were easily susceptible to demagoguery. Personal and political rivalries within the labor movement also impeded progress. Trade-union leaders have become increasingly responsible, but they are sometimes faced with stiff competition from violent agitators like Tubal Uriah Buzz Butler of Trinidad.

The following handbill issued by him in the course of a water-front strike conducted by another, long-established union illustrates his techniques: [18]

" 'Touch not mine Anointed and do my Prophets no harm'

BUTLER GIVES NOTICE!

STATE OF EMERGENCY DECLARED.

SHALL THERE BE PEACE OR 'WAR'?

"MEMBERS OF THE BRITISH EMPIRE WORKERS PEASANTS AND RATE-PAYERS UNION in every industry in this Country are hereby notified that the Union's Executive have, in view of their insistent and universal cry for 'MORE PAY AND BETTER WORKING CONDITIONS,' declared that a State of Emergency now exists in the Union following upon the drafting of Demands upon Oil, Sugar, Transportation, Shipping, Housing and Planning and every known employer of Labour (including Government and the American authorities) in the country, for more pay and better working, living and dying conditions for members of our Union specifically, and everybody in the Colony generally. You are also notified that this Union shall in no way give support to strikes of the 'Unofficial Brand' and that they must wait for the order to Strike which can only come from Butler and Butler alone—in the name of the Executives of course. To those who are yet outside our Union we should like to say this: JOIN OUR UNION NOW or you are bound to be sorry if you don't. We do not believe in a closed shop. But we do most certainly believe in Justice and in Right, and it is not just and right that Caesar should enjoy the things that are Won at the Price of Liberty and the Life of Uriah Butler and his warrior-workers. So join with us now in the great fight now on. Share with us the heat and burden of 'D Day' and you shall enjoy as by Right the fruits of the Victory that God Himself shall give us. Yes, sir, Victory Shall be Ours. For GOD IS WITH US.

> Issued by U. Butler,
> President-General B.E.W.P. & R. Union"

The employers were not generally helpful. Too many gave only lip-service to the idea of collective bargaining. A rise in wage rates seemed to outrun the value of articles produced, and to be accompanied by a reduction in the number of hours worked, which made the income of the workers as low as before. One of the most tenacious social attitudes is the indifference to opportunities for earning more than enough to satisfy the most immediate wants. Steady work at reasonable or agreed-upon wage rates should gradually develop habits of regular attendance. This has occurred in some industries.

There are many common social attitudes which hinder economic and political development in the West Indies. Outsiders have been appalled at the lack of parental care for children, the comparatively degraded position of women, the dangerously unoccupied youth, the chronic indebtedness, and the absence of community spirit.

The British working in the Caribbean have been evolving a "social welfare" program to counteract these conditions.

Development and Welfare has emphasized the case work approach through trained social welfare workers instead of the ineffective (although locally popular) public institutions, such as orphanages. Through a variety of measures it encouraged community activities which would develop self-help, co-operation, and self-respect. Development and Welfare built on existing organizations and activities, encouraging voluntary welfare work wherever possible. It put much stress on "the service of youth," and in that connection aided the 4-H club movement for rural young people and youth councils in the towns.*

A most promising organization was Jamaica Welfare Ltd., which Development and Welfare encouraged and helped to finance. This organization was founded in 1937 through the initiative of Jamaican civic leaders to promote the economic and social improvement of lower-income groups. By agreement with the United Fruit Company a voluntary levy on each bunch of bananas exported financed the organization, until the war cut off exports. Then Development and Welfare took over its financing. Its administration was reorganized to include representatives of leading organizations interested in social welfare.

Jamaica Welfare Ltd. stimulated local communities to take group action for mutual aid; the "village betterment" program was an important part of its work. Among other activities, Jamaica Welfare has developed co-operatives, rural housing, and "cottage industry" services. The special contribution of Jamaica Welfare Ltd. has been to set in motion "business" projects which also serve "welfare" purposes. Thus it helped to meet the peculiar West Indian need for developing individual responsibility, local leadership, and

---

* Important penal reforms have also been taking place under Development and Welfare auspices.

a sense of community. The great success of the enterprise led Development and Welfare to help establish similar companies in Trinidad and Barbados.

The Caribbean Commission and Social Development

Development and Welfare concentrated chiefly on social measures in the British colonies; the Caribbean Commission, on the other hand, focused on economic development in trying to break the vicious circle of meager economic resources and low living standards.[19] The main exception was public health. The commission's outstanding contribution was to sponsor the establishment of the Caribbean Medical Center in Trinidad. The center began as a joint project for venereal disease control in connection with the military base.

The program was later broadened to benefit the local civilian population and to demonstrate the practicability of conducting a modern disease control program in the Caribbean. In addition to conducting surveys, treating patients, and educating the public, the center also undertook an intensive training program for local personnel in order that similar programs might be established in other colonies. The United States and Trinidad shared the original cost and the United States Public Health Service participated in the early stages, but the work was later carried on by Trinidad with financial assistance from Development and Welfare.

In all its activities, the Caribbean Commission has emphasized planned development in place of isolated and random development efforts. The activities of the individual governments have also exhibited an increasing awareness of the importance of co-ordinated, comprehensive programs. Implicit in the idea of planning is the premeditated determination of the results of a program. Constitutional limitations forbid the Caribbean Commission to consider directly the political development of the colonies.[20] The United States Co-Chairman delineated the Caribbean Commission's field of activity by stating that political developments in the British West Indies were "none of our affair, but our work is the affair of those who will guide the political destinies of this area, for idle hands, empty stomachs, and godless hearts can sustain no political system." [21] Indirectly the social and economic measures encouraged by the commission and undertaken by the governments have important political effects. That in varying degrees they tend to change the class structure and to alter the dependence of the colonies on the mother countries will be indicated in the following three chapters.

VI. Political Consequences of Social and Economic Measures: the Beneficiaries

DISCUSSION of development policies for the colonies has frequently concentrated on social and economic needs without explicit recognition of the political consequences. The desirability of increased productivity or of improved health, for example, is so generally accepted that attention is rarely focused on the changes in political influence which might result from working on one rather than the other. The social and economic measures undertaken in the Caribbean have tended to alter the distribution of power within the colonies, and between them and the outside world.

Although presumably adopted for the good of the colony as a whole, specific policies have in practice benefited particular groups. It is pertinent to inquire which groups have been so aided, in what manner they gained (e.g., in income, respect, or security), and whether or not such gains were at the expense of other groups either on the island or in the mother country.

Influence in the making of public decisions tends to be apportioned in accordance with the distribution of such values as those mentioned above (income, self-respect, security). Individuals living at a bare subsistence level, without status, and exposed to a variety of physical disabilities and low life expectancy, are political ciphers. Therefore, if further grants of autonomy to colonies are conditioned upon a more equal local distribution of political power than has existed in the Caribbean, those measures which make the mass of the people politically effective and do not unnecessarily enhance the influence of those already the most influential are preferable to those which have the opposite tendency.

In considering the effect of social and economic measures on the dependent status of a colony, the manner in which they were adopted and carried out is as important as their consequences for particular groups. The observation of any trend toward greater colonial independence in decision-making may start by determining who made the policies and who executed them, whether they are metropolitan or colonial in origin. If the mother country's goal is more colonial autonomy, the next question is whether or not the kinds of policies adopted and the method of their adoption and administration tend to increase the degree of colonial participation in government. This question involves not only the preparation of dependent peoples to assume new responsibilities but also the attitudes in the metropolitan country toward loosening colonial ties.

Still another political question concerns the increase or decrease in group violence within the colonies which may result from particular social and economic policies. A diminution in violent social strife is a measure of the growth of a constitutional consensus, vital to autonomy. The effect of social and economic development on existing or potential conflict between the colony and mother country is an equally relevant consideration.

Who were the beneficiaries? What did they gain? Who bore the cost? Some policies tend to raise the living standards of the poverty-stricken to a basic minimum, improving their lot greatly without changing their relative power position. Health measures fall in this category. For example, it was the lowest-income group whose productivity was most impaired by malnutrition and such diseases as tuberculosis and hookworm which preventive campaigns seek to control. Similarly, the extension of health clinics was intended to aid this class, which could not afford to patronize a private doctor even if one were available. Some measures have an egalitarian influence, spreading advantages which earlier accrued to a more limited group. The greater the facilities for higher education, for instance, the broader the base from which leaders can be recruited.[1]

However, the most important measures capable of providing a basis for greater autonomy—those increasing productivity—are likely by themselves to increase the power of the existing elite. The experience of other areas which have undergone extensive economic development indicates that such progress intensifies inequalities in income for a relatively long period.[2] A closer examination of economic policies in the Caribbean colonies will illustrate this possibility.

The Beneficiaries of Economic Development

Since industrial development is still in the planning stage in most of the colonies, little evidence is available now to show that a differential gain accompanies it. Industrialization in Puerto Rico, however, has proceeded far enough to draw some tentative conclusions. In the period 1940-44 the share of net income going to labor declined in the nonagricultural private economy, while the concentration of income was furthered by the wartime operations of private enterprise. The most striking increase in capital's share of net income was to be found in the liquor industry, but a similar trend occurred also in finance, transportation, trade, and real estate.[3]

Such a trend is to be expected, and is believed necessary to further development. Capital accumulation for additional industrialization must come from those who can afford to save. Furthermore, the incentive to greater productivity depends upon the expectation of a relative improvement in the economic position of the entrepreneur.

Economic measures increasing agricultural productivity in the Caribbean have tended to benefit a different group. The emphasis on agricultural reforms has been aimed at the smaller agriculturists. Unlike the large-scale producers, who require relatively little government assistance to improve their efficiency, the small farmers badly need aid to stimulate their very low productivity. They are harder on the soil and less able to cope with plant and animal diseases. As their efficiency increases, this class should gain in real income.

If British and American policy succeeds in getting the small farmers to co-operate in their producing activities, in buying, and in selling, the art of organization which they will have learned should make them a stronger group politically. Political growth should also ensue from the practical education they will receive through diverse government assistance to improve their agriculture. Since the small farmers are a more truly native group than the large estate owners and operators, their increased political influence should have important effects on the growth of autonomy sentiment.

Large-scale sugar producers have long been antagonistic to the spread of mixed farming and local food production, because they feared the diversion of local resources to less economically efficient uses than sugar cane as well as a reduction in their dependable labor supply. Actually these programs have not seriously interfered with sugar production.*

Because the scarcity of arable land demands specialization according to comparative advantage, improving the productivity of small farmers and non-cane-producers is only a partial answer to the economic problem of the Caribbean colonies. Despite many difficulties associated with the dom-

* For example, former sugar land used in Puerto Rico for other purposes had already been forced out of sugar production by the quota system.

inance of sugar production (which are aggravated, in colonial opinion, by sugar production's being controlled from the outside), government support for this industry seems essential to the economic survival of the Caribbean colonies.

The expanding and increasingly efficient sugar production in the British West Indies during the thirties was relied upon as the only means for absorbing the alarming increase in population. In Puerto Rico, too, the depression would have been much more calamitous without the expansion, subsidization, and price control in the sugar industry, for sugar proved to be an important factor of stability during that period.[4] While propping up this industry will not bring prosperity, it has avoided disastrous unemployment and distress due to population pressure.*

Supporting or raising sugar prices through market guarantees, tariff preferences, and other subsidies benefited the large sugar producers chiefly. They were also the chief beneficiaries of production control schemes.[5] The exception was in the Virgin Islands, where the more radical step of government operation partially replaced large-scale private producers who had long since retired from the industry.

Part of the benefits from government support of the sugar industry might trickle down in the form of higher payments to small cane farmers and higher wages to agricultural laborers, but their gains would not be in the same proportion to those of the large producers. These measures tend to spur producers to greater efficiency through mechanization, higher yielding cane, and similar means, which though of general benefit, would be partially at the expense of the agricultural laborers.[6]

* The general gain accruing to the majority of the Caribbean colonies was not shared by the small non-sugar-producing colonies of the British West Indies, which complained that favors to the sugar industry were actually disadvantageous to them.

The mechanism for carrying out the sugar quota system in the American territory involved apportioning quotas to particular parcels of land, which made them especially valuable to the property owners. Some government officials tried to arrange that subsidy payments compensating for crop restriction be used for the benefit of the industry as a whole. But the effort failed, and the payments were attached to the land, thus principally aiding large producers. While sugar growers received benefit payments for reducing production, many of the workers merely lost their jobs.

Both British and American policies have attempted to balance the large producers' gains by special treatment of others. For example, higher Agricultural Adjustment Act benefits were paid to small farmers in Puerto Rico than to large producers, and this has effected a reduction in "administration" cane.* Even so, in 1941, 72 per cent of the producers received less than eight per cent of the total benefits, while one per cent of the growers got 56 per cent.[7]

To pass on some advantage from the AAA to laborers, subsidized operators were required to conform to a minimum standard of wages. Commodity Credit Corporation support payments also were so apportioned as to pass on some benefits to labor. Both Federal and Insular regulations protected the Puerto Rican small cane farmers from exploitation by the sugar centrals by regulating the price to be paid for their cane when they brought it to be ground. When in 1947 the British West Indies secured a price increase for the bulk sale of their sugar to the British Government, part was required to be set aside for a welfare fund to benefit West Indian sugar labor.[8]

In Puerto Rico the small sugar cane farmers dominate numerically and in acreage, but the large companies produce

* Sugar cane grown by the interests owning the mills.

the highest percentage of cane, and four of the most powerful are American-owned. British-controlled companies are even more dominant in the British West Indies. Therefore, much of the benefits to the sugar industry provided at the expense of consumers and taxpayers simply changed hands within the metropolitan countries.

Regardless of the particular groups most benefited, these economic measures represent gains for the colony as a whole. By making more effective use of local resources they increase the productivity of the colony. The Puerto Rican hydro-electric power development is an outstanding example.

To the extent that economic measures meet the unemployment problem due to population pressure, there is a general improvement in living standards. Some measures will enable local enterprise to produce at least as cheaply and easily what was formerly imported. Thereby, the basis is laid for greater self-support, and dependence on the mother country is reduced.[9] To achieve this goal, local producers need protection from dumping by some large metropolitan competitors. Such protection would not bar legitimate trade. Neither would economic development as a whole necessarily reduce the international trade of the colonies. On the contrary, it could increase such exchange.[10]

Aside from these general advantages, economic measures inevitably help those most, and most directly, who have the skills and other qualifications to benefit by them.* In the majority of cases the beneficiaries are the propertied class and higher salariat, already the most powerful groups in the colonies.[11] Similarly, improvements in transportation facilities and other measures which lay a foundation for further economic development chiefly aid those who can afford to

* Thus the variety of Federal credit facilities available to rehabilitate Puerto Rican agriculture chiefly aided the growers.

use them. This unbalance in advantage cannot be immediately corrected. To attempt a greater equalization of income in the early stages of economic development would retard if it did not halt such progress.

Compensatory Social Measures

Metropolitan efforts to help the least privileged groups in the colonies antedated most of the economic measures undertaken in the Caribbean. According to some colonial specialists, such action put the cart before the horse. However, the colonies themselves could not afford to carry out the needed social reforms, either before or during the process of intensive economic development. Taken alone, economic development temporarily increases inequalities; it does not promote the egalitarian aim of British and American authorities to redistribute local political influence. Therefore social measures, which directly aid other groups than the elite, tend to compensate for the gains of the wealthy from economic development. This has been especially true of certain measures for labor and land tenure reform.

Labor Regulations

The labor reforms instituted in the colonies were expected to benefit laborers and to improve their status politically and in relation to their employers. In some cases, execution has fallen far short of intention or missed the mark completely. The establishment of minimum wages, though ostensibly a gain, has often been the least effective method of improving living standards among laborers.

Especially where wages were raised far above the ability of an industry to absorb the increase, there was a loss to labor. The Puerto Rican needlework industry was almost ruined by the application of the Federal Fair Labor Standards Act, until modifications were made to take into account local labor differences. Firms that could still make a profit in a non-sweated industry remained in business; the women could earn considerably more than before regulation began, but fewer were employed.

Minimum wages fixed for field workers in the Puerto Rican sugar industry were still insufficient to prevent constant indebtedness for such elementary needs as food. Experience in the Puerto Rican sugar industry demonstrated that higher wages meant shorter hours, so that workers' incomes were raised only slightly. In the British West Indies higher wages often resulted in the laborers' voluntarily working fewer hours. Competing pleasures outweighed their desire for more monetary income.[12] The unavoidable question continued to plague the planners—how to increase labor's productivity to compensate for higher wages. It must be answered if labor's position is to be improved.

The promotion of trade-union organization may be more effective in altering the political status of labor. Leaders of some labor organizations (not necessarily from the ranks of labor themselves) have already become politically powerful. In the elementary state of organization, laborers have shown themselves easily influenced by irresponsible demagogues. Jurisdictional conflicts have been common and violent, and unions have been used too frequently for the adjustment of individual grievances rather than those of the group as a whole.

Trade-union organization in the colonies may follow the unfortunate example of some metropolitan labor unions which are obstacles to economic development and models of despotism rather than of democratic self-government. Nevertheless, the opportunity to organize and to learn how to act collectively can be a valuable asset to a formerly submerged group, not only in preventing exploitation by employers and improving working conditions but also in influencing government action in its favor.* Labor organizations, if not too closely allied to political parties, as they are not in Puerto Rico, can provide an additional type of social segmentation and thus offset a tendency toward extreme nationalism.

Labor in the colonies would benefit most from more full-time jobs. Among the various methods of meeting the problem of unemployment, work relief has been the least effective and the most expensive. Wages high enough to satisfy workers were too high for the colonies to afford by themselves, and there was a perennial complaint from private business that they kept workers from other employment. At best a stopgap, work relief was much less satisfactory during a period of unemployment than carefully supervised migration of labor to areas temporarily in need of its services.[13] Ultimately, unemployment will have to be conquered by the expanded opportunities which economic development provides.

Land Settlement

As a partial solution of the problem of unemployment, especially to relieve pressure on urban employment, programs of land settlement have sometimes been advocated. The chief beneficiaries of such measures, however, have been small agriculturists, farm tenants, and landless agricultural workers rather than town laborers or the urban unemployed. Where land was simply divided up and its use uncontrolled, no group benefited. To disregard the quality of the land, its relation to the colonial economy, and the qualifications of

* Well-organized unions also benefit those who must deal with labor because they minimize the frustrations resulting from a chaotic labor movement where no one speaks with authority and undirected and sporadic strikes are chronic.

the settlers would bring a general loss.* Therefore, recent policies in American and British dependencies have coupled a redistribution of the use of the land with improvements in agricultural methods, rather than granting titles outright. In this fashion settlers may be satisfied and productive efficiency may still be preserved.

Not only has Puerto Rico made the boldest experiments in combining large-scale operation with small-scale holdings. It has also reached furthest down the scale to benefit the poorest portion of the population, the *agregados* (squatters), on house plots. Subsistence garden projects enabled under-employed workers to supplement their inadequate incomes by growing much of their own food. Puerto Rican land settlement activities have assisted other agricultural groups as well, including those operating medium-sized farms.[14]

Metropolitan policy for the British West Indies (in some contrast to local policy) has not emphasized land settlement. This was partly so because it was believed to compete with government efforts to aid existing peasant landholders. Although the British preferred to stress better agricultural methods instead of resettlement, they did urge moderate reforms to protect the rights of existing farm tenants. Redefining the rights of landlord and tenant in the West Indies to favor the latter would represent a loss in privilege to the large landholders. Yet land settlement which relieved large estates of responsibility for resident workers for whom they had little employment would not be to their disadvantage.[15]

In the Virgin Islands much of the land available for homesteading had not been cultivated for many years because of the barren soil. In Puerto Rico the redistribution of land

* There is not enough land for a universal apportionment of workable-sized plots. Furthermore, the peculiar nature of the sugar industry requires unified supervision over large areas in order to keep the mills continuously employed during the grinding season.

was also no hardship to large landholders until the enforcement of the Five Hundred Acre Law in 1941. Acreage restrictions connected with the quota system meant that much land was already withdrawn from production of large export crops.[16] The Puerto Rican Land Law of 1941, however, provided for the disposal of lands in excess of five hundred acres belonging to corporations, which in practice meant American-owned property. The Land Law was specific in declaring its purposes to be, among others, the abolition of "corporative latifundia" and the provision of means for *agregados* and slum dwellers to acquire land for homes.

Land, the most important economic asset in the Caribbean colonies, has been concentrated in the hands of a very few, who have had overwhelming political powers. Therefore, the redistribution of the land and the income from it has great political significance. Economic improvement which access to the land makes possible for the property-less is not their only gain. They also may obtain security of tenure.

Lord Olivier, an enthusiastic supporter of land settlement in Jamaica, declared that a harmonious mixed community required that the black people be economically and industrially liberated. The first condition should be that they have command of their food-supply by possessing their own land.[17] While outright ownership does not appear necessary to achieve such independence, re-settlers in the Caribbean colonies have progressed in status. With the right to use a piece of land they have moved another step away from the domination of the large landowners, characteristic of the days of slavery and serfdom.

Whether or not resettlement will actually improve the economic status of the intended beneficiaries depends on a number of factors. Among them is the provision of sufficient governmental supervision and agricultural education to insure an efficient use of the soil. Aid in constructing housing is also vital to the success of a project.[18] Provision of credit for capital equipment and co-operative arrangements for the use of equipment, for purchasing, and for marketing are all necessary to make new settlements economically successful. Guidance in supplementing income from the land is another requirement.

Very important to the success of a project are social welfare activities which will foster community co-operation and develop self-reliance. The lack of these services to aid land settlement caused earlier projects in some of the British colonies to fail. More recent Puerto Rican undertakings have provided for them. Since comprehensive land settlement projects are costly, there exists the danger, cited by the West India Royal Commission, that those who cannot be given the opportunity to enter a project will be utterly neglected. Much unfairness could be avoided if the improvements which accompany land settlement projects were made available to the neighboring population.

Experience with land reforms is still insufficient to permit major conclusions about the political effects, but some observations can be made. In many of the Caribbean colonies the desire to possess a piece of land is completely out of proportion to the economic justification. Land ownership may often provide only an illusion of security, especially because of heavy mortgaging or excessive subdivision among offspring. The high value put upon landownership indicates that the possessors feel a stake in the community, which is an important step toward accepting some responsibility for the social and economic development of the colony.[19]

Regardless of the economic and social success of existing land tenure reforms, some kind of well-rounded resettlement program seems necessary. Otherwise, the unequal distribution of wealth and income in the colonies will become even greater as a result of economic development. That families of very low income will actually gain from these programs will depend, as in the case of other policies intended to aid them, upon whether or not the potential benefits are soaked up by an increase in their offspring or whether the prospect and taste of higher living standards will be sufficient to start a decline in the birth rate.

Gains and Losses of Noneconomic Groups

Some noneconomic divisions of the population also benefit from particular policies for social and economic development. Women of the lower economic classes will have an opportunity to improve their status as a result of the expansion of handicraft and home industries. Public health measures for better prenatal care and protective factory legislation should also improve their position.[20] The elevation of the women to a position more nearly equal to that of the men is a democratic tendency which conforms to Anglo-American political beliefs. Similarly, children have been the object of special concern. Focusing attention on child welfare may lower the birth rate and the illegitimacy rate because of a new attitude toward the importance of the individual child.

Some policies have implications for the position of the church in relation to the state. Illustrative are British attempts to give the colonial governments greater control over the schools. However, Development and Welfare officials in the British West Indies have emphasized the necessity of supplementing rather than supplanting the activities of the churches in the field of social welfare.

With the expansion of governmental functions the colonial governments have become increasingly powerful in comparison to the municipal governments. Efficiency requires such an alteration in their relations. Because the municipal governments are more likely to be in the control of the most conservative elements, this shift toward centralization has important political consequences for the relative position of different economic classes.

Certain sections of the population have been left relatively untouched by the social and economic policies of recent years. White-collar workers at the lower end of the scale, shop clerks and equivalent groups, have not shared directly in the benefits of these policies, although attention had been directed to their problems by British investigators. Since they are components of the middle class, which has traditionally been the mainstay of democratic governments, overlooking their needs may weaken the effect of other efforts to democratize the colonies. Where little or no progress has taken place in industrialization, there has been no improvement in the economic position of the town labor groups, which could only profit indirectly by agricultural development if the latter caused a return to the soil of the recent influx of competing workers to the towns.

Economic Development and the Population Problem

Piecemeal additions to existing industries are unlikely to make an important dent in the urban unemployment problem. Some social scientists believe that a large-scale comprehensive program of industrialization appropriate for local conditions may under favorable circumstances be economically feasible and capable of supporting a dense population.[21] It should be synchronized with other devices to reduce the fertility rate proportionately to the lowered mortality rate. For the lag in the downward trend of the former as compared to the latter must diminish in the change from a colonial to a westernized economy. A population expert has observed:

The uses to which technologically backward regions have been put, and the nature of the policies of dominant nations toward them, have been such as to impede the transition to low fertility. Agricultural life has been promoted; native industries have faced the competition of established industries of technologically advanced countries. Industrialization and urbanization have developed very gradually. . . . There has been considerable protection of native customs, religions, and social organization, all of which foster the maintenance of higher fertility. In short, the technologically advanced nations have disseminated and imposed that part of their culture which reduces mortality, while withholding, or at least failing to foster the transfer of, that part of their culture out of which the rational control of fertility and the small-family pattern develop.[22]

The process of lowering the fertility rate could be aided by draining off some of the population. The Caribbean colonies appear to be one region where large-scale migration would assist in speeding up the rise in living standards and the change in the social milieu necessary to curb suicidal population growth.[23]

In none of these colonies has a policy of promoting large-scale permanent migration been adopted, and only Puerto Rico has entered upon a comprehensive industrialization program.[24] Puerto Rico was also the only territory with government-operated birth-control clinics, and even here political expediency has limited the funds available to an utterly inadequate sum. While a planned parenthood program is admittedly only a partial attack on the population problem and is unavailing by itself, there is evidence that where the service has been available it was effectively used to limit family size.[25]

To the extent that policy for these dependencies falls short of a full-fledged assault on the population problem, there will be insufficient social and economic progress to justify a high degree of autonomy for welfare reasons. Nevertheless, policies already adopted have contributed to that goal. Higher living standards are associated in Anglo-American policy with the granting of self-government. Several of the measures adopted in recent years in the Caribbean colonies have increased their productivity. Generally-diffused higher living standards will not necessarily result from the economic development of the colonies. Yet, without increased productivity, the level of living standards would not merely have remained stationary; it would have fallen.

Implications for Autonomy

Certain economic developments have brought important political gains to the colony as a whole. Developments in the means of communication and in the ideas and objects communicated have done this. Internally they have provided a necessary basis for an increased sense of community. Externally they have tended to break down the parochialism characteristic of the colonies. When reinforced by the regional activities of the Caribbean Commission, they have brought self-government closer.

Social developments have tended to even out the bulge in the population at the lower end of the income scale. Actual accretions to the typically small middle class may not have taken place as yet, for they are partly founded on attitudes rather than on economics. Nevertheless, more rural inhabitants have acquired the appurtenances of the middle class. The growth of this class will add weight to demands for greater self-government.*

* The effects of the newer colonial policy on social discontent will be discussed in Chapter VIII, where the problem of violence is examined.

Economic and social development may therefore be seen as mutually dependent for economic reasons, but also for political reasons. Since most economic development tends to enhance the power of those already situated at the top of the pyramid, social development can compensate by improving the lot of those at the bottom. Conversely, social measures must ultimately be supported by economic development if a reduction in dependence is to be achieved. If British and American social policies succeed in bringing about a more equal division of political power within the colonies while their economic policies increase the colonies' capacity for self-support, governmental autonomy will be justified.

Where the less privileged classes have improved their position through social and economic measures, their gain has been largely economic.* As will shortly be seen, the burden of social and economic development has been chiefly financial, and has fallen almost entirely on the metropolitan countries.† Besides metropolitan subsidies (including tariff preferences), another cost may be the increased price of colonial products due to improved labor conditions. Furthermore, there has been some local transfer of economic power, chiefly as a result of labor and land policies. Regarding the latter, however, the major losers were metropolitan landowners.‡

Private vs. Public Development

Before the shift in British and American colonial policy in the Caribbean, some economic and social development

---

* Changes in other aspects of the political power of the mass of the people will be discussed in later chapters, particularly those devoted to governmental changes.

† It was not, for example, the sharing of manpower or privileges.

‡ Changes in local taxation altering the incidence of development costs will be considered in Chapter VII.

had taken place under private auspices. For example, certain social services later assumed by the state, such as housing and medical aid, were provided for workers on many large estates. Roads, railroads, and other public improvements useful to large enterprises operating in the colonies were constructed directly by private companies. Expansion of state activity in these fields should mean the diminution of the influence which large property owners could formerly wield over those dependent upon them for social services.* Where private welfare services were formerly enjoyed chiefly by plantation workers, public welfare services have extended benefits to independent small agriculturists generally. State-supervised economic expansion should mean that the projects were the most appropriate to the general development of the colony. Different criteria would determine their choice from those which had dictated the choice of private corporations (namely, immediate profits).

In some cases the development in certain directions would not have occurred at all, if the state had not undertaken it or stimulated it.[26] Puerto Rican advocates of economic development through state activity have emphasized that this would substitute, for economic domination by outside private interests, control over the territory's economy by Puerto Ricans directly responsible to the people. There is no important evidence substantiating the fears of conservatives that public enterprise would frighten away further investment in the colonies by private enterprise. There is evidence that state activity has increased private investment. In the balance, it would appear that state-directed economic and social development represents a general gain for a colony when compared to earlier development under purely private auspices.

* However, public administration of these services might conceivably be so arbitrary or politics-ridden that the change would merely substitute dependence on one master for dependence on another.

Thus, the recent colonial policies in the Caribbean have brought new benefits to these territories, and they have aided different groups than were benefited formerly. In the laissez-faire era, development was mainly to the advantage of large investors and estate owners. Today's emphasis on governmental action includes a conscious effort to raise the economic status of the less privileged classes. The following chapter will show who is carrying the financial burden of these policies.

VII. Financing Social and Economic Development

GOVERNMENT support for social and economic development has varied in amount and in method. An analysis of the type and size of the subsidies and the source of the funds will suggest who ultimately pays for colonial economic and social development under various methods of financing.

British Development Subsidies

The outstanding departure in British and American colonial policy in recent years has been the great increase in direct loans and subsidies from the mother country. Most noteworthy was the British Government's novel policy in the Colonial Development and Welfare Act of 1940. This act provided for the expenditure from the British Exchequer of £5,500,000 annually over a period of ten years (including £500,000 annually for research). The total was increased to £120,000,000 for ten years under a 1945 act, which also provided that unassigned yearly balances would remain in the fund.*

A 1929 act permitted the British Government to loan or grant up to £1,000,000 annually for certain kinds of presumably self-liquidating capital projects for material development in the colonies.[1] Great Britain had also aided the colonies by guaranteeing colonial governmental loans.

---

* Partly because of the war, only a small proportion of the earlier Development and Welfare funds could actually be expended.

93

Another earlier subsidy to the British West Indies (which has greatly expanded in recent years) was the guaranteed payment for their major products of higher-than-world-market prices. Nevertheless, the traditional theory that the colonies should subsist for the most part on their own resources was not significantly modified until the 1940 act. For the first time funds could be spent on welfare activities such as education, the expenditures for which could not later be recovered, and for recurring expenditures. The emphasis on comprehensive plans for development was also novel. Unlike the British colonial grant-in-aid, the new type of financial assistance did not require detailed metropolitan control of the assisted colony's finances.[2]

In addition to grants, loans (often interest-free) have been made available through the fund. Although the act covers the whole British colonial empire, funds available to the West Indies have approximated the scale recommended originally by the West India Royal Commission when it proposed such a fund for the West Indies. Up to December 31, 1946, the total amount for all projects approved for the West Indies equaled £1,312,092 and the estimated expenditure for these schemes was £677,199 by March 31, 1946.[3]

The West India Royal Commission had argued that each of the colonies required large-scale financial assistance for a period of reconstruction, and that the metropolitan government should aim to bring about conditions for financial self-support. Since the Royal Commission's proposals for agricultural reforms and sugar benefits would still not meet certain crying needs, there was no way to avoid direct metropolitan expenditures to redress social evils and rehabilitate the West Indian people.

The Royal Commission believed that the West Indies were entitled to special consideration for several reasons: The inhabitants had long been cut off from their native African cultures, and their contact with prosperous white persons and propinquity to North America had stimulated a desire for social progress. The colonies were dispersed over a wide area, increasing administrative difficulties and costs. They were suffering from a particularly severe handicap—the glut of their primary products in the world market. Finally, there was a very serious deterioration in living standards from the already unsatisfactory level of the 1920's. The Royal Commission urged that recurring annual grants for a long period were much better than one large grant or an annually voted subsidy. The former would avoid the frequent miscarriage of reforms caused by lack of continuity. The latter met only immediate needs, and reforms sometimes failed to find financial support for their completion at the most critical period of their development.[4]

Following the recommendation, the office of Comptroller for Development and Welfare in the West Indies was established. The Comptroller and his staff advised and otherwise assisted colonial governments to work out long-term programs of social reform to be submitted to the Secretary of State for the Colonies. The Comptroller recommended grants to the Colonial Office for acceptable schemes and supervised their administration. He also kept the British Government informed of West Indian conditions.[5] As the local ten-year plans were reaching completion, in 1948, the office of Comptroller was eliminated. In its place the British Co-Chairman of the Caribbean Commission, who also headed the committee working for closer association of the West Indies, assisted the colonial governments with their development problems. He was advised by the functional specialists on the staff of the former Comptroller.

As indicated earlier, the Colonial Development Corporation helped to meet the criticism that the British policy insufficiently emphasized colonial economic development as against admittedly inadequate welfare expenditures. Unlike the Development and Welfare fund, this corporation was intended to be self-supporting through the commercial enterprises it aided or operated.

British emphasis on continuity and upon planned and integrated long-term programs of social and economic development is an important contribution to colonial policy. The British system avoids wasteful expenditure of public funds and promotes a fair distribution of benefits.[6] Balanced development should ensue from the long-term planning. Finally, the British method is psychologically valuable, because it gives colonial peoples a sense of security and hope for the future.

American Subsidies

Since the early thirties the United States has made lavish expenditures in Puerto Rico and less generous contributions to the Virgin Islands. On the Federal level, however, there is an absence of the continuity and integration of the more recently inaugurated British method.[7] With the exception of the ill-fated Puerto Rico Reconstruction Administration, the Virgin Islands Company, and the 1944 Virgin Islands public works appropriation, most of the Federal funds spent in these dependencies were allocated by individual Federal agencies, such as the Farm Security Administration or the Federal Works Agency, much as if these territories were part of the mainland.

The Puerto Rican Organic Act provided that, except for revenue legislation, laws passed by Congress were applicable to Puerto Rico unless the island was specifically exempted. However, Puerto Rico has not automatically received aid from every Federal agency operating on the continent. Governors have usually taken the initiative in securing assistance, and in some cases special Congressional action was necessary to extend aid, as in the case of the public health sections of the Federal Social Security Act. As in continental United States, local contributions of varying percentages were usually required to be combined with Federal relief and grant-in-aid funds before projects could be approved.

From the date when Puerto Rico first became an American territory to June 30, 1945, direct financial aid from the Federal Government amounted to about $580,000,000. Of this total, 94 per cent was appropriated in the 1934-44 decade.[8] This does not include loans from Federal agencies, which (from 1929, when they were first made, through June 30, 1944) totaled $82,600,000.[9]

The above figures do not include the large sums spent in veterans' benefits since the war. These were part of the total of $739,000,000 expended in Puerto Rico by the Federal Government from 1942 through 1946, a period of large wartime expenditures. This sum amounted to $74 for every man, woman, and child on the island. Grants-in-aid alone reached a record total of $74,000,000.[10]

During the dynamic period of the Puerto Rico Reconstruction Administration (1936-40), Federal expenditures for relief and public works were co-ordinated by this single agency, whose work was closely meshed in with the Insular Government. In addition to its economic projects, PRRA spent funds on research, training, and the building up of social institutions. According to Governor Tugwell, PRRA's disadvantage was that it combined all Puerto Rican relief in one conspicuous agency, and thus facilitated repudiation by an unsympathetic Congress. Since 1942 it has struggled along on its small revolving fund originally made available through Presidential allocation.[11]

Among the largest Federal expenditures in the Virgin Islands were "emergency" relief allocations by the Public Works Administration and the Works Progress Administra-

tion. These funds helped to meet grave social problems arising from unemployment and hopeless destitution; they contributed substantially to social and economic rehabilitation as
well. Still, such measures could not eradicate the accumulated
social ills of the dependency or produce a prosperous industry and fiscal self-support. More permanent and continuous
provision was necessary. The Virgin Islands needed the aid
of many Federal functional agencies which had not extended
their work to the Virgin Islands. This deficiency has been met
in part by the $10,000,000 public works appropriation of
1944. Although very slow to materialize, these funds
promised to meet some of the dependency's most pressing
problems.

Another large Federal expenditure was for the capital and
operating expenses of the Virgin Islands Company. By Congressional enactment the company was required to pay annual
sums to the local treasury in lieu of taxes. Any profits made
by the company were to be deposited in the United States
Treasury. For several years it operated at a loss.

Important among Federal subsidies to the Virgin Islands
was an annual contribution covering the deficits incurred by
the municipalities of St. Thomas and St. John and of St.
Croix. Economic improvement in St. Thomas due to the war,
especially the rum industry's new prosperity, permitted this
municipality to operate without Federal subsidy in 1942. In
1948, however, Congress voted a deficiency appropriation of
$500,000 for the whole dependency and authorized it to
borrow $100,000 from the Reconstruction Finance Corpora-
tion. In addition to the deficit contributions, the Federal Government also paid for the central administration of the territory, consisting of Federal officers (the majority of whom
were Virgin Islanders).[12]

The Virgin Islands have long been seeking the same privilege accorded Puerto Rico—of receiving all Federal internal

revenue collected on local products sold in the United States, Alaska, and Hawaii. The United States Tariff Commission regarded this as a direct subsidy to Puerto Rico from the Federal Government and added it to other direct contributions to reach the total given above. The amount assumed spectacular proportions during World War II, when the curtailment of the mainland liquor industry provided a rum tax windfall for Puerto Rico.[13]

The Insular Government's economic program was framed to take advantage of this temporary good fortune. Since Virgin Islands rum sales soared proportionally, that territory was more eager than ever to obtain the internal revenue collected on its rum, for which it would have gladly traded the annual deficit contribution voted by Congress. The source of the rum funds has been the subject of much discussion. Some American officials maintained that they were a gratuity from American rum consumers to Puerto Rico. However, the real controversy centered not on the source but on the right to control their expenditure.

In addition to the remittance of internal revenue collected on Puerto Rican products, Puerto Rico also received United States customs fees collected on foreign goods entering Puerto Rico. In the fiscal year 1941-42, United States customs collected and paid to Puerto Rico amounted to about $2,085,000 and United States internal revenue to $13,939,989. That year, the receipts from internal revenue constituted about 37 per cent of the general revenues, while customs receipts equaled about five per cent.[14] The percentages varied considerably during different periods of the war.

Besides the Federal remittances to Puerto Rico, listed above, that territory received an indirect subsidy in another form. Individuals in Puerto Rico deriving half their income from a local trade or profession, or receiving all their income from an insular source, were exempted from the Federal income tax.[15] Puerto Ricans were also exempted from paying Federal excise taxes on articles consumed locally. Whether or not these indirect subsidies were "Federal money," they would not have been available to a state. It has been estimated that in the fiscal year of 1943 $33,000,000 out of approximately $41,500,000 of general revenues would have been turned over to the Federal Treasury had Puerto Rico been a state.[16] In the Virgin Islands, Federal income taxes are collected and retained locally. In 1942 the income taxes amounted to about $403,890, which was approximately one-half the total Virgin Islands Government income.[17] Federal excise taxes and inheritance taxes did not apply.

American Tariff Arrangements

A very important indirect subsidy to the Puerto Rican sugar industry (as well as to minor Puerto Rican products) results from Puerto Rico's assimilation into the United States tariff system. Without the privilege of entering the American market duty-free, it is doubtful that the Puerto Rican sugar industry could survive in competition with lower-cost areas. That this tariff assimilation was an unmixed blessing, or a blessing at all, has not been admitted on all sides. Many Puerto Rican leaders have assailed it in the past. A typical argument was that made by Luis Muñoz Marín long before he established the Popular Democratic Party:

> American dollars paid to the peons are so many tokens, redeemable in the American market exclusively at tariff-inflated prices. The same tariff that protects the prices of sugar and tobacco, controlled by the few, sky-rockets the prices of commodities that must be consumed by all.[18]

Careful consideration of the tariff arrangement led the United States Tariff Commission to this reasonable conclusion:

Tariff assimilation of Puerto Rico by the United States has imposed burdens and conferred benefits on various interests in both the island and the United States. Nevertheless, the Puerto Rican economy has clearly gained much more than it has lost by the tariff arrangement, whereas the economy of continental United States has lost more than it has gained. Unfortunately, there are no satisfactory indexes for arriving at quantitative estimates of the respective gains and losses.[19]

According to the Tariff Commission, duties waived by the United States represented both fiscal losses to the United States Treasury and gains for the Puerto Rican economy to a much greater degree than in the reverse case of duties waived by Puerto Rico on imports from the United States. This was principally because of the importance of sugar and other highly protected articles among Puerto Rican shipments to the United States.

Free entry was coupled with high prices. Puerto Rico was encouraged to produce almost exclusively for the United States market where the best prices were paid. Because of the tariff on foreign goods, however, Puerto Rico has virtually been compelled to get most of its imports from the United States. But many of these have been purchased at no higher cost than if Puerto Rico could have imported them duty-free from any source. For most of the rest, the prices have not exceeded world levels by the full amounts of the United States duties. Many of Puerto Rico's principal imports from the United States were among those the United States exported all over the world in competition with similar articles produced in what critics of the tariff arrangement called "cheap foreign markets."

Caribbean countries not maintaining preferential trade relations with other countries generally obtained at least half their imports from the United States regardless of the small proportion of their total exports sold to the United States. A chief exception was rice, for which Puerto Rico has normally paid a much higher price than if it came from the Orient. In addition, a number of other Puerto Rican imports, such as meat, dairy products, dried peas and beans, most textiles, and salted and cured fish, have been much higher priced because of United States duties, although few were above the world price by the full amount of the duty.[20] The Tariff Commission believed that even with the most liberal estimates for "price premiums" paid by Puerto Ricans on all varieties of imports from the United States, the aggregate could not equal more than a small fraction of the "price premiums" received on sales to the United States.

Concerning the claim that the real beneficiaries from tariff assimilation were nonresident owners of Puerto Rican properties, the Tariff Commission argued that the net outward payments to nonresident owners of sugar properties did not offset the economic benefits which the island derived. The total payments of dividends and interest to all nonresidents (which included interest on government obligations) were $9,000,000 in 1942 and $5,100,000 in 1943, sums not large compared with the island's receipts of Federal excise taxes, which were about $14,000,000 in 1942 and 1943.[21]

The Virgin Islands have had a different tariff arrangement. Free trade existed between them and the mainland, but foreign goods coming into the Virgin Islands paid only a local customs duty, which was a flat six per cent.[22] In the middle thirties (between the deepest part of the depression and the war) the percentage of the total Virgin Islands exports which went to the mainland was higher than the percentage of the total imports which came from the United States.* Since the

---

* Thus, there was no question raised about "price premiums" on Virgin Islands imports. The preference system clearly favored the islands.

chief export was highly protected sugar, this tariff subsidy to the Virgin Islands was a very important benefit. While their trade is not channeled by tariff assimilation, the Virgin Islands nevertheless obtained the major part of their imports from the continent.

British Tariff Preferences

Indirect subsidies to the British West Indies from Great Britain have been neither so numerous nor so complicated. The only important indirect subsidy was preferential tariff treatment.[23] In contrast to the free trade arrangements which existed between the United States and its Caribbean dependencies, the British West Indies and the United Kingdom exchanged preferences on their respective products. These preferences came to form part of a reciprocal system for the whole empire following the Ottawa Agreements. The preferences were commonly expressed as percentages of the general tariff on foreign imports, and the general tariffs were raised proportionately; duties on imperial products were not lowered. Sugar, citrus fruits, and bananas from the West Indies have been especially favored by such preferences. Canada had given preferential treatment to sugar and bananas long before there was an imperial preference system.[24]

The desperate condition of the West Indian cocoa industry could not be relieved in this fashion, because empire production of cocoa greatly exceeded empire consumption. Much pressure has been exerted on the British Government to increase preferences for West Indian exports whose principal market is the United Kingdom. The West India Royal Commission concluded that in most cases this was not feasible, partly because of the Anglo-American Trade Agreement of 1938.

In the case of sugar, however, the West India Royal Commission had proposed even larger preferences than existed. It was the third West Indies commission to recommend continued or increased preferences for West Indian sugar. In 1922 the Wood Commission had urged continuance of preferences given after World War I. The commission had recommended this aid to the sugar industry particularly because it would support the "European element" in the West Indies, whose preservation the commission regarded as essential to stability and progress.[25]

In 1930 the Olivier Commission had proposed three short-run expedients: increased preferences, a guaranteed price, and a single British purchasing agent. Lord Olivier's commission believed that long-term solutions through international action would be necessary to remove the disturbing factors of high tariffs and subsidies. Following this report, an increased supplementary preference was granted to colonial producers in 1934. It resulted in a substantial expansion of sugar production.*

In 1939 the West India Royal Commission recommended that the colonial preference system be liberalized and made more flexible. It hoped thereby to raise and stabilize prices. Thus sugar producers in the West Indies not only would receive a more economic return on their capital but would be able to pay better wages to laborers and higher prices to cane farmers. The West India Royal Commission linked this recommendation with a plea to increase the quota for West Indian sugar. Thus it recognized that under present-day quota restrictions, tariff protection and preferences may be of little benefit to the producers when quotas set absolute limits to production.

Tariff arrangements between the dependencies and the mother country and between the mother country and other

* The other recommendations were not accepted at the time, but wartime conditions brought them into effect.

states have been an effective obstacle to a proposed customs union among all the Caribbean colonies. The American and British governments, through the instrumentality of the Caribbean Commission, failed to favor such a union. However, they also opposed additional trade barriers and advocated a reduction in duties on imported foodstuffs. Furthermore, they disapproved of any further preferential tariff arrangements within the Caribbean.[26]

Whether or not there is free trade between the colony and mother country, as in the American dependencies, or merely preferential assistance, as in the British West Indies, it is the metropolitan consumers who ultimately bear the burden. They must pay higher prices for the protected products, and, in their role of taxpayer, they pay another fraction of the cost, because the loss in customs duties must be balanced by other levies. Since sugar production in both the American and British dependencies would be ruined without such subsidies, metropolitan consumers may still have an interest in making the contribution.

Military Expenditures

Military expenditures made in some of the Caribbean colonies have sometimes been counted as additional financial contributions. In comparison to other governmental expenditures they were enormous during World War II. The Caribbean dependencies, because of their proximity to the Panama Canal, can expect a continuing moderate inflow of money for supplying goods and services to the military establishments. Nevertheless, since these expenditures have been made without reference to specific colonial policies and since the United States made them in both American and British dependencies, they are not particularly significant in determining who is paying for social and economic development. Heavy military expenditures were temporary, and the contributions they made toward social and economic development were subordinate to their main purpose of metropolitan defense. These advantages also tended to be offset in part at least by the disruptions in the social life of the community accompanying military installations.[27]

Local Revenues

Many plans for social and economic development have called for expenditure of colonial funds in addition to or in place of metropolitan subsidies. Where metropolitan subsidies were necessary, policy-makers in the mother country usually wished assurance that the local government was doing everything in its power to finance measures to meet its own needs. No matter how good this policy is in principle, it is pertinent to inquire what effect the method of raising local funds had on the objectives of the economic or social program in question.

In Puerto Rico the chief local source of revenue has been the income tax. The rates were lower than on the mainland, but had been substantially increased and collections were improved during the war. Beverage taxes also yielded considerable revenue. Here again, the rate was lower than on the continent. Excise taxes have assumed important proportions. They were levied not only on luxuries such as jewelry and radios and semiluxuries such as cigarettes and gasoline, but also on sugar, matches, kerosene, and fuel oil. Another large source has been the general insular property tax, which was a basic one per cent, upon which municipalities could add as surtax another one per cent. Several million dollars have been raised through the national lottery, a source which was also available to the Virgin Islands.

At Federal instigation, important tax reforms took place in the Virgin Islands during the thirties. They were intended to increase local revenues and eliminate regressive features in the local tax system. The largest yielding tax has been the federally collected income tax, deposited in the local treasuries. There was also a uniform real property tax of 1.25 per cent, fixed by Congress in 1936. Adoption of this tax resulted in repeal of a St. Thomas tax based on use rather than value. It also repealed a particularly unsound tax in St. Croix which taxed sugar land in cultivation 300 per cent higher than acreage not in use, and it eliminated a series of taxes on personal property in St. Croix. Both municipalities have had a gasoline tax, and small luxury taxes were imposed in St. Croix.

Despite efforts of the governors, the St. Thomas legislature refused to impose a tax on rum. There has also been a "burgher's brief," which is a license to carry on a business. The lottery, pilotage fees, and customs duties (a flat six per cent on foreign imports) collected in St. Thomas complete the list of significant revenue sources.[28] A very burdensome and discriminatory export tax on sugar, originally imposed by Congress at the rate of eight dollars a ton, was repealed by the local legislature in 1942, not long after Congress finally gave it permission to do so.

For local revenues the British West Indies relied principally on indirect taxes, particularly customs duties. The West India Royal Commission reported that 80 per cent of the indirect taxes came from such duties. Preference was given to goods from British Empire countries, which were usually taxed at between one- and two-thirds of the duty on foreign imports. None of the most commonly used imported food-stuffs nor any principal imports were exempted from customs duties. The tax systems in the British West Indies have thus been regressive; the tax burden has fallen heavily upon the mass of the people, and thus further lowered their standard of living.

The West India Royal Commission suggested that financial aid from the British Government should be conditioned upon certain local tax reforms. Although the tax base was admittedly smaller than in the United Kingdom, the Royal Commission believed that local taxes could be increased to some level considerably closer to the rates in the United Kingdom. Regarding customs duties, the Royal Commission pointed out that although the per capita annual contribution in import duties was high compared to the standard of living, the figure was much lower than the average in the United Kingdom. Thus any substantial reduction of existing West Indian rates was difficult to justify in view of the higher United Kingdom rate. Nevertheless, the Royal Commission opposed any material increase in tariffs which would fall on the necessities of life.[29]

Since the West India Royal Commission reported, the tax systems of the West Indian colonies have been somewhat modified to accord more closely with the ability to pay. Thus in British Guiana the governor's program for social reforms included steep increases in direct taxes partially offset by decreases in indirect taxation. Specific taxation of capital and of profits going out of the colony, and other new sources were looked to in order to pay for the "very expensive ideal" of social security. In 1943 the Trinidad Government compelled all trades and businesses in Trinidad legally resident in the United Kingdom to pay the local excess profits tax, while giving relief from double taxation.[30]

Jamaica has been in more difficult financial straits than the other important West Indies governments. Early attempts to raise more revenue increased excise duties. Later a substantial increase in the company income tax was sought and personal allowances for income taxes were reduced. The

Benham Committee's report on economic policy for Jamaica recommended a new tax to meet the increased demands for government expenditures along social and economic lines.[31] It would add to the existing income tax a flat 10 per cent on the income of all those receiving more than two pounds a week. The committee believed that this section of the population could most easily carry the burden, and pointed out that many thousands in this category had up to then paid no income tax at all.

The committee also proposed changes in the excise and import taxes. However, it urged that no further restrictions be placed on imports, which would result in higher prices for goods of general consumption. It further recommended that as soon as public finances permitted, duties on foodstuffs should be lowered. Widespread opposition to the report prevented adoption of the proposed taxes, but it served to call attention to the need for heavier taxes on the middle class.

West Indian tax systems have also interested Development and Welfare, which conducted a tax investigation in 1944, advised by an official from the United Kingdom Internal Revenue Department. The British Government has been pressing for more equitable, scientific, and flexible taxation in the colonies generally. In particular it has emphasized the development of direct taxation, and has provided a model ordinance as a basis for modern colonial income tax systems.

The foregoing description of the sources of funds for economic and social development indicates that the money came chiefly from the pockets of metropolitan taxpayers and consumers and that the contributions were very extensive. A definite development policy accepted by Parliament and by the unified administration of the Colonial Office would seem to insure that British contributors would get their money's worth. In terms of effective planning, the Puerto Rican Government has the outstanding record, which gives assurance that the expenditure of subsidies within the control of the local government will not be wasted. However, the clear sense of direction and integrated administration of the Puerto Rican Government's program have had no counterpart on the Federal level. The lack of a settled legislative policy regarding colonial development and of administrative co-ordination have been obstacles to economical spending for colonial development.

In none of the dependencies have taxes been high compared with metropolitan rates, but most observers believe that they cannot be greatly increased without defeating the social purposes for which they were intended. Not only were rates low but there was also a general tendency in many colonies to rely for local revenues on regressive taxes. This system is gradually changing under metropolitan pressure.

The combination of subsidies in the American dependencies has been so intricate that the full amount of subsidization has not usually been apparent and was subject to no centralized control.* Some argue, especially in Puerto Rico, that unregulated kinds of subsidies help to compensate through local budgetary freedom for the lack of self-government or for full Congressional representation. They say such subsidies are no more than equitable in view of the value of Puerto Rico to the United States.

Others (in the United States) declare that regardless of possible exploitation in the past, Puerto Rico is now more indebted to the United States than the United States is to Puerto Rico. They are, of course, talking about different kinds of value. In recent years the chief controversy has been less

* Control here refers to co-ordinated administrative supervision over the use of funds already made available by legislative decision. Minute legislative interference with colonial administration would be antithetical to the prevalent philosophy regarding home rule. Administrative control, on the other hand, insures that the general will of the metropolitan government regarding aid to colonial development will be fulfilled.

over the source than over the kinds of things accomplished with the subsidies. Thus, Popular party leaders and Governor Tugwell sought control over funds for long-term development toward greater self-support, in place of stopgap expenditures primarily of a relief nature.

This conflict over ways of spending public money is part of the larger question: What is the relation between particular methods of social and economic development and the ultimate achievement of self-government?

VIII. The Effects of Social and Economic Development on Autonomy

PREVIOUS chapters have considered the social and economic measures which were taken in the Caribbean colonies of the United States and Great Britain, how the benefits were distributed, and at whose expense they were carried out. Discussion of their political effects has concentrated chiefly on changes in the political structure within the colonies. It is now pertinent to inquire further what effect these measures might have on the dependent status of various colonial· governments.

Where development activities have tended to render a colony more economically self-supporting, the effect has already been noted as a step in justifying the demand for greater self-government.* Particular methods of determining policy and carrying it out also affect dependent status. Who took the initiative in inaugurating individual measures? How was co-operation secured? Who was responsible for administering the measures? Equally relevant questions may be asked about the differential effect upon autonomy when the mother country directed social and economic development in varying ways. For example, some measures depended primarily on

* The goal of self-support should be distinguished from self-sufficiency. Self-sufficiency might be established by such protective means that most necessities were locally produced at too high a cost to justify the effort when compared to that obtaining when they were imported. Liberal policy aims at the less artificial state of self-support. It would provide the government assistance temporarily necessary to enable the colony to produce at home what it later could produce on a competitive basis without aid.

financial aid. Others involved educating and instructing colonial peoples to enable them to carry out programs by themselves.

In order to guide development, metropolitan governments sometimes secured changes in rules within the colonies governing relationships between groups. The outstanding case of this method was metropolitan-stimulated labor reforms. The reduction or prevention of civil disorder is another continuing objective of colonial policy. It has been used as one standard in determining fitness for greater governmental autonomy. What effect may social and economic development have on the degree of violence within a colony? All the above questions are closely related to constitutional changes in the dependent status of the colonies.

Source of Initiative

The mother country has taken the initiative for inaugurating many social and economic measures in both British and American dependencies, especially in such fields as public health and labor standards. Nevertheless, some colonial governments (especially Puerto Rico's) have taken independent steps toward raising living standards in their own areas and improving their economic resources. The development of secondary industries is one field in which the colonies have assumed some initiative; land settlement is another. Even taking account of these local actions, however, recent development in the British West Indies is largely the result of the new colonial policy of the British Government. In the American dependencies, too, development was stimulated chiefly by the New Deal. In Puerto Rico, however, it gathered speed after the original impetus from the United States had died down.

More metropolitan direction has been inevitable because

of the recent trends in colonial development. Lord Hailey was a philosophical spokesman for the new British colonial policy inaugurated under the Conservatives.¹ In advocating a "trusteeship" doctrine of positive state action to raise living standards in the colonies, he frankly pointed out the implications for central direction. The new approach demanded a common policy for the colonial empire, systematic planning, and the use of specialist agencies. Implementation of these necessarily involved much closer guidance by the Colonial Office.²

More central direction was also advocated by the Labor Party spokesman for a socialist colonial policy, Arthur Creech Jones.* He complained that in the past generous and liberal expressions of policy from London had been ineffective when too much discretion was left to the man on the spot. Metropolitan officials in the colonies did not have the necessary means to resist local pressures. Furthermore, too much initiative had been left to private enterprise, speculators, and groups lacking a sense of duty toward the dependent peoples.³

The Colonial Development and Welfare Act required that the Colonial Office give final approval to projects assisted under this legislation.⁴ In carrying out the terms of the act, West Indian Development and Welfare adopted procedures which aimed to leave as broad a field as possible open to local initiative.† Whether or not the original suggestion or recommendation for a particular measure came from colonial authorities or from the Comptroller's Office, there was full consultation with all interested groups, and favorable public reactions were sought before action was taken. In certain cases Development and Welfare surveyed a problem and urged

---

* Appointed Secretary of State for the Colonies in 1946.

† Similarly, the Colonial Office has emphasized that the more recently established Colonial Development Corporation will be required to work in the closest co-operation with colonial governments.

a particular course of action. In any case, the Comptroller emphasized that the West Indian peoples should do as much of their own planning and execution as possible.[5]

Prior to the Labor administration, Secretary of State for the Colonies Stanley enunciated the following policy in explaining the creation of the office of Adviser on Development Planning: There would be no detailed planning on the part of the United Kingdom, for it was wrong to impose a "prefabricated heaven" from London. Nevertheless, metropolitan authorities would have to insure that contracts were properly drawn up, that proper steps were taken to get estimates, and that technical advice had been taken. Over-all supervision was necessary for a sound and proper division of funds among colonies; it was necessary for the proper allocation to various projects within each colony, in order to keep a proper balance between development and welfare. Metropolitan officials were also expected to see that experience gained from development in one colony would be available to others.[6] Later a Colonial Economic and Development Council was established for co-ordinated planning of development in the colonies as a whole.

The kind of metropolitan initiative involved in the Development and Welfare program was in contrast to the earlier British methods of metropolitan influence, which it supplemented. Traditionally, changes in local policy came through such means as the Colonial Office circular dispatch recommending a policy to colonial governors.[7] Conferences between particular colonial governors and the Colonial Office were another way to influence local policy. So also were white papers resulting from investigations of particular problems or particular colonies, such as those of the West India Royal Commission and the Commission on Higher Education in the Colonies. Leadership in the Development and Welfare program was different because it was made continuously effective by subsidies and by gentle pressure from the Comptroller for the West Indies.

While the mother country was embarking on its development and welfare colonial policy and partly because of this policy, local initiative was increasing in the British West Indies. For instance, Trinidad made intensive inquiries into agricultural policy, health, and education, with the intention of instituting important reforms. Perhaps the most striking example of local initiative was the establishment of Jamaica Welfare Ltd. Although it has since required official aid from Development and Welfare, observers believe that Jamaica Welfare has retained the local initiative and enthusiasm which made it such a valuable example to other colonies.[8] Under the development and welfare policy, initiative in both the mother country and the colonies has grown because both the metropolitan and colonial governments increasingly favored state activity in social and economic fields.

Writing in the early thirties about the Virgin Islands, Luther Evans observed that a cry in favor of reform starting at home "would not get to first base; yet a cry against reform being forced on the Islands from above is always good for a home run."[9] Since this remark was made, a nascent local interest in improving social conditions has become evident. Nevertheless, there is not yet any remarkable instance of a social or economic measure spontaneously produced under local auspices in the Virgin Islands.

For Puerto Rico, American colonial policy has been so indefinite and was of such unco-ordinated authorship that initiative for particular measures is especially difficult to trace. Congress, in which ultimate responsibility rests, has on the whole played a negative role. The exception was its extension of certain Federal agencies' activities to Puerto Rico. These agencies have taken some part in instituting social and economic policies for Puerto Rico. The Department of the

Interior and, in special cases, the President have also given impetus to some measures.

However, as in the British West Indies, it was the governor who was the principal initiator of policy. Determining the need for aid from Federal agencies, he has sought an extension of their functions to Puerto Rico. Or, as in the case of the Puerto Rico Reconstruction Administration, he has worked for the establishment of special agencies. Through his budget messages and other means for influencing the Puerto Rican Legislature (such as his appointing power), the governor has persuaded the local lawmaking authorities to adopt particular policies for social and economic development. During Governor Tugwell's administration an unusual combination was formed between the governor and the majority party. They found themselves much in agreement on the need for initiating new social and economic measures, in opposition to some powerful local groups and to many Congressmen. Since Governor Tugwell's appointed successor was a leader of this party, continuing co-operation between the executive and legislature was facilitated.

Some Puerto Rican social and economic measures have originated locally, such as birth control legislation, which by its very nature could not have been instituted by mainland authorities. Local leaders in Puerto Rico and in some British colonies have pushed land settlement reforms more rapidly than they would have been promoted by metropolitan authorities. In all cases metropolitan officials have sought to apply the brake to simple subdivision of land, and to favor plans which would permit continued large-scale operation for efficiency's sake.

In both British and American possessions metropolitan initiative has usually been necessary for policies of a long-range character which require technical improvements and involve fundamental changes in methods. Thus the impetus for agricultural, fisheries, and forestry development has come largely from the mother countries. The emphasis on preventive health measures has also been metropolitan. On the other hand, policies promising immediate benefits, such as more schools and hospitals and the encouragement of tourism, are more likely to find a local origin. Many of the colonial governments have been inclined to stress the social reforms which are most popular with the electorate, such as old-age pensions and relief. They are less interested in reforms involving a basic reconstruction of the economy and of social institutions.[10]

No discussion of the sources of social and economic policy in the Caribbean colonies would be complete without mention of the Caribbean Commission. This organization exists primarily for the co-ordination of policy and for exchange and co-operation in ideas and facilities between the colonies. Nevertheless, it has played a more positive role in promoting social and economic plans than these functions might suggest. Improvements in communications and the development of fisheries, for example, received their impetus from this body.

Securing Co-operation

Not only has the Caribbean Commission taken the initiative in the formulation of some policies. It has also been an important instrument in obtaining co-operation from local authorities in carrying out policies which originated in the mother countries. For example, at its West Indian Conferences, delegates from the colonies come together with metropolitan representatives to discuss programs and plan for their execution. Since the commission's membership was broadened to include local officials it has become an even more important liaison body between metropolitan and colonial governments.[11]

Conferences of specialists in particular fields have been organized not only by the Caribbean Commission but also by Development and Welfare for the British West Indies. Conferences of this type are an effective way to achieve co-operation and a unified policy. They tend to gain acceptance for metropolitan ideas of social and economic development and help to bring up to an established standard those colonies which are less progressive than their neighbors.

Both American and British authorities have employed other public relations techniques to explain their policies, and have used the schools, radio, and other communication channels for such educational purposes. Similar techniques have featured execution of these policies. The rural health unit, for example, de-emphasized older public health procedures which depended principally on enforcement. Instead, it employed service, demonstration, and persuasion in order to stimulate health consciousness. Popular representatives on the Development Committees in the British colonies participated in formulating the ten-year development plans, thus facilitating local acceptance of the programs.

The groundwork for easier reception of ideas from the metropolitan country is laid in part by unofficial or semiofficial organizations from the mother country. This is one function of the British Council, which propagates knowledge and appreciation of British culture, and the Rockefeller Foundation, which emphasizes public health. The use of existing local agencies wherever possible also favors co-operation, and the British have followed this practice. Groups already functioning in the colonies, such as Jamaica Welfare, 4-H clubs, and Youth Committees, have participated in the Development and Welfare program.

The most potent means for securing colonial co-operation has been the offer of financial assistance which is conditioned upon certain local action, often involving local contributions to add to metropolitan subsidies. For instance, the Colonial Development and Welfare Act of 1940 included a provision that no colony could receive funds unless it had adequate trade-union legislation. In this connection, the International Labor Office has warned against indiscriminate attachment of social welfare requirements to loans and development credits. Standards set may be artificially high for local application or they may be resented locally as a new form of imperialism.[12] Where no subsidies are involved, patience with local legislators is, of course, especially necessary.[13]

The degree of co-operation which metropolitan authorities can easily elicit in a colony is partly dependent upon the composition and powers of the colonial legislature.* In Puerto Rico, where the House and Senate have large powers, social and economic policies have eventually been accepted when the majority party agreed with the governor and was sufficiently strong. However, legislative results could vary considerably from the intentions of the policy designers. At least until universal suffrage was established in the Virgin Islands under the 1936 Organic Act, vested interests represented in the legislatures there made any social advances very difficult if not impossible.†

Reforms in Bermuda and the Bahamas are still very hard to realize. Their legislatures are powerful and represent only the small wealthy group. Thus, Bermuda did not apply for financial assistance under the Colonial Development Act, which required certain minimum standards of labor legislation, and the Bahamas' participation was confined to some general West Indian projects not involving local labor.[14]

---

* For instance, the Puerto Rican Senate's confirming powers for administrative appointments even to minor offices was a special hindrance to the realization of many gubernatorial aims.

† The appointment in 1946 of a prominent and highly regarded Negro leader, Judge William B. Hastie, to the governorship of the Virgin Islands greatly improved the likelihood of co-operation.

Experience in these territories indicates that as colonies gain greater autonomy, metropolitan officials will need to exhibit much more finesse in securing local acceptance of their metropolitan policies than was earlier required.

Nevertheless, in the opinion of the British Colonial Secretary, Arthur Creech Jones, the good will and co-operation of the colonial peoples necessary to the success of social and economic policies depends upon some devolution of responsibility. Speaking of these peoples as willing partners, he said:

> In all the planning they should be consulted; their representative organs should be developed; responsibility must grow in executive as well as legislative machinery; they must be trained to play their part in administration and the services, and in the economic activities necessary for the building up of their country.[15]

Administrative Responsibility

Recent policies for social and economic development in the British and American dependencies meant new services, which in turn required technical and managerial specialists unavailable in the colonies.* This requirement ran counter to the general intention of American and British authorities to turn over as much administration as possible to local personnel. The resulting increase of metropolitan officials is locally very unpopular.[16]

The lack of qualified local personnel has been met in different ways, which in most cases do not appreciably increase local participation. Improved services in the Virgin Islands have been in federally directed hands. Thus, the St. Thomas market remained a Federal project for some years after its construction. Similarly, the problem of modern treatment for

* That local specialists were rare was partly due to lack of opportunity for qualifying experience.

the insane was solved by sending the patients to St. Elizabeth's Hospital in Washington. The Virgin Islands Company, chief enterprise in St. Croix, was also a Federal agency.

In Puerto Rico, Federal agencies administered their own programs, using much local personnel, and co-operating with complementary or duplicating insular agencies. Many Federal administrators would have preferred complete jurisdiction over their special function, although they conceded that local technical employees were often useful. They were suspicious of the efficiency, if not the honesty, of potential local managerial personnel.[17] Importing mainlanders for new public enterprises in Puerto Rico has sometimes aroused violent opposition. When Governor Tugwell appointed a continental American to head the Puerto Rican Agricultural Development Company at $15,000, there was a public furor; and the use of a few mainland glassworkers during a labor controversy in the new glass factory resulted in a costly strike.[18]

Numerous efforts are being made in Puerto Rico to meet the lack of qualified local personnel by special training of technicians. Some are sent to the mainland for study; others are taught in the huge new industrial school connected with the University of Puerto Rico. The University's School of Public Administration includes in its program in-service training for civil service employees as well as the training of future government officials. Training programs have also been inaugurated in some of the British West Indies to make local administration of new social and economic policies more feasible. For example, Development and Welfare funds have been spent on training of technicians in such fields as social welfare; local trade-union leaders have been taught by experienced British trade-union officials; and a million pounds have been especially allocated to prepare colonial inhabitants to qualify for higher posts in the colonial service.

Despite the practice of building on local institutions whenever possible, Development and Welfare projects have had to increase the employment of personnel from the British colonial civil service. Furthermore, the British Crown Agents, who act as purchasing agents and recruiters of technical personnel for the colonies, have played an increasingly large role since the projects have been undertaken.[19] There has been some difficulty in recruiting outside personnel for Development and Welfare projects because conditions in the colonies were not so attractive as elsewhere. As local candidates who can be obtained for lower salaries become better qualified, this problem will presumably diminish.[20]

Greater administrative responsibility was permitted Jamaica when Development and Welfare deviated from its usual procedure of approving grants for specific projects. It sanctioned an annual agricultural grant to the Jamaican Government. The grant was not allocated for a particular service but was merged with the ordinary agricultural expenditures of the colonial government.[21] This kind of concession is more common in Federal aid to Puerto Rico. Nevertheless, as long as Great Britain and the United States provide direct appropriations for their dependencies, they are unlikely to turn over administration of these funds completely to colonial personnel.

Methods of Influencing Change

Subsidies

Among the various methods by which the metropolitan government can effect social and economic changes in a colony, provision of funds involves the greatest problem in dependence. Not only is the mother country likely to control the way in which the money is spent (by administration), but, more important, it determines for what it shall be spent.

According to Sir Drummond Shiels, as long as there is some measure of imperial control over a colonial government, financial and other assistance will be available. But there will be a corresponding reluctance to provide funds when the appropriate control over their use and distribution is lacking.[22]

The West India Royal Commission opposed immediate and complete self-government because of the problem of administrative controls. The Royal Commission believed such controls necessary if the British Government were to give the amount of financial assistance which was regarded as vital to the welfare of the West Indies.

Development and Welfare has attempted to meet the problem of dependence by emphasizing that the expenditure of metropolitan funds should further the ability of a colony to help itself. Thus in providing housing funds, Development and Welfare insisted that the local governments also contribute to the program. Colonial governments were expected to stimulate private contributions as well. Development and Welfare did not wish to encourage the colonial people's expectation of getting something for nothing. It also adopted a strict policy concerning educational subsidies. Believing that "he who would be master in his own house must be able to meet his own bills," Development and Welfare disapproved of annually recurring subsidies for teachers' salaries.

These salaries constituted the most important and expanding educational expenditure. Under traditional educational organization they would be far beyond the resources of the colonies to pay if there were an increase of teachers sufficient to care for all school-age children. But if metropolitan funds were used to meet this permanently recurring and increasing expenditure, such subsidies might prejudice the growth of self-responsibility for which education was aiming. Therefore Development and Welfare proposed instead a radical reorganization of education which still depended in part on the use of pupils as teachers. This program was to reduce the cost of teaching to the point where it might be met by colonies whose economic development would begin to provide the necessary tax base.[23]

The Colonial Office has continued to define its development and welfare policy regarding the gradual decrease in financial dependence. It has declared that in the long run, social standards in a colony must depend on the colony's own resources, skill, and energy, and on the intelligent and full use of internal wealth. The 1945 Colonial Development and Welfare Act was intended to give the colonies the help they required to begin developing their own resources for themselves.

Illustrative of this policy was Development and Welfare aid to British Guiana to mechanize and modernize its rice industry in order to develop that colony as the rice granary of the Caribbean colonies. In like manner, subsidies were granted to the British West Indian Airways for necessary replacements in order to maintain service. With the adoption of the Colonial Development Corporation plan in 1947 the British Government took bold action to stimulate an increase in the wealth of the colonies themselves. This step the Government believed all the more desirable because of the foreign exchange position of the mother country.

Like the British West Indies, Puerto Rico has been advised to direct public expenditures as much as possible to projects broadening its financial resources. By such action Puerto Rico might ultimately provide for higher living standards and decrease its dependence upon outside aid as well. The emphasis on economic development—demonstrated particularly by the Puerto Rico Industrial Development Company's program— suggests a desirable solution to the dilemma of autonomy demands and financial needs.

Where funds have been spent in Puerto Rico by Federal operating agencies, the purpose for which they were to be used was originally decided by the Puerto Rican Government, since it sought the aid of a particular agency. However, the conditions under which funds were available and the conditions governing their expenditure were set by the Federal agency (or by Congressional act), and these sometimes involved close control. Thus, the wages paid by producers receiving Agricultural Adjustment Administration benefits were regulated by that agency, and the personnel system of the Insular Department of Health had to be reformed to comply with Social Security Administration regulations before it could obtain aid for public health from that agency.

The necessity for obtaining work relief presumably caused the Puerto Rican War Emergency Program to agree to turn over direction of that work to the Federal Works Agency in the spring of 1943, provided the latter agency was able to obtain the necessary appropriations from Congress. The superior organization of the Federal agency no doubt was also a factor in the decision, since some Puerto Rican work relief funds had already been allocated to the Federal Works Agency for administration.[24]

Many metropolitan Development and Welfare grants to Puerto Rico and the British West Indies were conditioned on local contribution to the funds. In spite of providing part of the money for some projects, however, the colonial governments did not have administrative control over its expenditure.*

Administrative controls are less serious than political controls. Some kinds of financial aid from the mother country involve much greater dependence in policy determination

* In the Virgin Islands, local contributions have not been customary, since they could not be raised. However, that territory has not shared in many grants-in-aid available to Puerto Rico and the States.

than those for development and welfare discussed above. Unless and until there is a general freeing of world trade, tariff preferences are essential for the survival of the economies of these colonies even at their present unsatisfactory level. Without the return of internal revenue funds, Puerto Rico would face a drastic restriction in its spending power. This type of financial assistance does not involve the metropolitan administrative controls characterizing development and welfare expenditures. But it depends upon the will of metropolitan legislatures, which may change at any time. If the change is unfavorable to the colonies the effects would be much more disastrous than the withdrawal of development and welfare expenditures.

Besides being unreliable, tariff subsidies are looked upon as a continuing source of expendable income, so that their use is not likely to be directed to capital improvements which help remove the need of further subsidies, as do development grants. Preferences on sugar have another defect. They work at cross purposes to the policy of promoting greater diversification of agricultural production.[25] The tariff relationship represents the kind of economic dependence which causes Puerto Ricans the greatest anxiety and frustration in their struggle for autonomy.

Tariff subsidies involve no administrative control over their use. At the other extreme is the British type of grant-in-aid over which administrative control is most rigid. If a colony becomes so bankrupt that it cannot meet even its minimum expenditures it may obtain financial aid from the British Government, but its budgetary freedom is lost to control by the British treasury. This is so drastic a measure that the threat of such action caused Jamaica to take radical steps to increase its own revenues in order to avoid further control by the mother country.

Education

Economic and social changes in the colonies can sometimes be brought about by education and instruction, rather than by metropolitan funds. When educational methods can be used, there is a pure gain for decreasing dependence. Ignorance of specific social and economic needs and ways to meet them has helped to prevent the colonies from achieving greater autonomy. When the mother country can pass on its superior knowledge of facts and methods to a colony it is making an indispensable contribution toward the colony's ability to govern itself.*

British and American governments have in recent years employed numerous methods of providing their Caribbean dependencies with the information, advice, and demonstrations necessary for carrying out social and economic policies. Such education is much broader than that conveyed through the public school systems. However, recent changes in school curricula and in the groups reached by the schools have also played a part. Increasing emphasis on vocational training and on various kinds of adult education courses has helped provide a popular basis for social and economic reform. To develop colonial leadership, British plans for a West Indian University will prove of great value, judged by the experience of the University of Puerto Rico.

In the past, some British colonial authorities, like those of other colonial powers, have feared that widespread extension of education would create a frustrated white-collar group, lacking employment opportunities and without a satisfying place in society. Such a situation would have explosive possibilities.

* The technical assistance to underdeveloped areas proposed by President Truman in his "Fourth Point" focused attention on the value of this approach.

This is a very complicated problem which involves, among other considerations, colonial attitudes toward what constitutes a respectable occupation. It also involves the suitability of the colonial education facilities for the kinds of jobs available. Development projects are now being held up in the Caribbean colonies for want of technically trained persons. If economic development proceeds intensively, an increasing supply of appropriately educated colonial inhabitants will find an ever-growing demand for their services. The existence of a body of well-trained colonial people will hasten development, and thus have important consequences for the reduction of dependence.*

To provide local agencies for social and economic development, British and American authorities have sought to stimulate the organization of producer, credit, and consumer co-operatives. In other areas co-operatives have proved useful for developing self-help habits and community responsibility, as well as for solving economic problems. However, the remarkably egocentric inhabitants of the Caribbean colonies have not joined immediately and enthusiastically in the co-operative movement. The metropolitan governments are faced with this dilemma: Co-operatives should be able to stand by themselves through the voluntary efforts of their members; yet they depend upon government aid in their establishment. Apparently much patience is required with the necessarily slow growth of this method of organization.

Through many different agencies the British Government has helped the West Indies to obtain the requisite information for dealing with their social and economic problems. These agencies have advised them on proper courses of action,

---

* The government must provide the desired technical training for the economic development of backward areas because particular private enterprises are unlikely to do so for fear that, once trained, their employees would desert to newly established competitors.

and showed them how to carry out social and economic policies. West Indian Development and Welfare has especially served the colonies by its detailed investigations, surveys, and other kinds of research on particular West Indian problems.

The Comptroller's advisers on economics, engineering, education, housing and planning, labor, social welfare, and health, have also counseled individual colonies. In addition, Development and Welfare has arranged for outside specialists to aid in dealing with particular problems. It has helped colonies to organize modern systems of collecting vital statistics and has contributed to the educational work of such local organizations as credit institutions. Development and Welfare has engaged in experimental activities to demonstrate new methods and organizations. It has also promoted community welfare activities, emphasizing rural health units, to show people how to help themselves. Especially important have been the Development and Welfare projects for training local personnel, some of them through special local institutes and permanent training establishments, others through scholarships and similar aids to study abroad.

Numerous imperial institutes, councils, and advisory committees have provided advice and information for the West Indies.[26] There have been special investigating commissions on particular problems such as nutrition and higher education; the West Indian Royal Commission has been the most important general investigating committee dealing exclusively with the West Indies. The British Crown Agents provide consultants for the colonies on such matters as water supply and engineering. These organizations usually assisted the colonies by request of the colonial governments or Colonial Office authorities.

Information and advice come to the American dependencies in a less extensive and much less highly organized fashion, but it is provided in numerous ways. For example,

United States agricultural and forestry experiment stations have carried on local research for Puerto Rico and also for the Virgin Islands. Consultants from the National Resources Planning Board and the Civil Aeronautics Board have made surveys and advised Puerto Rico and the Virgin Islands on special problems. Federal agencies carrying on extension services and home and farm demonstration work for individuals have included the Farm Security Administration and the Puerto Rico Reconstruction Administration.

As in the British colonies, the messages and recommendations of the governors have been the customary instruments for informing and advising local government officials on policy and administration. Lacking the requisite funds, personnel, and authority, the Department of the Interior, (legally responsible for supervising the dependencies), has been unable to give such extensive direction as is possible in the case of the Colonial Office in the British colonies. Congressional committees have from time to time investigated problems in the dependencies. However, their reports in the past supplied little useful instruction to the colonies.

The most important multinational instrument for providing and co-ordinating information and advice has been the Caribbean Commission. Its Caribbean Research Council, with subsidiary committees on such matters as agriculture, forestry, and building methods and materials, has brought together information on these subjects for the use of all. In 1948 the commission organized a centralized research information service and provided that original research in indicated fields be concentrated in single institutes in the Caribbean in order to avoid duplication and be most effective. Thus governments faced with particular problems could benefit from the previous experience of others.

The organizations mentioned above are official bodies. Several private or semiofficial groups in the United States

and Great Britain have also extended their welfare activities
to the colonies. Information, advice, and training have come
from many organizations like the Carnegie Corporation and
the (British) Inter-University Council for Higher Education in the Colonies.

All this assistance in educating the colonial peoples to
help themselves has important political consequences. Without such knowledge they cannot expect to move toward a
more autonomous status. With it, failure to permit them
more self-government will prove hard to rationalize.

Changes in the Rules

Besides subsidies and education, there is a third method
by which the metropolitan government can influence social
and economic development in the colonies. It may obtain
changes in the rules governing the distribution of power locally and between the colony and the outside world.

In the Caribbean colonies British and American authorities
have effected alterations in the fields of labor relations, land
tenure, taxation, housing, co-operatives (both producer and
consumer), and public ownership or regulation of such enterprises as transportation, power, communications, and sugar
mills. Such changes are likely to be promoted or actually imposed by the mother country. They seldom originate in the
colonies because they tend to affect adversely the traditionally
most powerful local groups. The metropolitan government
has usually been able to secure these changes indirectly by
persuading the colonial government to legislate in the desired
direction. Occasionally the colonial government may even
take the lead.* If the mother country does not need to take

---

* Some locally instituted rule changes in Puerto Rico have met with
opposition in Congress, where several committee members concerned with
the dependencies have had a general bias against public ownership.

direct action, that fact already reveals a reduction in dependence.

Where the immediate effect is to redistribute local power by benefiting formerly less potent groups, there may be long-range consequences for decreasing the dependent status of the colony. With a more egalitarian division of political power locally, the mother country will have less justification for retaining the governmental control, one rationalization for which was the necessity to protect submerged groups and preserve a fair balance. Furthermore, within the Caribbean colonies the strongest demands for greater autonomy have come from the formerly submerged groups. For example, labor leaders in both British and American dependencies have also been leaders in the fight for greater independence, while the vested interests of business, commerce, and large-scale agricultural industry have sometimes sought even closer ties with the mother country.[27] Failure of the mother country to stimulate a gradual breakup in the rigid colonial class structure might lead ultimately to its violent shattering through local rebellion. The ensuing civil disorder would then give real cause for perpetuating close metropolitan controls.

Other kinds of rule changes, such as in export, import, and production controls do not greatly affect the distribution of power within the colony; rather, they alter the position of the colony relative to other areas. When the metropolitan government sponsors such changes it may arouse the suspicion that the action is less for the colony's sake than for the mother country's. Colonial people may fear that the effects will increase rather than decrease the dependent status of the colony. The various devices for limiting sugar production in Puerto Rico and the British West Indies have not been popular locally. Conceivably, these controls might in the long run work in favor of the colonies, who might otherwise be lost in the scramble for a share in a market falling due to overproduction. Nevertheless, the colonial people know that they are powerless to set their share of the quotas. Colonial peoples may even suspect that fear of growing competition in particular fields causes the mother country to maintain controls of this type.[28]

In general, changes imposed by the mother country in the economic relations of the colony with the outside world have not been a reliable way to reduce colonial dependence.

Actually, British and American authorities have imposed few controls of this type other than wartime measures.* The Caribbean Commission has urged the elimination of many of the existing barriers to trade between the colonies. It has also favored easier importation of certain kinds of machinery and other implements necessary to develop greater economic independence within each colony and for the area as a whole. Some controls have been initiated locally. Thus, in the British West Indies, there has been a movement to restrict the import of edible oils as a protective measure necessary to the building up of a regional industry.

The methods used by Development and Welfare in the West Indies seem to give greatest promise for the ultimate reduction of colonial dependence. Although much of the initiative must still come from the mother country and metropolitan administrative controls are necessary as long as there is subsidization, the emphasis has been on the development of local resources which can eventually support the social development proceeding simultaneously.† Furthermore, Development and Welfare has employed advice, information and training—not merely subsidies—to help the

---

* A noteworthy exception was the restrictions on the British colonies in making dollar purchases, an apparently unavoidable control maintained by Great Britain in dealing with the postwar monetary crisis.

† This was also Governor Tugwell's main theme.

colonial peoples solve their own problems. At the same time, the financial aid it offered has been a strong stimulus to local co-operation, and the actual decisions for undertaking particular projects approved by Development and Welfare and the Colonial Office have remained in local hands.

The Reduction of Internal Violence

The "colonial problem" is a problem partly because its existence leads to violence in one form or another.[29] What effect have recent social and economic reforms had upon violence and conflict in the Caribbean colonies? This question gains pertinence because in the British West Indies the new policies were a reply to "disturbances" serious enough to call for radical changes in colonial policy. The riots in the various West Indian colonies appeared to arise out of economic difficulties; they were rooted in dissatisfaction over low living standards which were falling still lower.

In Puerto Rico the violence took the form of extremist nationalist agitation—the high point was the assassination of the American head of the Insular police. However, misery formed the background. Nationalist conflict has somewhat subsided since 1937-38, but labor conflicts in Puerto Rico have become more marked.

The situation in Jamaica has been especially difficult. The colony was the scene of some of the rioting which led to local and Royal Commission investigations in the late thirties. After five years of Development and Welfare and constitutional reforms bringing a new group to power, violence again became critical. This time, however, there were different groups in conflict. Political and industrial warfare between rival unions has continued to flare up frequently in this colony.

While living standards in the Caribbean colonies were so

abysmally low that individual and group rebellion would
have been understandable, the people had long been inured
to their "fate." Not until they were faced with still further
deprivations or saw the possibility of improvement, were
they likely to revolt. The first effects of social and economic
programs promising a larger share of an increasing supply of
goods and services might therefore be not less but more violence. Illustrative were the labor conflicts arising at United
States bases in the British West Indies.[30] A rise in living
standards—better housing, medical care, and nutrition—is
not in itself sufficient to reduce conflict. What is needed is the
provision of a sense of security and a feeling of respect.[31]

The United States has guaranteed external security for the
Caribbean colonies as far as possible, as a corollary to its own
defense.* Except for a brief interval of submarine warfare in
the Caribbean shortly after the United States entered World
War II, this has not been a major problem to the colonies.
But internal security will continue to be threatened as long as
there is racial discrimination making invidious class distinctions (this applies especially to the British West Indies with
their large black and colored populations). Abolishing racial
bias would not by itself rid the Caribbean colonies of violence,
but domestic peace is unlikely to come until there is a change
in racial attitudes.†

Virgin Islanders and British West Indians have been very
sensitive about race differences, partly because in the past
they have had unhappy experiences with the crude prejudices
and disdainful attitudes of some metropolitan officials.[32]
Racial friction in the British West Indies has been stimulated
and kept alive, often unconsciously, by the attitudes of white

* In this respect the colonies do not differ from the Caribbean republics.
† The problem of maintaining order in Puerto Rico presented by turbu-
lent nationalists arises not out of color discrimination but, in part at least,
from cultural conflict.

newcomers, whose very presence at the top of the power pyramid aggravated the class differences determined by shades of color. The most acute racial conflicts have been between "black" and "colored," not between colored and white, and the difference between them was in good part economic. The possibility of an improvement in the living standards of the black masses has sharpened this antagonism. The democratic values held by the mother countries will not sanction repressive measures to subdue the conflict. Therefore prudence would seem to demand social development which will reduce gross economic differences as rapidly as possible; else pressures for disorder will continue to accumulate.

Better living conditions may also reduce the mutual suspicion between individuals, often remarked upon by outsiders, which prevents the growth of co-operation and therefore opposes economic progress. Praedial larceny in the British West Indies, a legacy of slavery among the poverty-stricken, is not only a crime among neighbors. It has also noticeably retarded agricultural development. Social welfare policies emphasizing community activities, group recreation, and co-operatives may lead to a diminution in this personal distrust.[33]

Racial hatred has been employed by unscrupulous nationalist leaders in Puerto Rico, but here again animosity was partly due to the fact that the Negro population occupies the lowest economic status, and this was very low. Sympathetic observers have nevertheless noted in both the American and British Caribbean colonies that crimes of violence were surprisingly few considering the provocations. Accustomed to economic insecurity, many of the colonial people had developed a system of social values that compensated for property loss by minimizing the importance of wealth and economic competition.[34] There were, however, explosive possibilities in the problem of the returned veteran. These men had received technical training and had become accustomed to higher living standards. Internal security required that they be suitably employed.

The same means which insure a sense of security may sometimes be used to create a feeling of being respected. This is especially true of measures removing racial discrimination for jobs and social position. However, the most potent weapon is the provision of a place for everyone, for the individual's belief that he is needed is basic to his contentment with his status. Thus economic development policies which will open up more and more employment opportunities should prove valuable in producing this sense of respect. So will broadened educational programs which provide vocational and other practical training.

Full extension of civil liberties and the development of peaceful means for expressing discontent are essential not only for reducing dangerous pressures but also for increasing individual respect. Thus, encouragement of trade unions, especially as it is accompanied by training in peaceful trade-union procedures, should prove valuable in this regard. Labor conciliation as practiced and taught by metropolitan officials in the colonies would have the same effect in decreasing discontent and providing a fairer distribution of respect.

In cultures such as the Jamaican, where possession of a piece of land increases self-respect, land settlement programs will be effective in reducing sources of conflict. Individual prestige may sometimes be enhanced by the heightening of national prestige. Therefore, community good will should arise from such efforts as Rexford G. Tugwell's and Luis Muñoz Marín's to foster pride in Puerto Rico and faith in its potentialities, in place of self-pity and a hopeless view of the future.

Experience with the new social and economic policies is still not sufficient for drawing more than tentative conclusions about their effect on the incidence of violence. However, these policies seem to be pointing in the right direction, toward eventually peaceful communities in which a constitutional consensus can flourish. An immediate result may be increased violence, characteristic of the beginning of the upswing in prosperity for previously submerged groups. Class conflicts may be augmented and sharpened as these groups become more conscious of divergent interests. Undisciplined nationalism may also develop. Such conditions are not ideal. Nevertheless, they represent an advance over the subhuman privations of an earlier period, the undemocratic subservience, and the repression of discontent. A rise in living standards is certainly necessary, although not in itself sufficient to promote peaceful conditions in the colonies. Giving formerly underprivileged people a stake in the community tends to convert them into defenders of the public order.

Developing Local Responsibility

However, social and economic policies determined chiefly by the metropolitan government are not enough to insure the desired development. Among other problems there remains that of choosing the proper techniques for carrying out these policies. As Lord Olivier wrote of the Jamaicans, colonial people must be approached through their own interests, their own culture, their own ideas of liberty and well-being, religion, and education. In that way they can be helped to build the structure of an efficient and civilized community capable of supporting governmental institutions from which so much is being required.[35]

Development and Welfare successfully employed techniques for realizing new agricultural policies through public discussion of underlying principles and collaboration with people in all walks of life. A former Social Welfare Adviser to the Comptroller has given his recipe for changing undesir-

able customs: explanation, persuasion, and example, not co-
ercion or moral lecturing or criticism.[36]

A sociological study of the Puerto Rican community of
Comerio stressed the need for evaluating "economic" cause
in terms of "noneconomic" attitudes and social adjustments.
The low level of living and nonmaterial aspects of the culture
grew up together, and cause and effect were blended into a
strong social inertia dominating both economic and noneconomic adjustments.[37] Some progress is made when colonial
people begin to desire a better life. The creation of the "social
will" which will demand and work for the kind of social and
economic conditions regarded as valuable by the mother country is a difficult but necessary development.[38]

Anthropologists have been considering the problem of the
appropriate means for developing local responsibility. A
specialist in the Pacific area has emphasized that the task of
colonial control and direction is in subtle fashion to develop
incentives and evoke and guide drives to self-motivated
choices, rather than to try to impose alien forms. Colonial
authorities should keep open channels of public information
and understanding, and influence groups through their accepted leaders. Responsibilities should be devolved upon the
people in a measure commensurate with their capacity, leaving a margin where they can experiment and make the mistakes that are vital to learning.[39]

A South African anthropologist has written that the "welfare" approach sometimes seems to visualize colonial man as

consisting of a body that has to be adequately fed,
clothed, housed, cleansed of disease and dirt, and turned
on to maximum output, plus a blank cerebral cortex
that can be stamped with any pattern of skills and
knowledge we deem necessary by a long enough ex-
posure to schooling.[40]

He continued that "maximizing productivity and material welfare is merely a means to political ends. It can end up in fascism as easily as in democracy." [41]

Social and economic development is not the whole answer to the colonial problem. It is therefore necessary to consider some constitutional questions and, in particular, how governmental reforms are related to social and economic development.

IX. Constitutional Changes and Political Power

"TO educate a man is to raise not only his knowledge and skills, but also his hopes and his ambitions, his claims for full citizenship, and the sense of his personal dignity." [1] Social and economic measures cannot be divorced from constitutional development. Increasing knowledge of the mother country's free institutions came to the people in the British and American possessions along with improved living standards and, especially, education. Inevitably they demanded an extension of political liberties for themselves. However, colonial powers have insisted that further grants of autonomy should be conditioned upon greater social and economic development and should not hinder such development.

Modifications in Governmental Status

Constitutional changes modifying the locus of governmental authority may take different forms. There may be alterations which shift the center of governmental decision-making between the metropolitan country and the colony, between different groups within the colony, and between different colonies. These changes are often interdependent. For instance, the British have usually regarded closer union of the British West Indies as a prerequisite to extensive grants of freedom from metropolitan control.

Constitutional Relations between
Mother Country and Colony

Considering first the relations between mother country and colony, what modifications in constitutional status are possible in the British and American Caribbean dependencies?

Varying from one colony to the next, intricate governmental systems have regulated the relations of the British West Indies with the mother country. Each detail of a system might be involved in grants of increased autonomy. For example, the governor often named a certain number, sometimes a majority, of the legislature. Some of these nominees were also administrative officials. All administrative officials were chosen by the governor or, in the case of the highest posts, by the Colonial Office. The latter appointees have usually come from outside the West Indies. The Executive Council, which acted as a cabinet, was usually composed of varying proportions of official and unofficial members, all nominated by the governor.*

Legislative initiative was frequently confined to the executive, especially in money matters. Very significant has been the "reserved power" of the governor to override a majority vote of the legislature in matters which he regarded of "paramount importance." † The Secretary of State for the Colonies had an important role in the metropolitan supervision

* In the crown colony terminology classifying legislative council members, "official" members are metropolitan-appointed administrative officers nominated to the legislative council by the governor. (A few of these may be automatically entitled to a seat.) "Unofficial" members are of two classes: either nominated by the governor from outside the government or elected by the people.

† This was not merely a veto, but a power to take positive action despite the opposition of the legislative body. Some of the West Indies had once had larger legislative powers, which were taken away in the second half of the nineteenth century because of their abuse in the hands of a reactionary oligarchy.

of colonial administration, especially as his approval has been necessary for many kinds of activities. On the other hand, the colonial legislature had the power to approve appropriations which included determining the salaries of the administrative officials. It also had the power of taxation, which embraced determination of customs duties. Elected members of the Jamaican legislature long had a special power to veto any budgetary item for supplies. Barbados, like Bermuda and the Bahamas, has ancient powers making the legislature much more independent of the governor than is the case in the other colonies.[2]

Before the 1936 Organic Act for the Virgin Islands, its government somewhat resembled the British crown colony government. However, in place of the more extensive reserved powers of the British governor the Virgin Islands governor had an "absolute veto" and the local legislatures had more initiative.[3] Since 1936 the municipal councils have been entirely elective. The principal means for metropolitan control lay in the appointment of the important judicial and administrative officials, including the governor; in the governor's veto powers; and in the reserved powers of Congress to annul local legislation.[4]

Both houses of the Puerto Rican Legislature have been entirely elective, but up to the 1947 amendment to the Organic Act the Governor, Attorney General, and Commissioner of Education were appointed by the President. The Auditor and Justices of the Puerto Rican Supreme Court remained Presidential appointees. If a bill repassed the legislature by two-thirds after a veto by the governor, it could go to the President for final action, a procedure which has been tried only three times; in each case the President upheld the governor's decision. Congress has never exercised the power to annul an Insular act, although its use has been threatened.

Heads of departments other than those named above have been appointed by the governor with the advice and consent of the Insular Senate. Together all the department heads formed an Executive Council which acted as cabinet. In 1941, for the first time, it was composed entirely of Puerto Ricans. In 1948 Congress vested complete authority in the Puerto Rican Government to determine the salaries of all Insular officials. As in the Virgin Islands, the Puerto Rican judiciary is part of the Federal system.[5]

In both British and American colonies, the ultimate legislative authority has been Parliament or Congress, and in each case these bodies could legislate directly for particular colonies.* In addition laws passed by the United States Congress were extended automatically to Puerto Rico unless expressly or obviously inapplicable. However, none of the colonies being considered has had direct representation in the metropolitan government, as in the French colonial system. Puerto Rico came the closest, with its Resident Commissioner in Congress. He is elected at large in the island, and has the status and duties of a Congressman except that he lacks the right to vote.

The Governor of the Virgin Islands has acted as representative of that dependency in Washington when seeking legislative or administrative action. Witnesses from the American dependencies frequently have appeared before Congressional committees considering legislation applicable to the colonies. However, the British West Indies have had no such direct access to metropolitan legislative bodies, and in general their interests had to be presented through the Colonial Office. Nevertheless they could often count on the aid of

---

* Note that changes in the government of the American dependencies usually had to be by act of Congress; in the British West Indies, constitutional changes customarily have been made by administrative order.

sympathetic members of Parliament to ask questions of the Government in Parliament.[6]

Certain practices have tended to soften and blur the authority of the American or British governor. Thus, in the past, if a bill went through the Puerto Rican Legislature against the wish of a strong fighting minority which might continue its opposition and blame official powers for what they disliked, the governor found it convenient to leave for Washington on urgent business, leaving the acting governor, if a native-born Puerto Rican, to act on the bill in his absence. If a popular measure seemed to require a veto, the same device could be used to save the governor from bearing the full blame.[7] In the British colonies, as Lord Hailey declared, the attitude of local executives had shown a growing measure of response to legislative influence. In many colonies a convention had arisen whereby the governor, after previous consultation with legislative members, obtained legislation which frequently involved an important compromise of administrative attitudes.[8]

Typical of the explanations which colonial powers have made in the past for retaining close governmental control over their dependencies were those presented in 1922 by the Hon. E. F. L. Wood (later Lord Halifax) after his investigation of the West Indies. According to his report, responsible government could not be granted in a measurable time for this area for the following reasons:

(1) The population was too varied in color, religion, and race, and much of it was backward and politically undeveloped. The Secretary of State acted for them as the responsible trustee, and he could be counted on for impartiality and integrity.

(2) There was no leisured class which could take an active part in political life. This deficiency made necessary a supply of official services which was independent of local ties and

which could provide the necessary detachment for effective conduct of government services. There was the further risk that responsible government might merely entrench in power a financial oligarchy which would use its position only to benefit its own class.

(3) The controlling influence of the Secretary of State was necessary to secure some uniformity of administration among adjacent colonies.

(4) Finally, there was too small a proportion of the electorate exercising the franchise.[9]

Besides irreconcilable local divisions, the danger of dictatorship by a powerful local minority (either colored or white), and the absence of independence in a local civil service, other rationalizations have been reiterated from time to time. They include administrative incompetence which might result in bankruptcy; the possibility that other independent powers might seize control of a weak government; susceptibility of politically ignorant and immature populations to demagoguery; and the likelihood that legislation demanded in the public interest would not be passed by the local legislature. More recently, other reasons have been given for not granting further autonomy.[10] They included the necessity for maintaining financial controls if aid in social and economic development is to be made effective; the lack of concerted local opinion on constitutional changes; and the difficulty of getting progressive legislation approved by some conservative local legislatures.[11]

What are the major complaints leveled against the kinds of metropolitan government control described above? For Puerto Rico they have been phrased in very general terms: dislike of "colonialism"; the Atlantic Charter's unfulfilled promises of self-government; and inconsistency with the American theory of popular sovereignty.[12] Puerto Rico's war record has been cited as evidence that it deserved more autonomy. There have also been more particular dissatisfactions inherent in a government system which divided responsibility and where outsiders had high authority.[13] An especially frustrating condition proceeded from the failure of the Federal Government to fill Puerto Rican administrative posts under its jurisdiction, either through Presidential neglect or Congressional hostility to Presidential nominees. The prolonged period of "transitional" government in Puerto Rico has also caused many to complain that uncertainty of the island's future political status prevents long-range planning.

In the Virgin Islands, as elsewhere in the Caribbean, much hostility and distrust arose because administrative power was in foreign hands. It was aggravated there by the difference in color of the metropolitan officials. As elsewhere, blame for every kind of difficulty and public dissatisfaction has been shifted to the outsiders in the government.[14] Deadlock and inaction were frequent where—as in the American dependencies—the division of governmental authority between the metropolitan governor and the colonial legislature gave the colonial body wide powers.

In the British West Indies the chief complaints have centered around the impotence of the legislative body to do much more than approve the governor's will, since disapproval could be so easily overridden. Lord Olivier described in detail the unfortunate consequences as they appeared in the 1930's. He declared that the elected and unofficial members of the legislature regarded it as useless to talk and urge what they believed to be the right course when the governor had already made up his mind or had instructions from the Colonial Office. The official yes-men would not even listen to them; after the discussion was over, the nominated members (both official and unofficial) voted as they were bid, not as they thought. This position was uncongenial not only to elected and unofficial members but to intelligent official members also, who found it very humiliating. It tended to demoralize them, discouraging and blunting their sense of personal responsibility. It also diminished their readiness to express their own real judgment when they differed with the governor.

This system fostered an impatient and supercilious attitude among the governor's appointees, especially when all the unofficial members were elected. Since the Legislative Council was relatively impotent compared to the governor and his administrative officers, the implication was that the unofficial members were of little or no importance. Therefore, official members (especially imported civil servants) were likely to despise and ignore their arguments. The official members also tended to regard the opposition as habitually unreasonable and factious. Of course, this behavior would exasperate the unofficial members. They came to believe that such an attitude existed even when there was no cause for suspicion. In reaction they might well be provoked into manifestations which actually were obstructive, defiant, or intemperate.[15]

In addition to the general dissatisfaction with alien rulers and the particular criticisms of crown colony government there have been other complaints. Some governors and other administrative officials were inadequately qualified for their positions.* That these posts did not always attract the most competent men was partly due to the uncongenial atmosphere. For the administrators were subject to much personal abuse because of their official position. Colonial governments have also suffered from lack of administrative continuity owing to a constant turnover. The continual stream of newcomers was additionally unwelcome because many had not yet learned to treat colored people with the desired respect. Critics have also complained that intelligent and disinterested

* For example, British West Indians often resented the appointment of officials whose previous experience had been confined to Africa.

citizens were deprived of direct responsibility and a chance to participate in their government; the positions they might fill were held by outsiders.

Despite the theory that government nominations to Legislative and Executive Council posts were necessary to insure that all sections be represented, the practical results have often been quite different. The conservative character of these appointees has often simply reinforced the unprogressive attitudes of the elected members who were chosen through a restricted franchise and had to have certain property qualifications. Nominated officials have sometimes held office for several terms, thus limiting opportunities for newcomers with more liberal views. A most damaging accusation has been that in these colonies, with their white, colored, and black classes, the colored elite has tended to fawn on the white officeholders, because the latter were the dispensers of power. Meanwhile the colored group ignored or rejected the needs of the black masses. Such a situation has antidemocratic implications and revolutionary dangers.

Even before the war, some of the colonial governments were detaining "agitators" who spoke out against the existing system. They were sometimes held without bail or trial— evidence for the accusations of the "Nazification of British justice." [16] The practice reinforced suspicions that the slowness of constitutional change was due not entirely to a disinterested concern as to the competence of the colonial people to govern themselves, but partly to the determination to preserve the existing distribution of power.

Constitutional Reforms in the British West Indies

In the evolution of crown colony government toward fully responsible government, one stage is the removal of the nominated and official elements in the legislature. Another step is to eliminate the exercise of such restrictions on the legislative authority as the governor's veto and reserved powers. Finally, the legislature gains full control over executive functions through its own ministers.[17]

Illustrative of these possibilities are the moderate constitutional changes made in Trinidad and in British Guiana in 1942.[18] In the former colony, three-fourths of the official members of the Legislative Council were eliminated; the only remaining official members were the Colonial Secretary, Attorney General, and Colonial Treasurer. The total number in the Legislative Council was decreased from twenty-five to eighteen; half of these were elected and the remainder were nominated. The governor remained president and could cast a vote in case of a tie.[19]

A slightly bolder constitutional change was made in British Guiana, where the elected members of the Legislative Council were made the majority, fourteen out of twenty-four. Official members were three, and the number of nominated members was increased from five to seven to permit a wider field to be represented. From the Legislative Council came the unofficial members of the Executive Council. Another recommendation of the West India Royal Commission was followed in setting up administrative advisory committees of members from the Legislative Council to function with the executive officials of the several departments. The chairmen were usually unofficial members of the executive committee.

A similar step toward responsible government was embodied in the new Jamaican constitution, which, after several abortive attempts at revision, was finally granted and accepted in 1944. It provided for an entirely elected House of Representatives of thirty-two, a Legislative Council of fifteen, all nominated (some of them officials), and an Executive Council of ten. Half of the last was elected from the House of

Representatives, the other half nominated by the governor, including the three highest officials.

The Executive Council was the principal instrument of policy; it prepared the budget, initiated all bills, and was responsible for administration of the government. An embryonic ministerial system was created with the establishment of several committees in the House of Representatives to deal with such affairs as agriculture and education; their chairmen formed a general committee of the House. Jamaican leaders in the campaign for greater self-government did not succeed in eliminating the governor's overriding power. Neither did they gain greater local control over the civil service nor secure a majority of elected members on the Executive Council.*

Several improvements in the government of the West Indies do not have to wait for constitutional change; in fact, most of the suggestions made by the West India Royal Commission were alterations in the practices of the Colonial Office and of Parliament. For example, they recommended fewer changes and longer terms of office in the West Indies for colonial service officers, including governors. This reform was to be accompanied by better salaries and improved public relations with the local press and organizations. They also urged that the West Indian governments combine their administrative services. Such unification would facilitate, among other things, the development of more local appointments to the administrative services.[20] While recognizing the impracticability of appointing colonial representatives to the House of Commons, the West India Royal Commission suggested the "association of colonial delegates with the work of any standing Parliamentary Committee which may be created to consider colonial affairs." [21]

* One of the major reforms was the institution of universal suffrage, to be discussed presently.

In 1947 some procedural changes in Barbados not involving legal amendments brought that colony closer to "responsible government." The governor selected the House of Assembly leader most likely to be supported by the majority, and asked him to submit the names of House members for the Executive Committee. The members of this committee had charge of general policy in particular government departments. Thus they became rudimentary ministers in the pattern of the British cabinet system.[22]

Constitutional Reforms in Puerto Rico

Constitutional changes have been envisaged for Puerto Rico chiefly in terms of the following alternatives: increased Insular powers under the present system, statehood, "dominion status," or independence. Until recent years the most vociferous Puerto Ricans have demanded independence. Some were as extreme as the leader of the Unionist party, who declared at a meeting in 1930:

> I do not know where destiny will carry me, but wherever I go my voice and my soul will always support a nation free, sovereign and independent. . . . I prefer the liberty of my country before everything else. I prefer it although we die of hunger.[23]

Following the decline of violent agitation by the small Nationalist party in the middle thirties, a more moderate attitude came to prevail. Nevertheless, *independentistas* have continued strong enough to embarrass the Popular party chiefs. Responsible leaders have recognized that the economic dependence of Puerto Rico upon the United States was so pervasive that complete independence might bring not only unbearable poverty but also political chaos. As will shortly be seen, Puerto Rican opinion is not at all united on the particular form of the island's future political status—statehood, independence, or some other alternative. However, it is firmly united on the desire for a change in the present arrangements and for a voice in the change, whatever it may be.

Senator Millard E. Tydings, has since the middle thirties repeatedly sponsored legislation which would give outright independence.* In 1945 he permitted a modification to be introduced containing important amendments suggested by Puerto Rican leaders. This bill provided for a Puerto Rican referendum to choose one of several alternatives: the first was independence as outlined in the original Tydings bill with certain economic amendments; the second was statehood; and the third was a dominion form with full local sovereignty, but with limited power in external relations and the retention of American citizenship for Puerto Ricans.

The principal amendments to the Tydings conception of independence were the following: free trade between Puerto Rico and the United States should remain, but might be limited on occasion by mutual agreement rather than by a fixed schedule of percentages and dates; internal revenue taxes should not be collected by the United States on Puerto Rican products; instead, Puerto Rico would impose export taxes at the same rates (continuance of the present system but with different mechanics). Finally, economic aid to Puerto Rico should be tapered off only by mutual agreement. Under the dominion alternative, existing Federal aid would have been continued indefinitely, but immigration would not have been restricted, as it would under the independence alternative.

The Puerto Rican leaders emphasized that if the proper economic conditions were satisfied, the exact nature of the political framework would be of secondary importance.

---

* He was Chairman of the Senate Committee on Territories and Insular Affairs, which became part of the Public Lands Committee under the Congressional Reorganization Act of 1946.

Despite Presidential urging that Puerto Rico be permitted to choose among permissible alternatives, Senator Tydings declared November 27, 1945, that a survey of senatorial opinion had revealed "little or no sentiment here either for statehood or for a dominion status for Puerto Rico." He therefore canceled the public hearings which had been promised and declared that the Puerto Ricans had no choice but outright independence as envisaged in his original bill, or continuation of their present status.[24]

After a false start in 1943, Congress (four years later) passed the bill making the office of governor elective and empowering the governor to appoint two of the administrative officers formerly chosen by the President.[25] This moderate but important step toward autonomy by no means completely satisfied Puerto Rican demands for more governmental freedom. Muñoz Marín has argued for a temporary special status of autonomy which would permit Puerto Ricans to work out their economic problems before making a final choice on statehood or independence. He would have this temporary status terminate at the will of the Puerto Ricans expressed in a plebiscite to be determined by the legislature when it regarded the economic situation suitable.[26] (Resident Commissioner Fernós-Isern has suggested that Puerto Rico might become a "federated republic" or an "autonomous state.") President Truman also continued to urge self-determination for Puerto Rico, and the Democratic party platform in 1948 contained such a plank.

As for the Virgin Islands, since the transfer from naval to civil administration in 1932 and passage of the Organic Act of 1936 with its important changes in governmental organization, there has been no intensive agitation for a major alteration in political status. However, there is still some pressure locally and in Washington for further autonomy. In 1946 Federal officials began to support legislation which would give the Virgin Islands a resident commissioner in Congress and unify the legislative councils of the separate municipalities.

The Congressional appropriations committees sponsored a fiscal survey by the Public Administration Service (a private group), which recommended extensive governmental reorganization and consolidation. Such changes, which would make Federal subsidies more effective, would require amendment of the Organic Act. Virgin Islanders would also like to eliminate the Presidential veto by permitting bills to become law over the governor's veto if passed by three-fourths of the Legislative Assembly. In 1946 President Truman appointed Judge William Hastie as Governor. A renowned continental Negro leader, Judge Hastie was the first governor of the Virgin Islands of the same race as the inhabitants, and had had close personal and official connections with the Islands.

Regardless of constitutional status, there are practices open to colonial peoples which somewhat modify their political dependence because they refuse to operate according to metropolitan understandings. Thus local custom had whittled away the Puerto Rican governor's powers of appointment for many years prior to the Tugwell administration. The party in power would present a list of two or three names for every position to be filled by the governor, and his choice was restricted to them if he was to secure the necessary confirmation by the Insular Senate.[27]

An example of the poverty of power sometimes evident in the West Indies was the technique used many years ago in Grenada and Dominica to oppose the governor. At one period no one would run for office, all elected legislators retired, and public wrath was visited on any individuals accepting nomination to the Legislative Council.[28] In Trinidad the Calypso (popular song-making with contemporaneous references) was subjected to some censorship because of its use to criticize the government, with the result that the forbidden Calypso went underground.[29] Another practice was described as follows:

> Knowing that an unofficial member of the Council has more power to voice grievances than to remedy them, he [a particular popular leader] would speak in a voice that could be heard all over the hall, deliberately digress from the point at issue and enlarge the scope of the question under debate. Whenever asked by the Acting Governor how this was relevant to the discussion, he would come back to the main point again, before wandering off in another digression. In this way the Council Chamber became a platform for the dissemination of ideas that might not have been tolerated elsewhere.[30]

Changes in Local Distribution of Power

Shifting the center of governmental decision-making between the metropolitan government and colony has often involved a change in the local balance as well, and may be conditioned upon it. Constitutional changes in the local distribution of power generally take the form of broadening the franchise and easing restrictions on eligibility to serve in the legislative body. Universal adult suffrage has long prevailed in Puerto Rico, and there were no property qualifications for officeholding. These rights have obtained in the Virgin Islands since 1936.*

Franchise and Officeholding Qualifications in the British West Indies

In most of the British West Indies, however, there have been limitations on voting and on officeholding which are

---

* Prior to that date, restrictions on voting were also limitations on officeholding, which depended on the right to vote.

only gradually being removed. For example, in 1938 the registered electorate was only 6.6 per cent of the population of Trinidad and in Barbados it was 3.3 per cent.[31] The West India Royal Commission concluded that ". . . the present qualifications have had, as they no doubt intended to have, the effect of restricting the electorate to the comparatively well-to-do." Some colonies did not even provide for woman suffrage, while in others the age at which women were eligible to vote was higher than for men, and there were also restrictions on their holding office. In the Bahamas (which do not consider themselves part of the West Indies) the principle of the secret ballot was accepted for the whole colony only in 1946.

Qualifications for membership in the Legislative Council have been much higher than those for voting.[32] This situation led the West India Royal Commission to recommend a narrowing of the difference between the two kinds of qualifications.[33] However, it did not unanimously recommend immediate removal of property qualifications for voting but merely a gradual elimination after careful local consideration and consultation among the different colonies.

Modifications have been made in the franchise and office-holding qualifications since the West India Royal Commission reported. For example, in Trinidad universal adult suffrage was established in 1946 for Legislative Council elections; women were made eligible for election to the Legislative Council; and the qualifications for candidates were reduced about one-half. Qualifications for local elections were also liberalized, and universal adult suffrage instituted.[34]

In the same year changes in income and property qualifications for voting in British Guiana quadrupled the electorate. A compulsory literacy test did not require that English be used; thus it did not bar the large East Indian population from voting. In Barbados the property and income qualifications for holding office and for voting were merely reduced to the point where many agricultural workers could vote, and woman suffrage was introduced. The new Jamaican constitution provided for universal suffrage without a literacy test. Membership in the entirely elected House of Assembly did not require any property qualifications. However, candidates had to post election bonds which were forfeited if they failed to receive a certain percentage of the total vote.

One rationalization for not extending the franchise has been that minorities might go without protection; fear of this also justified the retention of the system of nominated official and unofficial members in the legislative body. Voting by a system of proportional representation might answer this problem. Protection might also be secured through such legal measures as making unconstitutional any legislative or administrative measure which discriminates against any group for racial or religious reasons.[35] Another rationalization for withholding the franchise has been the ignorance of the masses. Such ignorance may be partly the result of the system. The difficulty might be remedied by education and training. Furthermore, the removal of income and property qualifications might provide the practice which is essential to learning good citizenship.[36] A further reason given for a restricted franchise has been the lack of interest in voting among those already qualified. Indeed, why should the people bother to vote for candidates seeking office in an impotent legislative body? [37]

Municipal Government

Governmental changes, besides altering the balance of power between a colony and the mother country and between classes within a colony, may also modify the distribution of power between the municipal governments and the colonial government. Conforming to the pattern all over the world, the smaller units of government have shown their incompetence to handle modern social and economic problems, and in the case of such services as public health or education, the retention of jurisdiction in municipal hands may retard the colony's whole social and economic development.

The inability of local governments to meet these problems effectively has not only been a matter of size and lack of resources (the latter could be remedied to some extent by subsidies from the central government); the character of the members of the municipal government has also contributed to the incompetence of local administration. Municipal officials have been inclined to be excessively conservative (this is encouraged by qualifications for voting and office-holding) and to have such close personal and business interests in the affairs to be decided that they lack the desired disinterestedness and concern for the public welfare.[38]

Dissatisfaction with municipal administration in Puerto Rico led Governor Tugwell to sponsor the centralization of several services in the Insular Government, including even fire protection, traditionally a local concern.* Such a step may be regressive from the point of view of training for democratic self-government, however, since the local community has long been regarded as the seminary for such experience. The value of this training was recognized in a report on local government made for Jamaica in 1943 by a British authority, L. C. Hill.[39] The report recommended municipal retention of certain activities such as road maintenance, but urged colonial assistance and supervision. At the same time it emphasized that voluntary responsibility for many local activities should be stimulated, and it held up the English system as a model. The social welfare program

* More recently the Puerto Rican Government has been making a municipal survey to form the factual basis for a reallocation of governmental functions.

of Development and Welfare, in its efforts to develop community attitudes and a community spirit, may also have a beneficial effect on the quality of local government.[40]

Changes in Intercolonial Relations

Another kind of governmental change which affects the chances for greater autonomy (as well as the social and economic development of the Caribbean colonies) is that which brings the colonies closer to union. Specifically, the most likely modification is some form of federation among the British West Indies. British authorities have long discussed the desirability of federation, but whenever they made serious attempts to secure local consent in the past, they concluded the "time was not yet ripe." They emphasized that the sentiment for federation must come from the colonies themselves. In recent years, however, the British Government has more actively encouraged such a movement, and indicated that further self-government would in part be conditioned upon closer association.

The advantages of federation would be many. Not only would it eliminate the inconvenience to outsiders, metropolitan and otherwise, in dealing with so many little governments.* Federation would also tend to reduce excessive overhead administrative charges. It would free the circulation of administrative personnel and counteract the tendency to stagnation. While important administrative savings might not result, funds made available for social services could be more effectively spent under unified West Indian control, and services could be undertaken under a uniform plan. Better-qualified administrative personnel would be available, since higher salaries could be paid when the expense was spread

---

* For instance, the existence of a separate customs schedule for each of the West Indies definitely hinders their international trade.

over a number of colonies. There would also be a broader base for recruiting specialized talent.

Another advantage would be free trade among the separate communities. Political stability and administrative efficiency over a broader area could also facilitate economic development projects on a large scale.[41] Finally, a federated West Indies might be listened to somewhat more seriously in international discussions than the insignificant voices of the separate islands.

The chief obstacle to federation has been insular pride which amounts to excessive parochialism. There have also been geographical, cultural, and economic barriers, some of which have already been overcome. Wealthier colonies were reluctant in the past to share their resources with poorer colonies. The fear that closer union might solidify and perpetuate metropolitan control has also impeded progress toward federation. This fear has expressed itself in some colonies by demands that the inhabitants be given a greater voice in their government as a condition for closer union. An important obstacle to any governmental change has, of course, been the unwillingness of those in existing positions of power to risk their status under a new scheme.

In spite of these impediments, progress in bringing the West Indies together has been made since the West India Royal Commission recommendations for closer association. Development and Welfare is laying the economic and social groundwork for possible future governmental change. Not only has it worked for the adoption of uniform plans for housing and other specific developments. It has also stimulated the kind of co-operation which leads to closer political relations through such means as intercolonial conferences on specific problems. Furthermore, its training centers have been a step in the direction of unified administrative services. In some instances, the more favored colonies have shared their superior services with neighboring islands lacking the appropriate personnel and resources. In like manner the establishment of the West Indian University should provide further foundation for closer union of the West Indies.

In 1945 the Colonial Office sent a dispatch to the West Indian governors urging consideration of closer union and asking for local debate. The Windward and Leeward Islands began to move toward federation of those groups, and unification of the currency systems of the British colonies in the eastern Caribbean got under way. Most of the British West Indies seemed ready for further steps toward a general union.

In 1947 the Secretary of State proposed a conference to consider the desirability of federation and various methods for achieving closer association. It was composed of delegates nominated by the respective legislatures of the various British West Indian colonies. At the conference, the delegates expressed themselves in favor of the principle of federation, provided it was accompanied by further steps toward self-government. They arranged for a West Indian committee to work out the details of closer union, and make a report within a stated interval.* In the fall of 1948 the British Home Office sent a colonial negotiator to help the "Standing Closer Association Committee" work out details, with special emphasis on unified currency and a customs union.[42]

Closer political union of the American dependencies is highly unlikely.† The economic, cultural, and political differences are far too great, and the Virgin Islands would strongly

* The conference also called for the appointment of committees to plan for agriculture, industry, unification of currency, and a possible customs union. It recommended a British Caribbean trade commissioner in London.

† The absence of tariff, currency, and migration barriers has meant that there is considerable economic interchange between the two territories under the present system.

resist being merged with their more powerful neighbor.* In any case, until recently most Puerto Rican leaders spoke in no terms short of independence, and independence would be out of the question for the tiny Virgin Islands.

The work of the Caribbean Commission may significantly alter nongovernmental relations between all the dependencies of the Caribbean, even though the commission is not competent to touch constitutional questions. By promoting and co-ordinating social and economic development in the colonies throughout this area, it may produce many of the benefits which might otherwise be achieved through political union.

There are limits to voluntary co-operation in solving problems that cross jurisdictional boundaries. This has been demonstrated in the United States, where interstate co-operation cannot equal the effectiveness of Federal action. If the Caribbean colonies want greater autonomy they must get together on some basis. It is still true that "Where the units are small, federation is almost necessarily a preliminary to independence for practical reasons." [43]

The Inheritors of Power

The most common current reason given for withholding further grants of autonomy has been clearly put by Lord Hailey:

> There are some territories . . . in which sections of the population most closely in contact with European influences have attained a development out of all relation to the rest of the population. There should be no disposition to deny to the former a due place in the political institutions of their country, and it must inevitably be

* In fact, metropolitan officials have had difficulty in trying to merge the two Virgin Islands "municipal governments" because of the insular pride of St. Thomas and St. Croix.

determined rather by their social and intellectual attainments than by their numbers. But to allow them at this stage to exercise an undue share of political control might seriously prejudice a majority, which is often still living in primitive conditions and has interests different from those of an urban or industrial society. The chief characteristic of the rule of dependencies in its classical form is that it involves the control by a very few over very many. It is common ground that the objective in view is that the very many should eventually rule themselves. But it would be a misfortune if, in pursuance of this objective, the present few abdicated in favour of another group of very few, less likely than themselves to advance the interests of the many, and to devolve full authority on them.[44]

Representative of this general point of view are the following remarks of another colonial observer:

It has been my personal experience in the Caribbean countries and in the East that, although there is always a great deal of discussion about freedom and autonomy, the people who are the most vocal in their own behalf are the very ones who already enjoy a large measure of freedom, and they usually represent only a small fraction of the population. Many of them are politicians who hope to gain something by a change. Others have had a small amount of education, which has given them an urge to rule. . . .

To the majority of the population freedom means the ability to do what they want, and it does not make the slightest bit of difference whether the government is Dutch, English, or local, so long as it is equitable. But there are many native peoples who have learned that there is more true democracy in enlightened colonial government than there is in government by their own politicians.[45]

This is a key problem in relating constitutional change to social and economic development. How far does it prevail in the Caribbean colonies? To answer this question it is pertinent to discover what groups have favored particular governmental changes. It is equally important to know which groups will most benefit from constitutional revision.

Class Structure

Sharp class divisions, based on color and income, have characterized the British West Indies. Political arrangements facilitated the supremacy of the white residents and absentee white interests. The social contacts of high officials were primarily with wealthy white inhabitants. Besides these officials, who came from abroad, the governments were largely composed of lawyers, merchants, bankers, shippers, and planters, most of whom were white. Colored persons (as distinguished from black) could and did occupy most of the remaining governmental positions.[46]

The character of the colored middle class in Jamaica is clearly depicted in a sociological study, *The Marginal Man;* the portrait may be regarded as representative of other colonies in the British West Indies.[47] Those of mixed blood have formed a buffer group between blacks and whites, absorbing shocks from both sides and simultaneously binding the two races together.

> By giving the mixed bloods a middle class status, the British have developed a safety-valve for ambitious and discontented individuals. A restless black man may rise into the middle class, marry a mulatto, and so become effectively incorporated into the existing social structure.[48]

The colored individual has felt acutely the white man's underlying attitude of superiority but, admiring him, has accepted his superiority as inherent. Below the surface there has been an uneasy, sensitive, even obsessive spirit of race consciousness which, because it is inhibited, produces a conformist type of behavior and diverts ambition into social and economic success rather than into artistic expression or political innovation.[49]

The colored class has resented the black masses because it has been anxious to receive recognition as white though very much aware that such recognition is never complete. Thus there has developed the desire to protect this precarious status, which has been done by drawing a sharp line, political, economic, and social, between colored and obviously black. As might be expected, the black people resented this assumption of superiority by the colored.[50]

Where there are large groups of Chinese and East Indians, these (unlike the Negro groups) have resisted easy assimilation. They have formed separate classes not only racially but also economically, since the small property owners tend to be of such origin. Thus the Chinese and East Indians have been important factors in the lack of homogeneity which is cited frequently as a reason for retaining the present governmental arrangements.

Beginning in the late thirties this static situation began to disintegrate, and the color composition of the colonial governments grew darker. Leaders of the black masses came forward and gradually secured some recognition for the groups they championed.[51] Unionization of the black workers has proceeded rapidly, although the organizations are still of an unstable character. The new labor unions rapidly became political groups, although they did not become unified in a single labor party as in Great Britain. Labor members have appeared in the legislative bodies. In Trinidad and British Guiana the change was sufficiently noticeable to cause chambers of commerce to complain that business was no longer adequately represented in the councils of the government.[52]

A noteworthy phenomenon in Jamaica was the growth of the People's National Party, which was associated with the British Labor Party. It was chiefly a middle-class movement which espoused socialist and self-government views, and was allied with a group of unions composed largely of government and skilled workers. Under the new constitution this party was expected to inherit the government, but it lost out in the first elections to a rival leader who controlled large unions of the masses through sheer personal magnetism.*

Much of what has been said about the power of various classes in the British West Indies would apply also in the American Virgin Islands. A very small, ultraconservative sugar planter class ruled the territory, although merchants and real-estate owners have long since replaced this group in St. Thomas.[53] The constitutional props were removed from under this class by the Organic Act of 1936. Universal suffrage and the abolition of property qualifications for officeholding did not automatically alter the composition of the power pyramid in the Virgin Islands. Nevertheless, within a few years a new political movement arose, the Progressive Guides. This group was composed of darker-skinned Virgin Islanders, who professed much more liberal views than the former political leaders. In less than a decade they captured political power in St. Thomas.[54] The party has split into rival groups, but the general tendency toward younger, more social-minded leaders has become clear. In St. Croix a union leader successfully challenged the old ruling clique in 1946.

The Puerto Rican elections of 1940, which brought the Popular party into office marked a significant change in the political balance of that dependency. Until then Puerto Rico had been dominated by an oligarchy linked with the sugar industry. The earlier Spanish elite had lost its exclusive con-

* Right wing groups helped to elect this union head.

trol, but absentee interests from the continent were a significant political factor despite local resentment which compelled them to remain in the background.[55] Political, social, and economic ascendancy had been lodged in one group at the top, though political expediency required some lessening of the distances between classes for "the rich man needed the poor man's vote" and therefore had to pay him some attention.[56]

The success of the *Populares* is reputed to have been due, at least in part, to the *jibaro* vote.* In contrast to the customary purchase of votes or granting of "favors" such as poor relief and free medicine from the governing party, the Popular Party based its appeal on concrete social and economic reforms, "bread, land, and freedom." After the election it rapidly introduced some of these changes, and thereby consolidated its power among the propertyless.[57]

Color is not a vital issue in Puerto Rico, and the number of those with Negro blood is very much smaller than in the other dependencies, yet it has some political implications. As elsewhere, race and economic status are interlinked, with the blackest Negroes at the bottom of the economic scale. In spite of a dark skin, these colonials can sometimes effect entrance into more favored classes by improvement of economic circumstances.[58] Negroes have supported the Popular party, for it provided them with political and economic opportunities not formerly available to those of a darker skin.[59]

The rise of a party supported by and devoted especially to the masses presents a short-run problem of recruiting experienced and competent governmental officials. Governor Tugwell had to search elsewhere than in the Popular Democratic party for many administrative appointees—a difficult political dilemma.[60]

* The rural proletariat.

Group Opinions on Constitutional Change

People in the Caribbean dependencies have not been united in favoring one governmental change over another. They have not even agreed on the desirability of change. Sentiment of particular groups depended largely on how they estimated the effect which a change might have on their own status. In the past the British Government has given this division of opinion as a reason for postponing change. However, the absence of action was in itself partial, since it favored some interests over others.[61]

In general, British West Indian demands for greater autonomy have been most vociferous from labor and leftist groups, and from the darker-skinned elements in the community. Earlier, some members of the middle class had made moderate (and ineffective) appeals for more local powers. Nevertheless, this class tended to identify itself with the existing government. Only middle-class individuals who had experienced rebuffs from the ruling groups were likely to turn to subordinate or "oppressed" groups, often assuming leadership of them and thereby gaining status and self-respect.[62]

In Jamaica both left-wing factions originally demanded greater self-government. Led by a Rhodes scholar and respected colored barrister, Norman Manley, the People's National Party has constantly fought for more home rule. This position was later abandoned by the rival trade-union party under the leadership of Alexander Bustamente, the labor agitator who was twice imprisoned before he became "boss" of Jamaica.*

In the prolonged negotiations with the Colonial Office

* It should be noted that within the West Indies themselves autonomy demands go only as far as eventual "dominion status," not outright independence.

for a more liberalized constitution, however, these groups were joined by the middle-class Federation of Citizens' Associations, in order to prove to the British authorities that the governor was incorrect in stating that the desire for greater autonomy was not strongly supported. In fact, the first concrete proposals for a new constitution during this period were approved by the elected members of the Jamaican Legislative Council in 1939, most if not all of whom would have been regarded as middle-class representatives. In Trinidad and British Guiana, labor leaders have been the most outspoken proponents of more self-government. One demand upon which most local groups have been united was that which called for a greatly increased percentage of native West Indians in the higher brackets of the civil service.

Unlike many American colonial officials, whose positions were temporary, British colonial administrators were often apathetic to, when they did not actively resist, attempts to expand self-government. Radical changes would have greatly narrowed their career opportunities.[63] British colonial administrators have been essentially technicians rather than politicians. They tended to apply metropolitan standards of administrative perfection to local situations. Failing to envision any compensations, they inevitably concluded that the quality of government would seriously deteriorate in local hands.

One index of the existing governments' opposition to change was the censorship they imposed on the utterances of radical labor leaders, some of whom were also imprisoned for "seditious libel" even before the outbreak of World War II. This was also an index of the extreme behavior of those most anxious for constitutional changes. These curtailments of civil liberties were upheld by the British Government.[64]

There has been a notable absence of demands for greater autonomy coming from the chambers of commerce. Barbados and especially the Bahamas and Bermuda (the latter two do not regard themselves as part of the West Indies) are notoriously more conservative in their policies, and their laboring groups and black inhabitants have had little political voice. In these colonies there was scarcely any agitation for more self-government, although autonomy sentiment has gradually increased in Barbados with the liberalizing of the franchise.*

As might be expected, labor and leftist groups strongly supported universal suffrage and lower qualifications for officeholding. Other groups have been less united in favoring these changes than in demanding greater autonomy. Indeed, at least one native West Indian has complained that the contempt of the colored middle-class members for the black masses was expressed in the refusal to extend the franchise to "the barefooted man," whom they regarded as unready for the boon.[65] However, in Jamaica elected and unofficial nominated members, who were essentially middle-class, obtained Legislative Council approval for universal adult suffrage in 1939. This concession was not immediately granted by the Colonial Office. Nevertheless, as the negotiations for a new Jamaican constitution proceeded, the Colonial Office's position altered. It seemed readier to accept this change than significant modifications leading toward autonomy; the Colonial Office then used the concession as an argument against other desired changes.[66]

In Trinidad and British Guiana, where the presence of a large Indian population has hindered a united labor movement, the question of universal suffrage has been complicated. In Trinidad the Colonial Office would have liberalized the franchise further than the local legislature desired, by remov-

* The ancient constitutions of these three colonies already provide for somewhat greater local powers than in the case of the other dependencies. Thus, in Barbados the governor cannot authorize measures not already approved by both legislative bodies.

ing the suggested English literacy test.[67] In British Guiana, however, the Colonial Secretary (under the Labour regime) decided to defer inauguration of universal adult suffrage in favor of modified qualifications for voting because of the "very large body of responsible public opinion desiring its postponement." Even the labor groups in this colony favored a probationary period before complete adult suffrage was instituted.[68]

It was the British Labor Party rather than the Conservatives who constantly advocated greater self-government and a wider franchise for the colonies. Nevertheless, many of the moderate concessions granted in the British West Indies took place prior to the victory of the Laborites in 1945. Continual pressure for greater autonomy has come from the Fabian Colonial Bureau, which has furnished intellectual guidance to the Labor Party. (The Bureau's first chairman became Secretary of State for the Colonies in 1946.) [69] It has specifically expressed dissatisfaction with the halfway constitution of Jamaica under which responsibility for public policy is confused and uncertain.[70] British groups, including the League of Coloured Peoples, have expressed well-reasoned views regarding greater autonomy. In contrast, some of the colonial societies in Harlem, New York City, composed of emigrated British West Indians, have demanded more radical solutions, including outright independence.

Many labor and leftist groups have actively sponsored closer association of the British West Indies. These groups have usually linked up federation with greater self-government and with universal suffrage, which they regarded as at least as important. Chambers of commerce have begun to welcome certain aspects of federation, and both the local chambers and the Incorporated British Caribbean Chambers of Commerce have supported demands for closer economic ties. Earlier sentiment regarding federation had divided partly on insular lines. The more economically and politically advanced colonies opposed any union with the more backward islands. However, at the conclusion of the Conference on Closer Association in the West Indies, in 1947, only the delegates from British Guiana (which considers itself a part of the South American continent) and from the British Honduras failed to give wholehearted support to the principle of federation.[71]

In recent years Puerto Rican opinion on the future status of the island has divided along class lines. In an earlier era, before the rise of a strongly organized leftist party, the cry for independence was found to be a perennially potent type of propaganda by many kinds of party leaders. The vagueness of the demand and the unlikelihood of its success made it especially useful for vote-getting. In the case of the extremist nationalists, it has been the expression of individuals who failed to find a place for themselves in the existing organization of society and were eager for some form of recognition. Many of them have been romantically inclined Hispanic-minded intellectuals. Some university students are particularly susceptible to independence propaganda.

Within the last decade there has been a discernible tendency for the wealthy, well-born, and well-educated elite to support closer union with the United States and to favor statehood as the ultimate goal, leaving the independence cry to others. At the same time, those calling for greater independence began to temper their demands. Their attitude changed regarding both the desired form of self-government and the economic ties with the mother country, whose financial aid they now recognized as indispensable to their social and economic goals.

There have been some powerful *independentistas* among the leaders of the Popular party who have continued to attack the United States whenever possible. The ranks of the *independentistas* were joined by a small group of Communists, who became outspoken advocates of "complete independence" following the war. Communist party members have actively participated in the work of one of the two large union organizations, the *Confederación General de Trabajadores*.[72] In spite of some outbursts by the extremists, the tendency is toward moderation. For many years Luis Muñoz Marín has frowned on independence agitation and emphasized instead the economic and social problems.

Many administrative leaders on the continent have urged more self-government for Puerto Rico. Theodore Roosevelt the younger, who was governor in the early thirties, favored dominion status. Presidents Roosevelt and Truman urged greater autonomy. Successive secretaries of the Department of the Interior were regularly sympathetic, and Governor Tugwell actively sought legislation granting more home rule. The chief obstacle was the conservative membership of Senate and House committees dealing with territorial and insular affairs. Senator Tydings was outstanding.[73] His insistence on the choice of outright independence or nothing blocked the definition of a policy which could be both feasible and acceptable to all concerned.[74]

Prior to the Virgin Islands Organic Act of 1936, which made substantial concessions toward greater autonomy, there was some sentiment for such a move among several groups, each expecting to profit from the change. However, the conservative classes, which formerly held what local power existed, did not welcome the elimination of property qualifications for voting and officeholding and the inauguration of universal adult suffrage which extended the vote to women. In fact, representatives from the municipal councils went to Washington to argue against these changes in the franchise.

Some Political Effects of Constitutional Change

The sequel to the passage of the Virgin Islands Organic Act suggests who may inherit political power when constitutional changes grant greater self-government and broaden local participation in government. In the initial period following enactment, the formal legal alterations did not greatly modify local practices and customs, which were slow to change. The number of registered voters increased from 1,501 in 1937 to 3,726 in 1938, but the actual increase was much smaller than the potential increase under universal suffrage. Gradually, the character of the legislatures began to be modified. Younger men who were somewhat responsive to the beginnings of organized public opinion came into office. Political organizations were started, but organs for the formation and communication of public opinion were still in the primitive stage, especially because of the irresponsible and immature character of the local newspapers.[75]

The traditional hostility to the governor expressed by the local legislators did not significantly abate under the new act, and the same legislative efforts to oppose the governor's will continued regardless of the nature of the issue. However, this constant effort to reach out for executive power, apparent under both old and new regimes, had now to be undertaken under laws fixing responsibility for conditions which formerly could be blamed on "the government."

Several reforms expected of the newly organized Progressive Guide party failed to materialize, but this younger group was at least credited with educating the electorate in the value of the vote. Very slowly the political hold of the older conservative elite was loosened, and power began to be assumed by newer, somewhat more liberal politicians.[76]

In contrast to the gradual transformation in the Virgin Islands, the constitutional changes in Jamaica, particularly universal adult suffrage, brought about a radical shift in local political power. In the first elections under the new constitution the so-called Labor Party, which was actually another name for the Bustamente labor unions, won an overwhelming victory. It defeated Norman Manley's socialist People's National Party, the more temperate group on which so many British liberals had placed their hopes. The conservative parties were also defeated; to keep Manley out, enough conservatives had supported Bustamente to insure his victory.[77] Only four members of the old Legislative Council were re-elected: one Labor, one People's National Party, and two independents.

Bustamente's growing opposition to "self-government," so strongly sponsored by the People's National Party, accounted for some of his conservative support; otherwise he was regarded as an irresponsible demagogue. Because he had expressed unpopular opinions officially considered seditious, he had earlier suffered a curtailment of his liberties and even imprisonment. This had made him a martyr in the eyes of the masses. Furthermore, in earlier years Bustamente had secured substantial benefits for his union. The first few months of his regime were marked by very moderate actions in public policy, especially from the financial point of view. But within a year he had ruthlessly attacked the rival unions of the Manley group and provided verbal evidence of his dictatorial attitudes.[78]

A bloody crisis came with the riots springing from a Manley union strike at the mental hospital in Kingston. Bustamente led a violent crowd against the strikers, and three fatalities resulted. He and one of his lieutenants were found guilty of manslaughter by a coroner's jury, but were finally acquitted after a sensational trial.[79] On several subsequent occasions, he has participated in (though he did not always initiate) violent conflicts with members of the People's National Party, and he has been brought to court for defying the police. Bustamente's behavior has scandalized outsiders, with repercussions on his political power. He still must reckon with the People's National Party, which his unscrupulous tactics have failed to suppress. In the municipal elections of 1947 he lost considerable ground to the People's National Party, and the largest number of seats went to independents. Part of his party leadership in the House of Representatives also split off to form a new organization.

An increase in newspapers and in popular interest in politics was a less dramatic by-product of the new Jamaican constitution. Compared with elections under the old system there was a tremendous increase in candidates.* Parties began to be organized, in place of loose combinations following particular individuals. What might be an ominous tendency not in the direction of liberal democracy was the alliance of rival groups of unions with opposing political parties. This kind of association intensified the conflict between unions and often moved them to violence. It reinforced a drive for power not in the public interest, but to the advantage of the leaders and of particular economic interests. These included the interests of conservative groups who fought one radical by supporting another.†

* On election day, however, only 55 per cent of the registered voters actually voted. Participation was greater in the first elections under a broadened franchise in other colonies.

† Except for the change in political leaders, the tendency toward wielding of governmental power by a narrow economic group continues under the new regime. Neither the old oligarchy nor the new dictatorship conforms to liberal democracy, in which the government is expected to hold the balance between different interests rather than to rule in favor of one. Perhaps the absence of a literacy qualification for voting helps to explain why, despite their sociological similarities, Jamaica's political development differed from that in the Virgin Islands. The ability to read and write

The fact that the governor, a metropolitan official, could referee between Bustamente and his labor rivals and prevent his developing into the familiar Latin American type of *caudillo* may argue for the retention of existing metropolitan controls. On the other hand, Bustamente's irresponsible behavior may reflect the halfway character of the Jamaican constitution, where neither metropolitan nor colonial officials have clear authority.[80]

In contrast to both Jamaica and the Virgin Islands is Puerto Rico where without constitutional change there have been significant political alterations. The rise of the Popular Democratic Party, which won a decisive majority in the government in the 1944 elections, marked a sharp shift in political power among local groups. It was evident not only in the composition of the governing party but in the policies adopted.

While the humblest *jibaro* had long enjoyed the franchise, he was likely to vote for the man promising a small but immediately concrete reward (such as a pork dinner or two dollars). With the rise of the Popular Party the *jibaro* exhibited a tendency to vote for candidates promising a larger but more remote reward, such as a plot of land. Though the wealthy were against them, the support of the masses enabled the *Populares* to legislate a strongly "socialistic" program with the encouragement of Governor Tugwell. The loud complaints of expropriation coming from the large sugar producers and similar groups showed that they, at least, believed their power lost under the new regime.

One tentative conclusion to be drawn regarding the inheritors of power is that legal changes intended to democratize a colonial government are not always the decisive factor in

may make for a more enlightened electorate. However, a literacy qualification would perhaps have been politically unfeasible in Jamaica, where the literacy rate is so much lower than in the Virgin Islands.

effecting political changes, either in the ruling groups or in the character of the legislation. Universal adult suffrage does not automatically insure wider participation in government and its benefits. Nevertheless it lays the legal foundation making such changes possible. As long as the people are enfranchised, the means exist for displanting a small aristocracy and establishing a broadly based democracy.

A second conclusion is that granting more powers of self-government to the Caribbean colonies will not strengthen an already too-powerful elite, provided the franchise is widely, if not universally, enjoyed. Greater autonomy is no longer conceivable without this condition. The laboring class' share in the newly granted power will be proportionate to its influence, and this has expanded substantially in recent years. The political experience in Jamaica demonstrates clearly the need to accelerate social and economic development throughout the area, so that when power is passed on to the hitherto ignorant mass of the people they will be able to use it wisely and benefit from it.

A further conclusion is that the "independence" slogans are no longer so powerful in eliciting mass support as are economic promises. Both Muñoz Marín and Bustamente soft-pedaled the arguments for greater autonomy. Colonial leaders have become more sophisticated about the possibility of gaining the advantages of constitutional independence without losing the advantages of economic dependence. Nevertheless, they cannot ignore demands for self-government which spring from a psychological need as great as the physical need for food and shelter.

X. The Effects of Governmental Changes on Social and Economic Development

CONSTITUTIONAL changes can redistribute power between the colonies and the mother country and among local groups. They can also have indirect political consequences because of their effect on the social and economic development of the colonies. Are governmental reforms likely to retard social and economic improvement or might they accelerate progress toward higher living standards?

Some conclusions may be drawn by comparing the attitudes of existing colonial governments toward social and economic development with those of the potential inheritors of power when further self-government is granted. Also relevant, when the location of governmental decision-making is to be modified, are the possible effects upon other kinds of decision-making which emanate from the mother country. Are these effects likely to assist or retard social and economic development in the colonies?

Group Attitudes toward Social and Economic Development

Diminishing Conservatism in the British West Indies

Recent social and economic progress in the British West Indies has largely been the result of metropolitan initiative. Nevertheless, it corresponded with an intense but unorganized demand in the colonies, where constitutional and legal means for expression were absent. Thus the incipient but legally unrecognized labor movement of the late thirties sought its objectives through direct action, to the distress not only of the propertied classes but of all desiring the solution of political problems through peaceful means. Metropolitan direction and persuasion were necessary for several years before the colonial governments adopted modern labor legislation.[1]

The inertia of colonial governments in social and economic matters has sometimes been laid to the lack of interest or opposition among the local legislators. This assumption led to the belief that giving such governments further legal power would hinder social and economic development. Striking examples cited were Bermuda and the Bahamas, where the relatively independent legislatures would not pass the most elementary social legislation. Their conservatism was hardly surprising, for these legislatures were composed of members with high property qualifications elected on a narrow franchise, and in one colony not even by secret ballot.

An examination of the actions of legislatures in the other colonies indicates that, at least until the late thirties, the elected members were particularly economy-minded on many issues and prone to charge the governors with extravagance. The legislators' reaction to suggestions for enlarged expenditures on social services could not be separated from the general hostility toward an administration which they could not control but could only block. Nor is there much evidence in most of the colonies that the governors were outstandingly progressive in their programs. Usually they lagged behind the policies of the Colonial Office.[2]

In any case, it was still true that legislative members elected on a narrow franchise were not inclined to push forward boldly as reformers. In most cases they showed little appreciation of the grave social crisis confronting them, caused by the progressive deterioration of living standards among

the less privileged classes and by the masses' growing awareness of how more fortunate areas fared.[3]

The revolutionary change in British colonial policy of the
last decade has been reflected in the policies of the West Indian governments. Like the Federal grant-in-aid system in
the United States, Development and Welfare subsidizing has
encouraged the colonial governments to attack their problem
much more vigorously than they would without this incentive. Now, none of the West Indian colonies could afford
constitutional changes which threatened discontinuance of
British financial aid under this program.

Although monetary inducements from the mother country
have been an important factor in the new emphasis on social
and economic development in the colonies, they were not the
only one. There were already stirrings in this new direction
subsequent to the outbreak of the "disturbances" and prior
to 1940. For example, Trinidad and Jamaica had embarked
on modest slum-clearance programs; labor advisers had been
appointed in some colonies; and some nutritional investigations had been made. Earlier, local reformers had tended to
concentrate on political demands rather than on social and
economic reforms. Then came the embryonic labor organizations and the Jamaica People's National Party, the first
thoroughly organized political party in the West Indies.*
These local developments, together with modest constitutional
changes and Development and Welfare funds, account for
most of the change in West Indian social and economic
policies.

The difference between Trinidad in 1937 and in 1947,
both years marked by violent labor disturbances, is evident in

---

* A possible exception was the earlier Trinidad Workingmen's Association, led by Captain Cipriani, a white Creole. Although he obtained a
governmental position of importance his group did not become powerful,
in part because of the limited franchise.

the reports of metropolitan officials in these two periods of turmoil. The Forster Commission of 1937 attributed the rioting to a general sense of dissatisfaction with social conditions. This discontent could not be articulated because of the lack of regular collective bargaining machinery. In the intervening years there was a discernible improvement in industrial and social conditions, and many of the Forster and West India Royal Commission recommendations were being implemented. Collective bargaining became the generally accepted procedure for settling labor disputes. The behavior of the police in the 1947 disturbances was judicious and responsible; and, unlike the earlier conflicts, these resulted in no loss of life and very few serious injuries.[4]

Jamaica is the chief West Indian colony where constitutional changes were sufficiently great to throw some light on what effect, if any, they might have on social and economic development. In 1939 Jamaica was still exhibiting the same kind of unprogressive reaction to its social troubles that was typical of all the West Indies. The chief complaint seemed to be that labor unrest was costing the government very large sums for maintaining public order.[5]

Gradually, Jamaica awoke to the possibilities of more positive solutions for its difficulties. Although the program of the People's National Party was the boldest, other holders of, or contenders for, government power were advocating somewhat similar social and economic policies, if of a milder form. The chief difference was the modified role of the government in achieving agreed-upon social and economic goals.

There has yet been insufficient experience under the revised constitutions and the new Jamaican government to draw definitive conclusions. However, during the first years of the regime there were no startling changes in social and economic policies. A decision by the elected members of the old Legislative Council to sell the government-operated telephone service to a private corporation (held in abeyance by the Secretary of State until the new government came into power) was not reversed. No raid was made on the public treasury, as some had feared would occur when the labor group came to power.[6]

The new legislation which provided security of tenancy to agriculturists under certain conditions, and some moderate education, labor, and land tenure reforms, was not out of line with Jamaican tendencies before the government changed. The Bustamente regime's interest in popular reforms of immediate benefit, such as free meals for school children, rather than in long-run plans for economic rehabilitation did not distinguish this government from its predecessors.

The Jamaican constitution did decrease active intervention by the Colonial Office and Parliament in local affairs.[7] Suggestions from metropolitan officials were still acceptable. Sir Frank Stockdale, while Comptroller for Development and Welfare in the West Indies, declared (without reference to the change in government) that Jamaicans desired to work out their own problems. The majority were nevertheless eager to have the facts ascertained and presented, and Jamaicans wanted guidance from authoritative sources.[8] Jamaican leaders have sometimes talked loudly of their independence, but their actions have continued to accord with metropolitan policy.

The new government did not set off a sharp conflict between the propertied and the propertyless. After Bustamente's victory, the real change was that the bitter and frequently violent rivalry between his unions and those of the People's National Party now involved the government as one contender, instead of as a neutral attempting to keep the peace. Social and economic policies did not take a radical turn, but the methods of government by a labor dictator were a distinct departure from traditional practice.

For the West Indies generally, class differences in attitude toward social and economic development are not quite so marked as they formerly were. In an earlier period the elite, interested only in a cheap labor supply, was not inclined to advocate wide educational opportunities for the masses. Where the need for training was acknowledged, the wealthy favored purely practical education. Vocational training has now begun to be appreciated at its true value by those who can best profit from it. Meanwhile the desire to improve education generally has become more widespread in all classes. Indeed, wherever expression is free the most insistent colonial demand for better government services is usually for more and better schools.[9]

The more privileged classes have often proposed emigration of the unemployed as a solution to economic problems in some colonies. Like similar groups elsewhere, they are most conscious of the dangers of overpopulation. The propertied classes seem to be more interested in plans for economic development than in those for social reforms, although even in the former respect they are often averse to change. The sugar interests, for instance, have long resisted such new policies as crop-diversification. The well-to-do have been especially interested in metropolitan tariff subsidies and marketing aids, but have been less eager for social development grants.

Development and Welfare officials drew no class distinctions when they complained of West Indian attitudes toward social measures. There was a general lack of foresight in preferring improved hospitals and other immediate medical benefits to a preventive health program. Appreciation of social needs far outran the understanding of their costs. Development and Welfare officials believed that West Indians generally relied too much on metropolitan financing rather than on their own efforts to improve social and economic conditions.

Since constitutional changes involving wider suffrage are most likely to produce an increase in labor's influence in the colonial government, the kinds of policies advocated by the West Indies Labour Conferences which began in 1944 may give some clue to possible legislative directions.[10] In addition to constitutional reforms, they have urged an eight-hour day and forty-four-hour week, machinery for wage-fixing by wage boards, an intercolonial steamship service in the West Indies, and reforms and uniformity in the administration of justice. They have also favored social insurance, workmen's compensation, factory laws, general improvements in conditions of work, water supplies, and free compulsory education.[11]

While labor groups are naturally more interested in labor legislation than are the groups now governing in many colonies, the framework of a modern labor code has already been legislated in the West Indies, and labor unions have not been alone in their desire for a social security program. A chief distinction of the labor programs in the British West Indies was their comprehensiveness. They differed from others also in the emphasis on immediate action for their social policies. And they were especially remarkable for their support of government-operated enterprises and nationalization of some industries.

Changing Scope of Government Activity in the American Dependencies

The Organic Act of 1936 produced no abrupt or startling changes in local legislative policy in the Virgin Islands. Earlier governors had hoped that the extended suffrage would result in more representative municipal councils less inclined to be stumbling blocks to progress. Their hopes were slow to materialize, but some modest advances in social policy have been gradually realized, particularly in homesteading, labor, and education.

In sharp contrast, social and economic policies in Puerto Rico have changed radically in recent years, without any constitutional change as a contributing cause.[12] Puerto Rico has come a long distance since the younger Theodore Roosevelt was governor, just before the advent of the Franklin Roosevelt Administration. Governor Roosevelt was criticized by Puerto Ricans when he sought funds to feed the children. They complained that his action would bring shame on Puerto Rico by exposing her poverty, keep tourists away, and injure the sale of her products.[13] The subsequent change in spirit came from a local, not a metropolitan, shift in power. However, the change was aided by New Deal agencies and very greatly encouraged by the last continental governor, Rexford G. Tugwell.

The more conservative local groups very bitterly opposed the program of state-stimulated economic and social development.* Even during the war they fought the idea of diversification of food crops in place of complete reliance on large-scale cash export crops. Some of the Insular Government's development activities which they deplored were justified on the ground that wealthy conservatives, who had capital to invest, had failed to provide the necessary funds for development under private auspices. Although a leader of this conservative opposition, Bolívar Pagán, had introduced the Insular five-hundred-acre laws into the legislature in 1935, he and his colleagues were strongly against the kind of land reforms undertaken. They preferred division of the land into individually owned family-size farms.

In opposition to the government's program, some commercial interests proposed a Businessman's Ten-Year Plan. This

* Many romantically inclined *independentistas* also had no concern for social and economic reforms.

included, *inter alia*, increased tariff protection for Puerto Rican industry; an increase in the sugar quota; industrialization under private, not government auspices; a different type of industrial development stressing handmade products, food processing, and novelties; rehabilitation of the coffee industry; and certain exemptions from the Federal Fair Labor Standards Act.[14] Like their opponents, however, they did advocate improvements in health, sanitation, education, and housing.[15] There seems to have been little class division regarding the desire for better transportation facilities and the encouragement of tourism.

With the Popular party in power, Governor Tugwell succeeded in realizing many of his ideas for social and economic development; he was less successful in achieving administrative reforms. No matter what the political complexion of the dominant party, it can be expected to be jealous of the official positions it controls and to resist efforts to strengthen the executive or promote the merit system. Nevertheless, important improvements in the administration of Puerto Rico have occurred in recent years, including reforms in the personnel system. Nor did progress stop with Governor Tugwell's departure.

Further shifts in local political power in Puerto Rico which might come with the granting of greater autonomy can only be speculated upon.* The first native governor, Jesús Piñero, has pursued policies similar to those established by his predecessor. If further autonomy were granted, could the Popular Democratic Party remain in power without the aid of Federal officials, which would then no longer be available? Not all

* This discussion assumes that statehood for Puerto Rico is politically unfeasible, because of opposition both in Congress and in the Popular Democratic Party, notwithstanding support for statehood among the *Populares'* opponents and in the Republican Party platform for 1948. The United States Tariff Commission also believed it to be economically a very disadvantageous constitutional change.

metropolitan officials were in harmony with the party program, for both the federally appointed Attorney General and the Auditor in office early in the Tugwell regime opposed the "experiments" of the new government. Even without outside support the Popular Party is strongly situated. Once in the government seat a party is difficult to dislodge, especially if it seems to make good its promises. If the program adopted under the *Populares* fails to any extent, much blame could be transferred to the last continental governor, Tugwell.

Leaving the present Puerto Rican regime to govern alone would probably have less effect on social and economic policies than on governmental processes. The lack of a politically effective opposition to the Popular Democratic Party carries two dangers: first, the government might degenerate into a one-party dictatorship along Latin American lines; secondly, it might fall apart into dissident groups, and, because of sharp divisions in popular support, resort to armed force to maintain its supremacy. However, recourse to violence would run counter to Puerto Rico's long tradition of settling political contests peacefully.

A more immediate question is whether or not Congress will make the desired concessions toward self-government when the Federal legislators most responsible for colonial policy are conservatives, unsympathetic to the Puerto Rican program because it is further to the left than they approve. Furthermore, certain Puerto Rican policies run counter to the immediate interests of some of their constituents. Congressional refusal to grant further autonomy would be a serious blow to Puerto Rican hopes. But a graver danger would be that, for economy's sake, a conservative Congress might cast Puerto Rico completely adrift without any economic assistance whatsoever.

Governor Tugwell feared that the social and economic

plans of the new regime would risk failure without certain administrative reforms, for he recognized that an outmoded administrative system could not bear the burden of increased government activity. That graft, nepotism, and inefficiency are much more common in the Caribbean than they are in the mother countries is well known.* Since the government is the largest employer in many of the colonies it is especially difficult to get rid of these defects.

Both British and American officials have deplored the colonial people's lack of a sense of public duty divorced from immediate and personal political advantage. Will the new groups coming to power with positive programs of social and economic development be sufficiently imbued with their avowed purposes to carry these out effectively? Good intentions are not sufficient. Well-trained and personally disinterested local administrators are also essential to extensive social and economic development; otherwise it is likely to fail with the relaxation of metropolitan controls. The testimony of numerous observers recently viewing the Puerto Rican political scene indicates that able, honest, and intelligent leaders are participating in the development program.

In the long run the benefits of such a program should reduce the popular tendency to value the government service chiefly as a private advantage, because money and security would be obtainable elsewhere besides in public employment.[16] Meanwhile, the administration of certain measures is held to metropolitan standards because they are supervised by Federal agencies extending their services to Puerto Rico.

The assumption that social and economic development requires metropolitan financing has led Puerto Rican leaders to consider further self-government only if aid from the Federal Government would be maintained. The problem of con-

* Nevertheless, there is a tendency in metropolitan countries to impose a double standard of administrative morality at home and in the colonies.

tinuing Federal subsidies is one aspect of another question. What effect would greater governmental autonomy have upon other metropolitan decisions which affect the colonies?

Metropolitan Decisions and Colonial Autonomy

Public Decisions

In addition to decisions regarding financial assistance to the colonies, there are many other governmental decisions of significance to them. They include the extension of trade privileges, the fostering of transportation and communications facilities, monetary regulation, and the conduct of their external defense and foreign relations, including relations with international organizations. Constitutional changes may also alter public decisions regarding citizenship and migration rights as well as the local application of certain metropolitan laws such as quarantine regulations, postal service, and the currency system.

In addition, there are private and semipublic decisions of consequence to the colonies, which might be affected by the grant of greater self-government. The continuation of capital investments may be involved (including the effect upon the colonial government's credit in the metropolitan market). Autonomy concessions may also extend or contract the activities of philanthropic, cultural, scientific, religious, labor, and similar metropolitan organizations which operate in the colonies.

Of comparable importance to the extensive direct subsidies made in the British and American colonies in recent years are metropolitan measures favoring their trade. The value to the colonies of these decisions is due to many circumstances. Although the sugar industry, mainstay of most of these colonies, is utterly dependent upon preferences in the metropolitan markets, this dependence is partly the result of historical trends for which the metropolitan countries are partly responsible. For example, the trade of Puerto Rico had gradually become monopolized by the mother country as a result of tariff assimilation. At the same time, free world trade, especially in sugar, was disappearing; as many countries subsidized local production, particularly in beet sugar, the Caribbean colonies became increasingly dependent upon metropolitan preferences.

When extensive government controls over trade are common throughout most of the world, colonies rely especially upon metropolitan protection to maintain their economies, so closely tied up with the sale of cash export products. If self-government concessions weakened the sense of responsibility in the mother country, causing disregard of the continuing need for economic aid, the increase in governmental independence would have disastrous effects on the colonies. On the other hand, when decisions have been made in the mother country allocating quotas, setting tariff rates, and making trade agreements, the needs of a particular Caribbean colony have been a negligible consideration compared with those of more powerful units or interests with Parliamentary or Congressional representation.[17]

Although potentially of economic value to the dependencies, metropolitan government actions relating to the provision of transportation and communications have not always benefited the Caribbean colonies. This is especially true of the American coastwise shipping law, which has been injurious to Puerto Rico. Greater independence might free her of this control, but exemption could also be secured without a change in governmental status. The colonies in this area have suffered in the past from discriminatory freight rates. The American rates were fixed with the acquiescence of the Maritime Commission. Puerto Rico, however, had little influence with the commission compared to that of the large shipping companies, which had a legal monopoly of the trade.[18]

On the positive side, government subsidies have improved transportation facilities for some of the Caribbean dependencies. Air transportation, so important to these widely separated islands, also depends considerably upon metropolitan government action. However, many of the airfields which might be available for civilian use were built by the United States for military reasons and would probably not be abandoned no matter what the governmental status of the colonies might be. Although regulated by the Civil Aeronautics Board, Puerto Rico's air service has been primarily a commercial affair. Air service for the British West Indies has required some British subsidizing. Radio communication has not depended greatly upon metropolitan aid, although the British Broadcasting Company provided special programs for the West Indies. Development and Welfare helped to provide receiving sets in some of the islands, and the Caribbean Commission has furnished programs.

The metropolitan countries might have provided more economic assistance than they have yet offered their Caribbean colonies in some fields. Nevertheless, the sum of the financial aid, direct and indirect, is far too important to the colonies to risk cutting it off for the sake of more local government power.[19] The colonies would doubtless prefer to have the aid continued without the administrative controls which accompany various kinds of assistance. Yet, in theory, when one government level assumes financial responsibility for a policy, it should also have administrative responsibility.

Contrary to the usual case, Puerto Rico and the Virgin Islands have long received important subsidies over which the metropolitan government has no administrative control. These have been in the form of tax remittances and exemptions not permitted the States. These arrangements, like those regarding tariff assimilation, are part of the organic law of the dependencies. Any constitutional changes granting further autonomy would have to take account of these unregulated subsidies. However, subjection to administrative controls has not been a particularly repugnant aspect of dependency to Puerto Ricans and Virgin Islanders. The real object of their hostility has been the symbol of a frequently arbitrary and absent-minded Congress.

Further autonomy does not necessarily conflict with continued administrative control by the metropolitan agencies now providing services locally. For example, the governor of Puerto Rico, both before and after passage of the legislation making his office elective, has had relatively little control over the administration of aid from Federal agencies. To satisfy colonial desires for more responsibility, however, the attitude of metropolitan officials administering local projects must be one of co-operation with colonial officials. Such an attitude is, in fact, replacing the paternalistic or authoritative deportment of some officials which was so hateful to the colonial people.

The problem of political and administrative controls is somewhat simpler in the case of subsidies to the British West Indies. There the general policy of development and welfare was set by Parliament for a long period. As soon as particular Development and Welfare projects have been approved by metropolitan officials, almost all administrative responsibility is put in the hands of the colonial governments.

Future aid for colonial projects in areas which had achieved considerable governmental autonomy would depend upon the mother country's continued sense of political responsibility. For both British and American dependencies there are metropolitan agencies (the British Colonial Office and the United States Department of the Interior) which speak for these colonies when political decisions are made concerning them in the mother country.* Presumably, greater autonomy would tend to relieve these metropolitan officials of their obligation. But metropolitan action is bound by no law. Even without further self-government there is no real assurance that the current unprecedented interest and generosity toward the Caribbean colonies will continue.

What are the forces which might cause the British and American governments to continue assisting Caribbean territories when they had obtained a marked degree of self-government? A preclusive concern with the military security of the area could make for a continued interest, especially with respect to American action in the Caribbean. This interest was, for the United States, wholly independent of the question of sovereignty. For example, the coming of World War II caused the United States to give many kinds of aid not only to her own dependencies but to independent Caribbean countries and the British West Indies as well.

There are also ideological forces. Both the United States and Great Britain have developed sensitive international consciences. Their national pride, their desire for the spread of democracy, and their sense of obligation for past performance might induce generosity despite the postwar forces of financial stringency. These tendencies may be reinforced by the fear of the spread of communism in dependent areas.

Economic forces might also operate in the direction of continued aid. The economic ties between the different members of the British Commonwealth are close despite governmental independence. American policy toward the Philippines, though it leaves much to be desired, also indicates a wish to prevent the economic catastrophe which sudden independence might bring. Conceivably, metropolitan investors

* The Division of Territories and Island Possessions performs a role similar to that of a Congressman's staff, with the dependencies forming its constituency.

and traders in the colonial areas would lend influence to the continuation of aid which would assure them of continued returns from their colonial enterprises. In the case of Great Britain, at least, the need for expanded export markets will produce strong pressure in the government for aid in industrializing the colonies in order to create purchasers of British goods.[20] In the meantime, British demand for food and raw materials from the sterling area has already stimulated public aid to colonial production.

The vicissitudes of the American Good Neighbor Policy toward Latin America are not reassuring to the Caribbean dependencies. The colonies cannot count on a constant economic policy should they become more autonomous. Neither have they been able to depend upon such constancy during most of their years under American tutelage. One point is clear. Legal assurances are not by themselves reliable, despite the encouraging clauses in Congressional bills for a more autonomous Puerto Rico.[21]

The Caribbean colonies have no real assurance that tariff preferences will continue. They have feared that fulfillment of the frequently expressed American desire for general reduction in trade barriers will affect them adversely regardless of their political status. In the Anglo-American negotiations regarding world trade policies, exceptions have ultimately had to be made permitting the continuation of special treatment for the British colonies.

The General Agreement on Tariffs and Trade made at Geneva in 1947 reduced the margin of preference for many colonial products from the British Empire and decreased the tariffs on sugar imported into the United States; it also prohibited new preferences or increases in present preferences.[22] However, the colonies were expected to gain ultimately by an increased volume of trade offsetting the losses in preferential margins. For the moment quantitative restrictions on imports from the colonies are more important than the rate of customs duties.

Should the British West Indies become more autonomous, their tariff position in the empire would probably become similar to that of the dominions. In the event of greater independence, the trade status of Puerto Rico might eventually resemble that of the independent Caribbean countries. Cuba, for instance, has especially favorable tariff arrangements with the United States which are not open to other countries.*

Many kinds of decisions made in the mother country have no very direct economic value for the colonies. Yet they are somewhat related to colonial development and might be affected by a change in constitutional status. The American dependencies have more of these decisions made for them than have the British West Indies. The United States census includes Puerto Rico and the Virgin Islands. Quarantine regulations are made in the United States. Lighthouse administration is Federal. When prohibition was the Federal law it was also extended to these territories. The same currency is used. The Federal civil service is open to islanders. Radio broadcasting is federally regulated. In some cases the same tax rates apply locally as in the United States. Customs collections are in Federal hands.

For the British West Indies there are variations on some of these decisions; others are completely absent. The British colonies are part of the sterling bloc, which places restrictions on their trade. For many purposes the British West Indies are expected to use the services of the British Crown Agents, who usually use British materials and patronize British firms. These services may be viewed as a privilege rather than as a

* There have sometimes been complaints that the United States has given Cuba greater trade favors than Puerto Rico has enjoyed.

restriction. The British colonial inhabitant's eligibility to the Empire's Colonial Service is definitely a privilege.

Superficially the list of decisions outlined above may seem purely administrative, but in practice many political considerations are involved. For example, whether or not to take a census and what to include in it are policy decisions important to social and economic development. The lack of up-to-date census statistics in the West Indies was a hindrance to development activities; in certain cases local desires to take a census were vetoed by the Colonial Office.[23]

Constitutional changes need not in every case affect the decisions mentioned above to the disadvantage of the colonies. For example, if Puerto Rico should become autonomous, some kinds of Federal service might conceivably be arranged for on an *ad hoc* basis or by intergovernmental agreement somewhat in the manner that smaller civil divisions on the mainland may contract with neighbors or larger divisions for certain services. The problem of modern standardized quarantine measures in the West Indies has been met by inter-colonial agreement sponsored by the Caribbean Commission.

The privileges of American citizenship and of free migration, which would be affected by constitutional changes, are an important economic consideration arguing against a radical change in Puerto Rico's present status. American citizenship is theoretically and potentially a great boon. In practice, however, Puerto Rican migrants have met such difficulties in overcrowded Harlem, the only community where they find compatriots speaking their own language, that the heavy emigration has been partly offset by the return of the dissatisfied.*

* On the other hand, Virgin Islanders, despite their color, have found an inviting refuge on the continent from seemingly hopeless conditions at home. For many years they migrated in numbers sufficient to keep the population down in the Virgin Islands. Now their place is being taken by enterprising Puerto Ricans, who have already significantly altered the social composition of St. Croix.

One kind of metropolitan decision which self-government would render unlikely is the decision of Congress, Parliament, or some administrative agency to investigate local economic, social, and political conditions when a situation became critical. Such investigations have sometimes produced very constructive results. The creation of the West India Royal Commission has been of great benefit to the British colonies, and the investigation of the Virgin Islands by the United States Bureau of Efficiency in 1929-1930 proved worth-while.

When metropolitan-colonial relationships with the outside world are considered, it seems unlikely that constitutional changes would greatly alter existing defense arrangements. Even the most extreme bill for Puerto Rican independence (the Tydings Bill) provided for the United States to retain military and naval reservations. The independence alternative in the Tydings-Piñero Bill provided that the United States would retain the right to establish and maintain bases, after consultation with the government of Puerto Rico, while the dominion alternative included a provision corresponding to that of the Tydings Bill plus the following provisions:

> Sec. 415. All laws of the United States now in force or hereafter enacted declaring a state of belligerency with a foreign nation, requiring service in the armed forces of the United States or otherwise pertaining to the national safety, insular, or hemisphere defense shall be applicable to Puerto Rico to the same extent as to the United States.
>
> Sec. 416. All treaties between the United States and foreign countries which are applicable to Puerto Rico shall remain in force in regard to Puerto Rico: *Provided*, *however*, that Puerto Rico shall, so far as their applicability to Puerto Rico is concerned, have the same options thereunder for termination or modification as are now enjoyed by the United States.[24]

The American and British possessions in the Caribbean and the United States are mutually dependent for defense. Although the colonies have great strategic importance to the United States, they also vitally need its protection and this dependence is clearly recognized by them and by Great Britain. Nevertheless, the West Indian colonies in which the United States leased bases resented the negotiation of the agreement between the two metropolitan powers without West Indian participation. The fact that the United States does not have possession of all the strategic territories in the Caribbean has not hindered it in securing the desired bases for defense.*

The usefulness of the Caribbean colonies as sources of military manpower is limited. However, there were large numbers of volunteers in both American and British areas, possibly a reflection of unsatisfactory economic conditions as much as of patriotic attachment to the mother country. Nevertheless, there have been no important or strongly disloyal movements in the Caribbean colonies comparable to those in other parts of the dependent world which would provide a basis for expecting divergent defense policies if self-government were granted. On the contrary, the West Indies made generous financial contributions to the British war effort until the Secretary of State requested that they cease in view of local needs. Thousands of enlisted and inducted Puerto Ricans served in all branches of the armed forces in every combat zone, although their chief service was to guard the Caribbean frontier, which they did creditably.[25]

The question of further autonomy will not affect military decisions concerning the colonies. Its importance to defense is in its effects on internal conditions. If concessions to self-

* These bases have incidentally been a direct or indirect economic aid to many local groups, although their construction deprived certain low-paying local employers of labor during the building period.

government do not keep step with colonial demands, and if social and economic development lags under more independent local administration, the resulting instability might be a military hazard.

Another aspect of metropolitan-colonial relations with other countries is the colonial dependence on the mother country's decisions in international organizations and multinational agreements. Even in the conferences of the International Labor Organization, where social and economic policy in the dependencies has been discussed, the colonies have had no direct government representation.[26]

Some observers believe one reason for lack of colonial compliance with agreements made by the metropolitan countries was the absence of colonial participation in the negotiations. The International Labor Office has been considering ways of working the colonies into its activities, since it would like to have more colonial interest in the social reforms it promotes.[27] One method by which these objects might be attained would be to change colonial constitutions in the direction of dominion status, with a broader local participation in colonial government.

The Caribbean colonies have had a very direct interest in international commodity agreements concerning products which they are best suited to provide. In the abstract, the colonies have favored such agreements, but the execution of the International Sugar Agreement of 1937 caused great dissatisfaction. The mother countries negotiated the quotas for themselves and their possessions. However, the Caribbean territories regarded the quotas assigned to them as much too small compared to those of other areas or to their own productive capacity. Were the colonies able to negotiate directly as self-governing entities, their relative influence would continue to be slight. They probably could not expect more favorable treatment than they now receive, even granting that their special interests have had no priority over more influential domestic or other political and economic claims. But if they could combine with each other for bargaining purposes, their influence would undoubtedly be increased.

The one international organization in which the interests of the colonies are likely to be paramount is the Caribbean Commission. Although the United States and Great Britain were the original sponsors and are still its chief support, the organization has moved toward greater colonial participation. The associated West Indian Conferences are composed of local delegates, and since 1946 the colonies have had direct representation on the commission. A change in constitutional status of the British and American territories would be unlikely to alter their position in the commission. And regardless of metropolitan decisions, the work of the commission will indirectly aid them in obtaining more self-government.

Private Decisions

Governmental changes may have important effects on certain private and semipublic decisions about the colonies which are made in the mother country. Among them the commercial and investment policies of metropolitan capitalists are of great importance. As observed in the Royal Institute of International Affairs' extensive examination of *The Colonial Problem:*

> The application of capitalistic methods to colonial production has made colonial communities the debtors of the investors, both public and private, of the countries which supply the capital. Colonial produce is sold in the world market, not simply in exchange for goods consumed by the colonial community, but for capital goods which enable it to produce for the world markets and so pay the interest on its borrowing. The decision to under-

take this indebtedness is in fact generally made, not by
the colonial community, but by industrialists and financiers in metropolitan and foreign countries.[28]

It has been characteristic of dependent areas that these
interests and the existing colonial governments have been
very closely allied, so closely that in Curaçao, for example,
a common expression has been, "The Government is run by
the oil companies." [29] One much-discussed question related
to the extension of self-government was whether or not
greater freedom would make the colonies less attractive to
foreign investors, since it might lead to an encroachment on
the privileges and opportunities formerly enjoyed by external capital. Along with the expectation of higher taxes and
restrictions on their operations, foreign investors might fear
instability and "disturbances" consequent upon a shift in
political power.

These misgivings about the effects of autonomy on the
future of foreign enterprise operating in dependent areas are
based on the assumption that such measures are necessary and
desirable for the social and economic development of the
colonies. Opinion is divided on the net value of private outside investments in the colonies. Some regard them as the
colonies' salvation; others believe they have brought at least
as much evil as good. The latter have argued that metropolitan investors have used political power to oppose economic
and social progress for the inhabitants of the areas.

The position of the United Fruit Company in Jamaica is
an example of the ambivalent attitude toward outside investors. The sale of one of the United Fruit properties in
this colony in 1943 aroused great fear among some inhabitants
that it was the signal for a general withdrawal of the company's business connections with Jamaica, which would have
catastrophic results for the banana industry.[30] On the other
hand, this company had aroused ill will because it successfully

opposed efforts of Jamaican banana producers to operate independently.[31]

The Puerto Rican sugar industry gives a prime example of the controversies over foreign investment. The four giant companies are American-owned, and about 40 per cent of the sugar cane production is controlled by continentals. The American companies have attracted unfavorable attention partly because they are the largest. The fact that they apply the most impersonal methods of corporate management in contrast to old agrarian traditions has also incurred dislike. Furthermore, since they are foreign they cause certain emotional reactions arising from the inevitable friction between different cultures.

Puerto Rico is faced with a dilemma: cutting off the flow of dividends to the continent would probably end American enterprise in the island and so reduce productivity that the result would be a net loss to Puerto Rico. If Puerto Rico were to seek further external investment for future industrial expansion, public policy regarding old investments would be a conditioning factor. Should Puerto Rico try to penalize the withdrawal of earnings by preventing profits from accruing, insular companies would be as adversely affected as the foreign investors. Many obvious difficulties would beset one alternative penalty—preventing exportation of profits. The net "drain" of absentee profits compared with the possible loss from any available alternatives (such as government acquisition) has not been really very important economically. The real problems arising from the operations of the American companies are social.[32]

Governor Tugwell was less concerned with the net economic "drain," which is hard to prove, than with the control over the sugar industry.[33] Since absentee ownership had reached such a stage of diffusion and remoteness, he believed that government supervision might be at least as careful in administering the industry as the private American concerns. Governor Tugwell could see no real distinction between overhead control by agencies of New York financiers and the heads of San Juan and Washington bureaucracies, except that the latter might be a little more humane. The real question for an efficient industry was whether or not there should continue to be large-scale management, despite a change in the character of the ownership.[34]

The question of control has frequently been discussed by liberal British commentators on colonial policy. They complained that the British Government gave much too free a hand to large monopolistic enterprises operating in the colonies, and the result was exploitation of the native inhabitants. Suggested ways of retaining the proceeds from native resources (human and physical) for colonial development included changes in the British taxation system.

The advantages and disadvantages of private metropolitan investment in the colonies have usually been discussed within the framework of the colonies' present constitutional status. If the colonies were given greater autonomy, the political influence in the metropolitan governments enjoyed by investors in the colonies might become less important.[35] The loss of this conservative influence might speed up the colonial governments' social and economic activities. However, as long as the colonies depended upon metropolitan financial aid, either public or private, some influence would probably be retained.

Some students of colonial policy (such as Wilfrid Benson and G. H. C. Hart) have pointed out that even where the metropolitan government has been gradually relinquishing administrative powers into local hands, the private enterprises operating in the colonies have not followed suit.[36] Even though there may be governmental changes toward autonomy, they would not necessarily be accompanied by similar, and equally important, development of local leadership in business activities.

If the nationalistic tendencies (more noticeable in colonies elsewhere than in the Caribbean) were to cause more powerful local governments to restrict unreasonably the activities of foreign investors because they were not native, rather than because they hindered social and economic development, the colonies would eventually be the losers. Among other losses, they would forego the beneficent political influence of metropolitan investors interested in securing advantageous quotas and other favorable treatment for their colonial products in the mother country.*

A London University economist, himself a native West Indian, has summed up the relationship of autonomy to foreign investment in the following conclusion:

> Industrial development in a backward country seems to involve the creation of monopolies, since when a new industry is being established monopolistic concessions of one sort or another have frequently to be given to particular people. This element of monopoly is well in line with the general economic structure of the colonies. Colonial economies are not "free." On all sides the native finds himself up against a combine of one sort or another. . . . Some of us point to the necessity of organising trade-unionism in the colonies, but that is a slow process and is not in itself a complete answer to the problem. We talk, too, of the need for developing cooperative associations, but that again is a long and difficult process. In the last analysis the most important check on monopoly must be provided by the colonial governments themselves in one way or another, whether by decent industrial legislation, by taxation, by controlling the profits of concerns, or by operating the industries

---

* Greater autonomy might, however, have the opposite effect. Freed of metropolitan controls, the backward areas might be able to offer better concessions to foreign capitalists than before.

themselves. But checks on colonial enterprises are unfortunately checks on colonial enterprise. Anything you do to control investment or limit its profits necessarily tends to discourage investment, and therefore the development of the colonies. Nevertheless, checks are essential, but who is to impose them? Who is the Government? To the native the monopolist is European and the Government also is European. He is not certain in his mind that all Europeans are not the same. For him to be satisfied he must feel that he has adequate control over his own government and is able to use it to protect himself from exploitation.[37]

The whole problem of outside capitalist investments in dependent areas is a very large topic in itself. Since it touches the subjects of the present study only obliquely, the question cannot be examined more intensively. Nevertheless, some observations regarding Caribbean experience may be pertinent.

Despite the legal independence of many Central American and Caribbean republics, extensive American economic enterprise in those areas means that they are economically dependent territories and potentially subject to political pressure. American enterprise in these areas has, however, had at least one favorable influence: it was accompanied by certain international law concepts which tended to prevent the denial of justice and discrimination against aliens and to maintain minimum standards of respect for life, liberty, and property. Political power did not depend exclusively on sovereignty in these republics; neither was sovereignty the conclusive factor in certain of the Caribbean colonies. In these dependencies dominating enterprise was often not even domiciled in the mother country, as in the case of the United Fruit Company in Jamaica and the bauxite industry in Surinam.

That constitutional changes and the contraction or withdrawal of non-native economic enterprises need not always

be closely intertwined may also be seen in the brief experience of Puerto Rico and Jamaica. In the former territory, a
rapid enlargement of the government's role in stimulating,
regulating, and operating commercial enterprises has taken
place without a wait for autonomy. And postwar private investment from the outside has expanded in the face of an
increase in self-government. Under the new Jamaican constitution, the important changes in the privileges and free
activities accorded outside enterprises actually favored rather
than restricted their activities. Further evidence that foreign
investors were not worried was the formation of a private
development corporation in Trinidad by Barclay's Bank
(D.C.O.) to foster new industries in the British West Indies.

Metropolitan and other outside investments are likely to
continue as long as they remain relatively profitable. There
was already substantial foreign disinvestment in the British
West Indies prior to the constitutional reform period, and
payments of interest and dividends to outside investors in
Puerto Rico had begun to shrink before the enactment of the
Popular Democratic Party program. The decline in returns
could not be attributed to these factors.[38] The tendency
toward government intervention in economic activities is
becoming so general, even in dependent areas, that the possibility of future restrictions in newly self-governing territories
is not likely to put these areas at a competitive disadvantage
with other areas.*

The colonial policies of the metropolitan governments and
the attitudes within the Caribbean colonies toward economic
development through public action do not differ enough to
provide the basis for expecting great changes with more
autonomy. The "socialist" experiment of the Virgin Islands
Company was a Federal Government policy; the Puerto

* It is conceivable that extensive government intervention may dry up
private capital sources in all parts of the world.

Rican development plans, though federally aided, were grounded in local politics; and the social and economic activities of the Development and Welfare organization have been in political tune with the policies of growing local mass-leadership groups.

If foreign capital does become increasingly cautious in the more autonomous colonies, the losses may be offset by other gains. The more diversified economic development probable under government stimulation might bring greater stability. This could be achieved without abandonment of the advantages of specialization in international trade. Furthermore, the colonies might well derive important psychological benefits from the increased local control over local interests.

The government credit of the Caribbean colonies, both American and British, has been good in metropolitan markets compared to the credit of many legally independent areas. Despite some conservatives' assertions that private funds would be timid about further investment in Puerto Rican agriculture and industry, public utilities like the Water Resources Authority have been able to borrow on favorable terms in New York. Presumably the absence of any extreme local turbulence has been one factor, and there may be some fear that the maintenance of order would not continue after the grant of more self-government.

A certain amount of violence might be expected during the period of uncertainty while it is determined exactly who will inherit the government powers relinquished by the mother country. This occurred in Jamaica. But it is doubtful that this danger is greater than the risk of violence if demands for self-government are not satisfied, especially since the impact in the former case is likely to be upon local rather than upon metropolitan groups and interests. Furthermore, if social and economic development can continue sufficiently fast to reduce the discontent which leads to violence, the

risks run by those lending to more autonomous local governments may be no greater than now.

What effect may autonomy have upon the activities of
other kinds of private metropolitan organizations operating
in the colonies? Political or agitational activities of such
Harlem groups as the Jamaica Progressive League and of
the (British) League of Coloured Peoples will probably continue after self-government concessions are made. These
groups will find a reason for existence as long as any kinds
of racial inequities appear in colonial areas.

Severance of religious bonds between churches in the
mother country and in the colonies because of a change in
government status is also improbable. The social conditions
which interest such groups will not automatically change,
and in any case such groups usually have a cosmopolitan
outlook which tends to ignore national boundaries. The
Protestant missionary societies in Great Britain have shown
an intensified interest in the West Indies in recent years. Even
if the connections between the continental Catholic Church
and Puerto Rico were weakened (which is improbable),
Puerto Rico might gain in one respect, for the strongest opposition to its birth control legislation came from the mainland church.[39]

The activities of foundations like the Carnegie Corporation and the Rockefeller Foundation, which operate internationally, and the need for their services in these areas will
not diminish with a change in government status. Their
operations require local co-operation, but since the value of
their services is so widely appreciated, a local government
might be expected to respond similarly to one controlled by
the mother country. Organizations conducting scientific research in the tropics would scarcely find their interest greatly
altered through constitutional changes. Thus greater autonomy for Puerto Rico would not be likely to affect the arrange-

ment whereby Columbia University has contributed to the support of the School of Tropical Medicine in Puerto Rico.

There are a number of imperial associations which have rendered scientific or commercial assistance to the British West Indies. Since many of these organizations also operate in the dominions, constitutional changes in the West Indies in the direction of dominion status should not significantly alter these relations. The British Council, which only recently extended the scope of its activities from foreign fields to the British colonies, has been undertaking useful projects in the West Indies.* Presumably the interest this government-subsidized organization has in spreading British culture will be unabated by the grant of greater self-government to the West Indian colonies.

British and American labor unions have affiliations with local groups in the Caribbean colonies and have rendered them various types of assistance. The metropolitan labor organizations also have international ties, which are extensive in the case of the American unions and Latin American organizations. In order to defend their higher standards of employment, if for no other reason, these metropolitan groups would be likely to continue their connections with the Caribbean unions regardless of constitutional changes. Since labor is becoming increasingly potent in the Caribbean colonies, the colonial unions could be expected on their side to expand their relations with other labor organizations capable of strengthening them.

When the factors determining the effects of constitutional changes on social and economic development in the Caribbean colonies are considered together, it appears that autonomy concessions are not necessarily impediments to such development. Concessions might even accelerate the progress

---

* These included taking over a regional library service centered in Trinidad, and the extension of island-wide library service in Jamaica.

of social and economic reform. The demand for social and economic rehabilitation is sharpest among the labor groups, who now seem most likely to inherit the governmental power; constitutional changes would provide means for the expression of their demands. These have taken priority over the earlier demands for self-government which ignored economic consequences.

The crucial question is whether or not the mother countries would continue to provide the economic aid indispensable for maintaining and improving the standards of living in the colonies after self-government concessions were made. Their decision may rest in part upon the appraisal of the administrative competence of the colonial governments under new constitutions. However, such competence comes only with practice, and the general improvement in social and economic conditions could have a beneficial effect in raising governmental standards as well.

Demands for self-government are intensified by the colonial peoples' appreciation that decisions vital to their development are frequently metropolitan in origin and quite outside their control. Many of these decisions are unlikely to vary with a change in constitutional status. Nevertheless, the psychological satisfaction of greater local self-government should not be ignored in weighing the economic risks, while the risks themselves may become less if the demand of the colonial peoples for control over their own governments is satisfied.

XI. Summary and Conclusions

A CENTURY ago the debate over colonial autonomy and independence was usually carried on without regard for the question of colonial economic or social welfare. Perhaps this was because self-government was a real issue only for colonies which already had a high standard of living. Today *imperialism* has become such a term of opprobrium that the colonies are able to demand before the bar of free world opinion that the imperial governments give them both freedom and higher living standards. But the underdeveloped and over-populated colonies of the twentieth century may in the immediate future be able to move rapidly toward only one of these two goals.

Governmental independence for such colonies might bring their economic collapse and a catastrophic depression of living standards. On the other hand, metropolitan efforts to improve living conditions in the colonies intensify the dependence on outside subsidization, and postpone indefinitely the day when they could reach self-government. How the balance might be struck when these two aims appear in the short run to conflict and how they might in the long run be reconciled will be briefly restated.

Summary of Economic and Social Developments

Preceding chapters have assessed colonial policies in the British and American Caribbean territories with respect to the interrelations of economic, social, and political measures. Just as domestic policies abandoned laissez faire for state activity in economic fields, the recent "new deal" in this colonial area (which the British call "development and welfare") has emphasized positive governmental measures for social and economic development subsidized by the mother countries. Activities primarily economic in nature tended to be of general benefit to the colonies in relations with the outside world; they aided in making more effective use of existing resources, and thus increased productivity in the direction of greater self-support. These governmental measures supplemented or supplanted unco-ordinated economic development by private enterprise, which had a tendency toward lopsided growth.

Counteracting measures were adopted which helped prevent economic development from unduly favoring already privileged groups, particularly the large sugar companies. If any specific group was most benefited by these measures it was the small agriculturists. While the economic measures were usually long-range in their ultimate effects, the social measures which were undertaken were not. They tended to produce immediate benefits for particular groups, principally laborers (especially rural laborers), and agriculturists lowest down on the economic scale. The increase in their wealth and security may help reduce their political impotence. In any case, the economic development of the colony as a whole requires a healthier, better-educated working class. In equal measure, future support for social services depends upon the economic development of the colony.

Metropolitan taxpayers and consumers have paid most of the bills for the economic and social development of the Caribbean colonies. They do this not only for economic, ideological, and humanitarian reasons, but because of the strategic value of these possessions as well. Since the chief financial support came from the mother countries, much of the initiative also originated there, although metropolitan

stimulus found a ready response in the colonies. The operation of subsidies was sometimes not sufficiently controlled to
produce any but very haphazard results.

Increased reliance on the mother countries for financial aid
seems to contradict the efforts to promote self-government.
However, financial aid rendered as part of a rationally con-
ceived program gives some promise of leaving the colonies
with a more viable economy; thus the day is hastened when
they might support autonomy without a disastrous drop in
living standards. Therefore the methods which the mother
countries use to assist the colonies are critically important;
choosing one means rather than another can obviate or decrease the conflict between financial aid and self-government.

Emphasis on types of economic development which might
ultimately lead to financial independence (such as agricultural
reforms and industrialization), and constant efforts to devolve more administrative responsibility seem a promising
combination. These methods offer more than do additional
tariff favors. Such trade preferences are likely to lead to
greater political dependence, even though they do not involve
administrative control.[1]

When the mother countries transfer knowledge and skills
rather than goods, the colonial peoples learn how to help
themselves. This appears to be the most effective way to
reduce dependence. Educational aid is all the more vital to
the development of democratic self-government because the
legal inheritors of power are unlikely to be the small, well-
educated elite historically in control of the colonies.

The much-debated issue of public vs. private development
is resolving in favor of the former. Public development
promises that economic benefits will more likely accrue to
the colonial people as a whole rather than to particularly
privileged groups, some of them outsiders. It also compen-
sates for the general decline in private investment. The idea

of the development corporation or authority has become increasingly popular both in the United States and in Great Britain. By this means comprehensive government-guided projects can provide technical aid and enlist both public and private capital to exploit colonial resources on a businesslike basis, again helping the colonies to support themselves.

Many observers of colonial societies have expressed the fear that improving living conditions is hopeless when the immediate effect of social measures is merely to increase the already too numerous population. This has led them to offer specific panaceas such as birth control and emigration. These are only partial solutions, however, and must be incorporated in a much more comprehensive program which goes to the roots of the problem.[2] The continuing high birth rates in the Caribbean colonies represent a cultural lag. They are an inheritance from an earlier period before the mortality rates had been reduced by modern techniques, a time when backward peoples bred to the biological limit to reproduce the population.

High birth rates reflect a fatalistic attitude of inertia and indifference nourished by the experience of many generations with low living standards. The hope of a better life proffered by the programs for social and economic development in the British and American colonies could conceivably stop this appalling increase in the population. To do so, such development must be carefully co-ordinated with education, birth control services, and organized emigration.[3] The political rise of the mass of the colonial peoples and an increased independence from the mother country depend upon such a comprehensive attack on the population problem.

Economic and social improvements in the Caribbean were described earlier as unlikely by themselves to promote the domestic tranquillity which is necessary to the development of a constitutional consensus. Such a development depends upon a wide enjoyment of both respect and security. To distribute these values more broadly requires constitutional reforms. Nevertheless, the by-products of social and economic development—the reduction in the radical differences in economic status between different parts of the population and between the colonial society and that of the mother country—help to spread the sense of status, in itself necessary for greater security. Increasing the stability of the colonial economies also contributes to a greater sense of security.[4]

Political Developments

Although the immediate effect of social and economic changes may seem to be more rather than less domestic conflict, it is not necessarily the economic improvements themselves which have caused the difficulty. As a British colonial specialist has pointed out, if productivity and economic incomes are increased without corresponding changes in the means of political expression or in education, social and personal frictions are created. One part of life is out of tune with another. "A stable social advance involves advancing simultaneously in all aspects of life, which must be geared one to the other."[5]

Social and economic development may bring increased wealth to particular parts of the colonial community as well as to the colony as a whole, and may lay the basis for greater security. However, development toward self-government is also necessary to produce the increased respect which is not only a component of political power but vital to domestic tranquillity as well.

Some steps toward self-government have been taken in the British West Indies, and Puerto Rico is on the threshold of a new autonomy. But constitutional change in the Caribbean has been generally much slower than social and economic reform. The latter nevertheless contributed to break down the old theory that the wealthy and wellborn elite would take over governmental powers relinquished by the mother countries.

Instead, laboring groups with middle-class leaders are coming to the fore to assume governmental authority or at least to share it with formerly more powerful groups. This development was partly a result of the economic and social programs. Extension of the franchise was another factor. Legal changes do not guarantee that there will be greater popular participation and more genuine self-government when metropolitan controls are loosened. Still, the legal framework at least sets the limits. In many colonies, liberalizing the constitution has facilitated a redistribution of political power which favors the mass of the people.

The chief danger to continued social and economic development under more autonomous constitutions would be a decrease in metropolitan financial aid or abandonment of it. It is hazardous to predict the future generosity of the mother countries, whether or not the colonies become more independent. However, autonomy which puts an end to metropolitan aid is unlikely to prove acceptable either to the colonial peoples or to some political forces in the mother country. So far, British financial aid has continued unabated or has expanded while certain colonies were achieving a greater degree of self-government.

The increasing influence of less conservative groups within the colonies should remove the customary fear that, left to themselves, colonial politicians would not press for the necessary social and economic reforms. Another common fear has been that the growth of self-government would endanger private investments in the colonial areas because of an increase either in disorder or in public regulation of economic activities. Actually, the danger of civil disturbance is at least as great where autonomy demands are ignored. Furthermore, the world-wide trend toward public ownership and regulation would seem to reduce the risk that more autonomy would put the colonies at a comparative disadvantage in attracting and holding private investment.*

When the consequences of increased autonomy are weighed, they do not appear to raise insurmountable obstacles in the path of social and economic development. Greater self-government can conceivably promote this development by giving expression to local forces desiring such changes; in any case, a higher degree of autonomy is in itself essential to any real improvement in the colonies. These conclusions, however, assume the continuation of metropolitan assistance, which is now taken for granted as necessary.[6] As Lord Lugard described it, colonial governors formerly felt economically responsible to their colonies and politically responsible to Great Britain; the direction of their responsibilities has now been reversed.[7]

Decreasing Dependence

While social and economic development takes place mainly through outside aid, there can be no real independence.

> So long as this assistance is essential . . . its [a colony's or "independent" state's] freedom will be limited or at best subject to the good will of the provider of material benefits. . . . If the broad political aim of a colonial community is towards self-government, the achievement of this aim will tend to be postponed so long as economic and social conditions are relieved from outside.[8]

* The possibility that further private investment in foreign areas may not materialize in the postwar world must be kept in mind. However, the International Bank for Reconstruction and Development may prove a valuable substitute for prewar investment patterns.

In any case, the mother countries can hardly be expected to subsidize the colonies heavily for an indefinite period.

A reduction in economic dependence, which is closely related to the goal of self-government, might be accomplished in one of the following ways. The first—intensive development of local resources through metropolitan aid until they could independently sustain a higher standard of living—has already been discussed. Because of the difficulties inherent in this approach, some policy-makers have also experimented with a second alternative—scaling down colonial living-standard demands to a point where existing or only slightly increased local resources could meet them. The earlier of two plans for the Virgin Islands was based on this second proposal, but when it became evident that a primitive subsistence economy was politically unacceptable, another plan had to be devised.

Development and Welfare tried to compromise in its educational reform in the British West Indies, recognizing that it might obtain a cumulative effect by attacking a complex social problem at particularly strategic points. In framing a desirable educational policy for the British West Indies, the Educational Adviser declared that many of their economic and social (including educational) ills were traceable to a preoccupation with a cash export trade. The foundation of good education was "the conservation and right use of the means by which the people ultimately lived," and "the conservation of the people themselves, by a stable home and stable family economy." [9]

He believed they should be self-supporting through self-subsistence and internal exchange at least as far as the economy would not be disrupted by changes in export markets. Therefore, in his opinion, the West Indies should increase their permanently recurrent educational expenditures in as moderate a degree as is consistent with steady development.

Experiments in educational dilution would help achieve this. Meanwhile, the new outlook in farming should be vigorously promoted. Economic reorganization would increase the purchasing power of the teacher's salary. Greater internal exchanges would provide a larger cash margin, thus increasing the tax resources available for educational services. In this fashion Development and Welfare hoped to solve the dilemma of the West Indies' schools. The education needed for developing self-responsibility could be provided without using recurrent subsidies from Britain which prejudice the growth of self-responsibility.[10] So far the British West Indians have been unwilling to accept this solution.

These approaches to the twin problems of poverty and dependence give some indication of the wide variations conceivable for implementing general policies regarding higher living standards and greater independence. The following comments of an anthropologist suggest further complications:

> The cliché "self-government" is no answer to the questions what kind of Government? what system of law? what patterns of ethics? what quality and standards of cultural values will the new colonial society have? . . . Equality in a state of common material poverty, dirt and danger from disease, where it goes with equality of rights and duties and deeply held common cultural values is not a disorganizing force in society. On the other hand, a high average standard of living and health, where it is associated with wide discrepancies of wealth, political power, and social privilege, in a society lacking vital common purposes and values, may have results only too lamentably familiar from our own history.[11]

He added:

> It is a fallacy to think that a transformation leading to a higher level of social integration, and capable of direct-

ing the driving forces of society into constructive new channels, can be effected solely by equipping a backward society with the end-product apparatus and end-product skills of our civilization. Literacy, the machine, and chemo-therapy are useful tools for adding to human welfare. They would, however, soon cease to exist if it were not for the extensive and historically deep-rooted network of institutions and cultural values of which they are an outcome. Literacy can be an extremely valuable tool in a previously-preliterate society. It cannot become an instrument of social transformation without the institutional matrix which gives it life and meaning; and poets and publishers are as important in this matrix as schools and colleges.[12]

Unlike Asiatic and African colonies, the Caribbean territories are already assimilated—though imperfectly—into Western European culture. Therefore, the conflict between the need to force urgent reforms and the desire for cultural self-determination is less present in this region.

However, the relative absence of this problem is balanced by another. The Caribbean inhabitants are loudly clamoring for the complex of values enjoyed in the mother countries, which is impossible to transfer intact. To try to reproduce exactly in the colonies the standards of a satisfying life in the mother country would not merely be impracticable; it would also be irrelevant. The real problem is to reconcile what the colonial peoples themselves want with what can actually be achieved. This compromise will not only involve vigorous metropolitan efforts to satisfy their aspirations; it will also require the colonial peoples to clarify and probably reshape their desires. The people in this area have learned too much about the outward form of the Anglo-American way of life to be satisfied with a qualitatively different existence, but they might be content with a modified version of our system.

One axiom in our democratic theory is that government

should be responsible to the governed. Only in a very attenuated way does colonial government conform to this principle. Trusteeship is honored more in theory than in practice. Members of the metropolitan legislatures are notoriously ignorant and unheedful of their colonial charges (who do not elect them). This is true even in Great Britain, with its strong empire tradition.* Furthermore, changes in the metropolitan party in power may bring changes in colonial policy and administration over which the colonies have no control. As the colonies move toward autonomy, governmental responsibility becomes even more diffused and uncertain. Power and responsibility, which should go hand in hand, become separated.

There is no easy way to insure that where constitutional authority is shifted to the colonial peoples political control will accompany it. It is possible, however, to give them a share in the responsibility for making the constitutional choice. In a Fourth of July address, 1942, Governor Tugwell stated:

> It is my view that Puerto Rico's future depends on closer rather than looser ties with the United States; but that that decision ought to be made freely by all citizens, not by a few capitalists who prefer no disturbance of their investments.
>
> This moral problem of the United States in Puerto Rico is surely as hard a one as ever confronted a nation. To put Puerto Rico outside the tariff and quota walls of the nation would bring quick ruin. To keep Puerto Rico inside without a clear showing of desire would always stand as a reproach to democratic professions. Sooner or later Puerto Ricans must be allowed to choose and must accept the responsibilities of choosing for themselves.[13]

---

* Once a year the colonies have their general problems presented in Parliament, when the colonial estimates are debated. This is a signal for the departure of most of the Members.

Giving a colony the responsibility of making some choice regarding its future status may help to reduce the tendency noted in Jamaica (but equally applicable in American territories) for local political leaders to treat the mother country alternately as milch cow and scapegoat.[14]

The promises of greater freedom made during World War II, and the wartime experience of necessarily increased local responsibility, had the effect to be expected. They stimulated colonial dissatisfaction with dependence, even though this discontent has taken a much milder form in the Caribbean than in the Far East. Nevertheless, concessions of self-government need to be made graciously to win colonial favor in the Caribbean; the people in this region are suspicious after a long experience with unfulfilled promises.[15]

The "stitch in time" which the United States and Great Britain prudently took in the Caribbean dealt with economic and social discontent more than with governmental dissatisfactions. It was true that the acute local unrest arose primarily from unsatisfactory social and economic conditions during this period. When colonial people demanded autonomy they did not usually express themselves in the blunt terms of outright independence or international administration.

Alternative Ways of Shifting Metropolitan Authority

Colonial policy regarding autonomy should certainly avoid repeating the proliferation exhibited by the Caribbean republics; that experience has had too many unhappy consequences. Strong-armed dictatorships alternating with chaos and revolution in this area of such strategic importance to the United States meant continual American responsibility without legal authority. World peace will not be served by increasing the number of formally independent states which actually are incapable of standing "by themselves under the strenuous conditions of the modern world."

This does not rule out a legal status of independence which still includes a certain degree of association with the mother country for the maintenance of security and economic stability.* Both Conservatives and Liberals in Great Britain have recognized that disintegration of the empire is no desirable solution to the colonial question, and they have talked in terms (somewhat varying in connotation) of "partnership" and "commonwealth." The new Philippine Republic (whose independence is somewhat nominal because of the close economic ties with the former mother country) will long be guided by the United States. Even the revolutionary Indonesian leaders seemed at times to be ready to recognize official Dutch leadership in many fields of government activity.[16] These relations have a legal basis which could be accepted by both sides. They differ from those of the Caribbean republics, where extralegal power was exercised unilaterally.

Does this tendency toward continued guardianship of newly self-governing countries simply perpetuate "imperialism" under a different cloak? (Few terms are more ambiguous.[17] Abandoning the word entirely would surely contribute to colonial progress; its use only obscures and confuses the real issues.) Great Britain and the United States have recognized financial responsibilities in developing their Caribbean territories. These are expensive possessions not only because their former sources of wealth are exhausted but because their living-standard demands are more in line with Western European standards than those of other colonial areas.

The mother countries cannot be expected to provide ex-

---

* Such a status is sometimes loosely and inaccurately referred to as "dominion." The term thus used is not synonymous with the status of the really independent members of the (British) Commonwealth of Nations.

tensive economic aid while completely relinquishing governmental controls. The reconciliation of the two goals of higher living standards and self-government requires a variety of innovations in metropolitan-colonial relationships, both legal and administrative. Important among them are the introduction of international arrangements, which weaken, where they do not obliterate, the vices of the colonial system.

The costliness of colonial development has been an additional inducement to British policy to recognize an international interest in colonial affairs, for through international media the cost may be shared by others.[18] The Labor Party has in any case long argued for some international accountability in the administration of colonies. An international interest has also accorded with American anti-imperial ideology, even if the recent American record with respect to the former Japanese-mandated islands has not reflected the customary antipathy to the idea of colonial possessions.

International interest in colonial areas may be expressed in a multitude of ways. For the Caribbean territories, at least, international administration is desired by no one. It would be a regressive step in an area where the demands for a shift in governmental authority are in the direction from the mother country to the colonial peoples, not to a supranational authority of which the mother countries are an important element.

Nevertheless, all colonial areas have a real (if not explicitly recognized) interest in certain kinds of international agreements. They are not served by compacts which simply solve conflicts between colonial powers without concern for dependent peoples or in which the dependencies are treated as pawns. However, a strong international organization to maintain peace would indeed be a benefit to these peoples, whose dependent status is most disadvantageous in time of war. Furthermore, having the United Nations to act as an arbiter between a subject people and its mother country could add to the strength of the weaker party.

That the independent nations have an international interest in the colonies was recognized in the United Nations Charter. The importance of an impartial umpire in a sphere which has always caused friction between nations is gradually becoming clear. Chapters XI to XIII are an expression of certain broad (perhaps too broad) principles regarding colonial administration which have been accepted internationally, together with some provisions for a mild degree of international supervision.[19]

Under Chapter XI, which contains the "Declaration Regarding Non-Self-Governing Territories," a very weak form of international supervision is being exercised over non-trusteeship dependencies. Under circumscribed conditions colonial powers have transmitted to the Secretary-General certain kinds of technical information regarding colonies other than trusteeships.* These reports have been examined by a special committee of the Assembly. This procedure is a step in the direction of international accountability. For the first time in history, for example, the United States has reported to an international organization on the administration of its territorial dependencies. These provisions facilitate the formation and strengthen the impact of world public opinion capable of producing reforms in colonial areas.[20]

Do these chapters of the Charter represent substantial progress or merely fine-sounding but meaningless promises? Whatever the answer, they are principally supervisory. As such, they offer less than the kind of international action which provides for positive collaboration in raising living standards. Within the United Nations there are the Economic

* Governmental subjects are not covered, but the United States has voluntarily included such information in its reports. The Soviet Union and other states have been trying to make this compulsory.

and Social Council and such specialized agencies as the Food and Agriculture Organization and the World Health Organization. The International Labor Organization has already proved its usefulness in pressing for improved living standards in the colonies.

Such agencies can aid in the solution of economic and social problems (such as commodity controls and the control of diseases) which can be effectively dealt with only on an international level. Some colonial reformers have recommended that an international colonial agency connected with the general international organization be given a budget to undertake development on its own responsibility. More likely to be realized are suggestions for the creation of international development authorities which would carry out extensive regional enterprises modeled on the Tennessee Valley Authority.[21]

The most promising international arrangement actually in operation is the Caribbean Commission, whose success has led to enthusiastic recommendations that it be copied in other colonial regions.[22]

This war-born agency grew in prestige because it proved itself capable of solving such emergency problems as insuring the delivery of minimum supplies to the Caribbean islands when they were in desperate straits. Although its terms of reference were directed to peacetime functions, the commission was established while considerations of military security as well as international conscience were predominant. However, the wartime momentum has carried over into a period of general colonial reconstruction on a peacetime basis.

The Role of the Caribbean Commission

The Caribbean Commission is neither a supervisory nor an operating agency. It is purely an advisory body. Working in an empirical fashion on specific problems, it has co-ordinated the activities of metropolitan and colonial agencies in practical programs; provided a clearing house for research; facilitated the interchange of information; organized conferences and made recommendations on special questions; and acted as expediter. In diverse and original ways it has stimulated the metropolitan governments to co-operate with each other and with their colonies in taking active and concrete steps toward social and economic improvement.

The chief weakness of the commission is its inability to deal with specifically "political" questions.* In practice the line between political, social, and economic questions is hard to draw, for, as previous chapters have labored to show, social and economic measures inevitably have political connotations. So reluctant were colonial powers to admit any outside intervention in governmental matters, that such questions were omitted from the jurisdiction of the commission as being too delicate, complex, and inseparable from internal politics.

The commission has therefore been somewhat handicapped because well-rounded recommendations regarding social and economic conditions must take into consideration local political and administrative situations, including the competence of the colonial administrations. Furthermore, exclusion of "political" questions had some tendency to arouse suspicion among the dependent peoples regarding the true purpose of the Caribbean Commission. This omission gives some colonial leaders an impression that the mother countries do not intend to relinquish any governmental controls. Fortunately, this agency has been able to proceed in such an informal fashion that it was unnecessary completely to by-pass political ques-

* Another weakness is its inability to arouse general interest in Puerto Rico, because most of its activities to date have been aimed at raising standards in the less advanced areas to levels comparable with those already achieved in Puerto Rico.

tions, which began to be approached obliquely as a result of the commission's work in the fields of social and economic development.[23]

Both economically and socially the commission has helped the formerly isolated dependencies by treating their problems on a regional scale. In this way it has laid the basis for more self-government. In addition it has worked toward the inclusion of the dependent peoples in the commission's activities. Prior to the appointment of colonial representatives to the commission itself, an important step had already been taken to associate the colonies with the commission's work. At the first session of the West Indian Conference, in 1944, half of the West Indian delegates were "unofficial" representatives. The subsequent Anglo-American statement on the conference's conclusions was the first instance in which two metropolitan governments had jointly formulated economic policies for their dependencies based on recommendations from those dependencies.[24]

At the second session of the West Indian Conference, attended by twenty-nine delegates and a Canadian observer, most of the fifteen local territories were represented by one elected delegate from the local legislative assembly and one appointed by the government. Twenty-three of the twenty-nine were natives of the Caribbean and sixteen represented legislatures. The commission invited the delegates to show how it could best serve the area, and asked them to suggest future agendas.[25] At the third session of the Conference the delegates showed that they were already learning a valuable lesson in international organization; they began to realize the importance of concentrating on specific programs in contrast to repeated generalities in promoting economic development.[26]

Because of its informal methods and experimental approach, the Caribbean Commission has been able to avoid many of the usual difficulties with sensitive national feelings about colonial affairs. While the Permanent Mandates Commission never did obtain the right of inspection in local territories and this right was secured only with great difficulty and under circumscribed conditions for the Trusteeship Council, the practical equivalent has been practiced in the work of the Caribbean Commission without arousing unfounded suspicions. The commission has enjoyed good public relations on all sides because it is a service, not a control, agency. In contrast to supervisory organizations, it can devote its energies to taking positive steps toward social and economic development, emphasizing collaboration rather than policing.[27]

The Caribbean Commission as a regional international organization dealing with colonial problems has proved itself capable not only of easing friction between the United States and Great Britain over colonial issues, but also of promoting the achievement of mutually agreed-upon aims in the Caribbean. It has been particularly valuable as a continual reminder to the metropolitan governments that they have colonial responsibilities in this region. Although this is not an area in which the third great power, Russia, is likely to attempt intervention, the kind of activities engaged in by the Caribbean Commission have significance also for American-Soviet and Anglo-American-Soviet relations.

Colonial Development and American Security

The organization of the Trusteeship Council will permit American and Soviet participation in colonial areas not under their own jurisdiction. That this participation is unlikely to be harmonious is very evident. Despite the great complexities of the problem and the many obstacles to achievement, the promotion of decent minimum living standards and the American ideals of democratic self-government seems worth attempting in colonial areas. It is worth-while not only for their own sake but also in order to decrease international friction arising from colonial discontent. The unsatisfied demand for economic, social, and governmental progress has created social frustrations and the rise of Messianic political leaders whose power interests are not those of the colonial peoples. The soil thus becomes fertile for Communist penetration.

Although there are serious gaps in the program, and practice falls far short of intention, British and American colonies in the Caribbean are experiencing a significant degree of social and economic development. This has brought new powers to formerly submerged groups and helped the colonies toward the greater self-support which is a prerequisite for autonomy. The inheritors of political power under constitutional changes are likely to be the mass of the people rather than a small elite. This emphasizes the need for more intensive social development than ever. It also underlines the desirability of metropolitan aid which passes on skills and knowledge instead of aid which continues indefinitely the dependence upon relief funds.

Recognition of colonial demands for self-government is as important as recognition of hunger and ignorance. These demands are based on the need for respect, and respect is as significant an aspect of political power as increased income. Greater autonomy is also likely to avoid rather than encourage violent class conflict within the colonies, because it accords with their changing political composition. It should eventuate in a greater security internally, and create a friendlier attitude toward the mother countries. Thus, it can also contribute to the security of the United States and Great Britain themselves.

Just as the premature grant of independence to weak countries may create a dangerous power vacuum, so may a social vacuum also be created. Social and economic development of the type being undertaken in the Caribbean can fill this dangerous void and produce healthy communities immune to antidemocratic doctrines. It will be completely effective, however, only if the colonial peoples are simultaneously granted increasing power to govern themselves.

Notes

CHAPTER I

1. One of the major differences is that the inhabitants of the Caribbean colonies (with minor exceptions) are not indigenous. Furthermore, these islands have been under the rule of European or American governments for four hundred years. In this respect, the "native question" in the Caribbean is unlike that in Africa or the Pacific islands. Nor, for the most part, is there a strong nationalist urge such as exists in territories like Indonesia or Indo-China. There is no real native civilization; Caribbean culture is a mixture of Western European civilization and remnants of ancestral African folkways. Thus the Caribbean colonies are considerably more "advanced"—integrated with the dominant world civilization—than the primitive groups in Africa or the Pacific. Unlike the Far Eastern colonies, they do not possess scarce raw materials like tin or rubber, valuable where free trade has broken down or there is a threat of war.

2. The following table of the rates of natural increase, in the period immediately before the war, indicates the gravity of the population problem in the Caribbean dependencies.

TABLE I

EXCESS OF BIRTHS PER 1,000 OVER DEATHS PER 1,000

Russia	23.2
Puerto Rico	21.0
Egypt	16.0
Jamaica	15.7
Philippines	15.4
Japan	12.5
India	11.5
Italy	9.3
Germany	7.5
United States	6.1

Source: Clarence Senior, *Puerto Rican Emigration,* University of Puerto Rico, 1947, p. 1.

3. Cf. T. S. Simey, *Welfare and Planning in the West Indies,* Oxford, 1946, pp. 48-117, for a detailed examination of West Indian society.

4. For an objective account of "Culture Conflicts and Nationalism," see Vincenzo Petrullo, *Puerto Rican Paradox*, University of Pennsylvania Press, 1947, pp. 126-58.

5. The following characterization of psychological traits in St. Thomas (Virgin Islands) is also valid to a large degree for the West Indies generally:

"The customary effect of the process of early acculturation in St. Thomas is to create for the child, particularly in the lower economic group which makes up the great majority of the population, a total situation which is distinguished by insecurity and a lack of dependable, protective, social relationships. From this psychological matrix there typically emerges an insecure, suspicious, egocentric adult. The adult situation provides relatively little opportunity for the satisfaction of the needs which have been traditionally recognized as paramount in St. Thomas, those associated with personal aggrandizement. While some individuals live within a context of very limited aspiration and a few others are able to realize their ascendant ambitions, for the majority the situation is one of continual dissatisfaction and frustration. To this they react by attempting to establish status through available forms of emulation, by retreat from social relationship into egocentric isolation, by aggression against those with whom they have social contact, especially those who appear in the role of competitor, and by the formation of relationships of dependence toward the church, toward the administrators of the island's government, and occasionally toward individual members of the white race." A. A. Campbell, *St. Thomas Negroes—A Study of Personality and Culture*, American Psychological Association, 1943, p. 89.

6. For an elaboration of this principle see Gunnar Myrdal *et al.*, *An American Dilemma*, Harper, 1944, pp. 1065-70.

7. Antidotes to the abundant publications treating colonial problems superficially and emotionally (many of them of American origin) are *Empire in the Changing World*, by an Australian economist, W. K. Hancock (Penguin Books, 1943) and *Colonies*, by a Cambridge historian, E. A. Walker (Cambridge, 1944).

CHAPTER II

1. For a concise discussion of the colonial problem in international relations see A. N. Holcombe, *Dependent Areas in the Post-War World*, World Peace Foundation, 1941.

2. On the question, "Do colonies pay?", see Grover Clark, *The Balance Sheets of Imperialism*, Columbia University Press, 1936; M. J. Bonn, *The Crumbling of Empire*, London, 1938; and Royal Institute of International Affairs, *The Colonial Problem*, London, 1937.

3. For an historical account of the interaction of economic theories and colonial policies, see Klaus Knorr, *British Colonial Theories, 1570-1850*, Toronto, 1944.

4. For a brief summary of this development see *Colonies and International Conscience*, A Report to the Fabian Colonial Bureau, London, 1945.

5. International Labor Organization, *First Report of the International Labor Organisation to the United Nations*, Geneva, 1947, Vol. II, Appendices, pp. 54, 260-307.

6. Others were the extent of international supervision, the powers of trustee states, and which states would decide international policies regarding the trusteeships. In setting up the new trusteeship system Great Britain and the United States disagreed on several points, but their differences have been reconciled. On the other hand, the Soviet insistence on a final determination of "states directly concerned" (which under the Charter were to give prior approval to the trusteeship agreements) and on banning military establishments in trusteeships, threatened to prevent even the institution of a trusteeship system. Finally, the Trusteeship Council was organized without Soviet approval of the trusteeship agreements, and it began to function despite nonparticipation by the Russians, who alleged that it was unconstitutional. When the Soviet Union finally decided to join, more than a year later, the reason was its desire to participate in the proposed plan that the Trusteeship Council should deal directly with the Palestine problem.

7. Thus in deliberations over the principles of economic development held by the Economic and Employment Commission of the United Nations, the Soviet Union unsuccessfully sought to include the declaration that governmental dependence was a major obstacle to colonial economic development and that the decisive element of such development was industrialization (New York *Herald Tribune*, May 1, 1948).

8. United Nations Charter, Article 73 a.

9. See, for example, International Labor Office, *Social Policy in Dependent Territories*, Montreal, 1944; and G. H. C. Hart, *Towards Economic Democracy in the Netherlands Indies*, Institute of Pacific Relations, 1942.

10. Article 73 b and c.

11. "Economic development may be regarded as an end in itself, with the implicit assumption that the social structure most appropriate for every stage of economic progress will, with a little guidance here and there, crystallize out in the historical process. It is as well, then, to be aware in advance of the price that will certainly have to be paid for this. If, on the other hand, raising the standard of living in the colonies is regarded as a means to social and political ends, it is desirable that these ends should be defined and the tactics of economic development closely related to them." M. Fortes, "An Anthropologist's Point of View," H. N. Brailsford *et al.*, *Fabian Colonial Essays*, London, 1945, pp. 227-28.

CHAPTER III

1. *The Caribbean Islands and the War*, United States Government Printing Office, 1943, p. iii.

2. G. St. J. Orde Browne, *Labour Conditions in the West Indies*, London, 1939. This was a companion study to his labor investigations in other parts of the British Empire. The British Government had also been making some general inquiries into colonial problems, including a nutrition survey and a survey of agricultural education.

3. West India Royal Commission, 1938-39, *Recommendations*, London, 1940. The full report, West India Royal Commission, *Report*, was not published until 1945.

4. Article IV, "An Agreement for the Establishment of the Caribbean Commission, Signed October 30, 1946, in Washington, D. C.," reproduced in *International Organization*, February, 1947, pp. 251-56.

5. The same restriction was retained in establishing the South Pacific Commission in 1947, an organization modeled after the Caribbean Commission for the South Pacific island territories belonging to the United States, the United Kingdom, Australia, New Zealand, France, and the Netherlands.

CHAPTER IV

1. The following comparative statistics give some conception of the relative poverty in Puerto Rico and the British West Indies.

TABLE II

PER CAPITA INCOME PAYMENTS IN PUERTO RICO AND IN THE FIVE STATES
WITH THE LOWEST PER CAPITA INCOME PAYMENTS, 1940 AND 1944

	Per Capita Income Payments (in dollars)	
	1940	1944
Puerto Rico	117	228
Mississippi	202	541
Arkansas	252	617
Alabama	268	677
South Carolina	286	652
Kentucky	308	701

TABLE III

NET INCOME IN PUERTO RICO AND IN OTHER CARIBBEAN ECONOMIES

Per Capita
Net Income 1942
(in dollars)

Puerto Rico	185
Cuba (calendar year 1943)	159
British Guiana	138
Jamaica	104
Barbados	102
Grenada	90
St. Vincent	57

These tables are reprinted from Daniel Creamer, *The Net Income of the Puerto Rican Economy, 1940-1944*, University of Puerto Rico, 1947.

2. During the period 1940-44 about one-eighth of the net income of the agricultural producers came from Federal subsidies. Creamer, *op. cit.*, p. 37.

3. Sometimes several agencies have collaborated, as in a program conducted under the Research and Marketing Act of 1946. The co-operating agencies were the Federal Soil Conservation Service; Bureau of Plant Industry, Soils, and Agricultural Engineering; Agricultural Experiment Stations; and the Insular Agricultural Experiment Station. Together they are promoting erosion control and more efficient food crop production on the small farms of the steep slopes so prevalent in Puerto Rico.

4. Credit facilities for these activities have at one time or another been made available to agriculturists and other entrepreneurs by the following Federal agencies among others: the Federal Land Bank of Baltimore, the Baltimore Bank for Cooperatives, the Puerto Rico Reconstruction Administration, the Farm Credit Administration's Emergency Crop and Feed Loan Office, the Reconstruction Finance Corporation, the Puerto Rico Hurricane Loan Section of the Department of the Interior, and the Commodity Credit Corporation.

5. A Federal Tropical Forest Unit manages the Caribbean National Forest, which is the only tropical national forest in United States territory, and co-operates with forestry agencies in Latin American countries.

6. It has been estimated that this restriction (which does not apply to any state) has made a difference of $20,000,000 annually in Puerto Rico's income, and in the ten years in which it operated, equaled the sum sought by the Industrial Development Company from the Reconstruction Finance Corporation to further its work (Letter to the Editor of the New York *Herald Tribune* from Resident Commissioner A. Fernós-Isern, dated March 30, 1948).

7. New York *Times*, March 24, 1948.

8. For a brief summary of industrialization in Puerto Rico, see R. G. and G. F. Tugwell, "Puerto Rico's Bootstraps," *Harper's*, February, 1947.

9. New York *Times*, April 4, 1948.

10. Creamer, *op. cit.*, pp. 23-24.

11. *Ibid.*, p. 24.

12. Illustrative of Development and Welfare aid for agricultural rehabilitation was a contribution of half of the £497,500 farm improvement fund established in Jamaica in 1947, the money to be spent on loans and grants for small farmers for clearing land, applying fertilizers, soil conservation, drainage, planting materials, and water supplies.

13. An example of intercolonial marketing arrangements was an agreement made in 1946 between the British islands of the eastern Caribbean and British Guiana for the purchase of stated quantities of rice from the latter for a five-year period (*Crown Colonist*, January, 1947).

14. An example of the criticism was that expressed by T. S. Simey, formerly attached to West Indies Development and Welfare, in *Welfare and Planning in the West Indies*, Oxford, 1946, pp. 125-45. Another critic was W. A. Lewis, a native West Indian economist at the London School of Economics. He took to task the report of the Jamaican Economic Policy Committee under the chairmanship of Dr. F. C. Benham, then Economic Adviser to the Comptroller, for disapproving of industrialization because current production costs were high ("An Economic Plan for Jamaica," *Agenda*, November, 1944).

15. Cf. the statement of policy of the Secretary of State for the Colonies, *Colonial Development and Welfare. Despatch to Colonial Governors*, London, 1945.

16. Examples are the interim reports of the House of Representatives Committee on Insular Affairs made in April and June of 1944 (78th Congress, Second Session, House of Representatives, Reports Nos. 1399 and 1676).

17. National Resources Planning Board, *A Development Plan for the Virgin Islands*, reissued, Puerto Rico, 1944; F. P. Bartlett, *Original Revised Draft, Report to the Governor of the Virgin Islands on Population and Economic Factors for Planning in the Virgin Islands*, n.p. 1947. An earlier inquiry was made in 1930 by Herbert Brown of the Bureau of Economy and Efficiency, under the Hoover Administration.

18. Appendix C of *Report of the Anglo-American Caribbean Commission to the Governments of the United States and Great Britain for the Year 1945*, Anglo-American Caribbean Commission, 1946, pp. 29-39. The statement also contained agreement on a number of social policies.

19. An example was a forestry research conference held in January, 1946, which discussed practical problems of conservation, forest planting, and the use of woods. This was the first formal convention on forestry ever held in the Caribbean.

CHAPTER V

1. The death rate of about 12 per 1,000 recorded for 1947 (contrasted with 27 per 1,000 in 1900) was the lowest in Puerto Rican history, but the birth rate rose to a record high of over 42 per 1,000.

2. Jacob Crane, "Workers' Housing in Puerto Rico," *International Labor Review*, June, 1944.

3. For a brief résumé of educational facilities and problems in Puerto Rico and the Virgin Islands, see L. E. Blauch, "Education in the Territories and Outlying Possessions of the United States," *Journal of Negro Education*, Summer, 1946.

4. Because of the language issue, Puerto Ricans were particularly gratified to have the 1947 amendment to the Organic Act make the Commissioner of Education a locally appointed office. Otherwise the demand for a Commissioner appointed by the Governor rather than the President was less an expression of specific dissatisfactions with the educational system than of a general desire to control education as a psychologically important element of self-government. (On this point as it applies to colonies in general, see Amry Vandenbosch, "The Provision of Education in Dependent Territories," *Journal of Negro Education*, Summer, 1946, p. 566.)

5. The sharp increase in unguided Puerto Rican migration to New York City following the war raised many problems, not only for the municipal and social agencies in New York but also for the immigrants. This very difficult situation has prompted a number of studies. A long-range research project on the population problem is being conducted at the University of Puerto Rico's Social Science Research Center (Senior, *op. cit.*). A survey of the Puerto Rican migrant in New York City made by Columbia University's Bureau of Applied Social Research (and financed by Puerto Rico) has exposed a number of misconceptions. It showed that the large proportion of migrants were not from the lowest classes at home and that they gave up jobs in Puerto Rico to get better ones in New York (New York *Times*, June 16, 1948). The problem of assimilation in New York does not disprove the desirability of large-scale migration but only of a particular type of undirected exodus from Puerto Rico.

6. Petrullo, *op. cit.*, p. 27.

7. A history of the 500-acre provision may be found in *Puerto Rican Public Papers of R. G. Tugwell*, Puerto Rico, 1945, pp. 291-347, which includes a report made to Secretary of the Interior Ickes.

8. The purposes of the law were as follows: "to take the necessary action to put an end to the existing corporative latifundia in this Island, block its reappearance in the future, insure to individuals the conservation of their land, assist in the creation of new land-owners, facilitate the utilization of land for the best public benefit under efficient and economic production plans, provide the means for the 'agregados' and slum dwellers

to acquire parcels of land on which to build their homes, and to take all action leading to the most scientific, economic and efficient enjoyment of land by the People of Puerto Rico" (cited in the Caribbean Commission's *Caribbean Land Tenure Symposium,* Washington, 1946, p. 143. Accounts of land reform may be found on pp. 18-28 and 132-49).

9. New York *Times,* March 27, 1948.

10. A recent report puts the illiteracy rate at only 2 per cent. John Collier, *America's Colonial Record,* London, 1947.

11. The Jamaica census of 1943 indicated a marriage rate of only 272 per 1,000 compared to 645 in Great Britain in 1931, and the illegitimacy rate was approximately 70 per cent. Even allowing for consensual marriages, such a rate (which is characteristic of other West Indian islands) is very high, and has actually increased in the last few decades (*Development and Welfare in the West Indies, 1945-46,* London, 1947). For the sociological effects of this phenomenon, see Simey, *op. cit.,* p. 88. He declared that "it is doubtful whether there can be said to be *any* effective father-substitutes at all for large numbers of West Indian children."

As for color prejudice, in the Caribbean it is more subtle than the crude Jim Crow practices in the United States, but since the dominant group is white and the vast majority of the population is at least partly Negro, it permeates every aspect of colonial life.

12. Simey, *op. cit.,* p. 160. An important theme of this book is the need for systematic rebuilding of West Indian society.

13. For an exposition of West Indian educational problems and methods of meeting them see S. A. Hammond, "Education in the British West Indies," *Journal of Negro Education,* Summer, 1946. In the same issue may be found a critique of British and American educational policies in the Caribbean by Eric Williams, "Education in Dependent Territories in America."

14. West India Royal Commission, *Statement of Action Taken on the Recommendations,* London, 1945.

15. For details see *Report of the Commission on Higher Education in the Colonies,* London, 1945.

The only other genuine institution of higher learning, the Imperial College of Tropical Agriculture at Trinidad, served the whole empire and it concentrated on specialized research and instruction for a limited number of students.

16. Among the Jamaican projects was an experiment in co-operative farming, where individual leaseholders operated a large area on a communal basis. Also established were a series of Agricultural Centers to train farmers in the intensive use of the land, which would later be settled by those responding satisfactorily to the instruction.

17. In some colonies multiplication of unions was out of all proportion to apparent need. For about 150,000 workers in Trinidad there were in 1947 seventeen unions, nearly half of them maintaining that they serve

all classes of workers in all industries (*Trade Union Organization and Industrial Relations in Trinidad, a report by F. W. Dalley.* London, 1947).

18. Dalley, *op. cit.*

19. The West Indian Conference has, however, discussed particular social problems at length and suggested courses of action. Similarly, special conferences called by the Caribbean Commission, notably the Land Tenure Symposium in 1944, have dealt with social development.

20. Oblique references to political questions have occasionally occurred. For example, in President Truman's message to the Second West Indian Conference, he listed among the fundamental tenets of American colonial policy, "strengthening the foundations upon which self-governing institutions may be developed." (*Report of the West Indian Conference, Second Session,* St. Thomas, V.I., U. S. Department of State, 1946, p. 64.)

21. C. W. Taussig, at the Fourth Session of the Fourth Meeting of the Caribbean Commission, held in Jamaica, June 23-27, 1947.

CHAPTER VI

1. About one-fifth of the students at the University of Puerto Rico have come from families with annual earnings of less than $500. Paul Blanshard, *Democracy and Empire in the Caribbean,* Macmillan, 1947, p. 226.

2. Lord Keynes wrote of the economic development of pre-World War I Europe: "While there was some continuous improvement in the daily conditions of life of the mass of the population, Society was so framed as to throw a great part of the increased income into the control of the class least likely to consume it. The new rich of the nineteenth century were not brought up to large expenditures, and preferred the power which investment gave them to the pleasures of immediate consumption. In fact, it was precisely the *inequality* of the distribution of wealth which made possible those vast accumulations of fixed wealth and of capital improvements which distinguished that age from all others. Herein lay, in fact, the main justification of the Capitalist System. If the rich had spent their new wealth on their own enjoyments, the world would long ago have found such a regime intolerable. But like bees they saved and accumulated, not less to the advantage of the whole community because they themselves held narrower ends in prospect.

"The immense accumulations of fixed capital which, to the great benefit of mankind, were built up during the half century before the war, could never have come about in a Society where wealth was divided equitably." (J. M. Keynes, *The Economic Consequences of the Peace,* Harcourt, Brace, and Howe, 1920, pp. 18-19.)

3. Creamer, *op. cit.,* pp. 44-45.

4. A. O. Gayer, P. T. Homan, and E. K. James, *The Sugar Economy of Puerto Rico,* Columbia University Press, 1938, pp. 40, 160.

5. Especially regarding the quotas under production control, the British and American colonies complained that they were discriminated against in

favor of other areas. Although the government support programs were intended to aid the industry in general, there was no assurance that they would aid producers in these areas in particular. In the case of Puerto Rico, mainland producers (especially the beet sugar industry) and those in Cuba have had priority in the execution of the quota plans.

Under the International Sugar Agreement, which established a quota for the whole British Empire, a proposed increase for the West Indies would have to be offset by losses in other British dependencies. A desire to aid colonial sugar producers was not the only reason that the British Government entered into the International Sugar Agreement of 1937. The loss of revenue due to increased entrance of colonial sugar with special preference, the fears of the London international sugar market over the relative decrease of foreign sugar arriving in the United Kingdom, and British interests in other international control schemes also favored the agreement (West India Royal Commission, *Report,* pp. 269-71.)

6. The West India Royal Commission admitted that the expansion of sugar production in the thirties was not accompanied by a proportionately equal increase in employment. On the other hand, if production had decreased the burden would have fallen heaviest on labor.

7. Puerto Rico Minimum Wage Board, *The Sugar Cane Industry in Puerto Rico,* Puerto Rico, 1943.

8. The West India Royal Commission recommended that its proposal for increased benefits to the producers should be conditioned upon local enactment of minimum wage legislation, acceptance of wage rulings by the producers, and welfare levies on sugar produced, which would be spent for the common benefit of the sugar laborers.

9. In computing comparative costs, consideration should be given to the social costs of superficially more efficient metropolitan enterprises which are borne by the state. Thus, small-scale decentralized colonial industries, because of their stabilizing effect on major business fluctuations, may contribute more directly to social security than large metropolitan industry, whose products may be priced lower (League of Nations, *Industrialization and Foreign Trade,* [Geneva], 1945, p. 54).

10. However, the character of the trade would differ from the earlier exchange of raw materials for food and clothing. For the possible effects on international trade see A. J. Brown, *Industrialization and Trade,* London, 1943.

11. Conservative politicians, businessmen, and estate owners in Puerto Rico did not regard government-operated enterprises for economic development as benefiting them but rather as competitors for limited markets, disregarding the fact that these enterprises were in new fields which they could have entered but had not. Those personally engaged in the government enterprises took a different view.

12. The unwillingness of many laborers to respond to higher wages by increased activity does not mean that they regarded their status as

idyllic. From his long acquaintance with Jamaica, Lord Olivier concluded that under proper circumstances Jamaicans would work energetically and capably, but that the average Jamaican did not think of himself as a laborer. He was therefore less interested than the Europeans concerned in working "for particular rates or wages, with particular assiduity, at some form of productive agriculture conducted by proprietors of estates or their attorneys or lessees or overseers, growing some form of exportable produce, by selling which these latter may obtain an income" (*Jamaica, The Blessed Island*, London, 1936).

13. British West Indians transported to the United States for work during the war sent back to their homes twelve million dollars from 1943 through 1946 in compulsory deductions from their pay. This sum did not include considerable amounts returned voluntarily or saved. Further contributions to the local economies were made subsequently.

14. The Puerto Rican experiment with the proportional benefit farm most significantly aided agricultural laborers. Since labor conditions were usually more favorable on the large estates than on small farms, an increase in the latter would not improve the lot of agricultural workers who had not been resettled.

15. Orde Browne, *op. cit.*, p. 17.

16. The Chardón Plan was specifically designed to plan other uses for land and labor excluded from production by the Jones-Costagan Sugar Act of 1934.

17. Olivier, *op. cit.*, pp. 326, 436.

18. As with the land itself, financial terms attached to the provision of housing should not be out of proportion to the resettlers' income. Otherwise their standard of living will suffer in other directions. This occurred in some of the earlier Puerto Rican projects, where higher rents meant less money for food. As in the British West Indies, Puerto Rican provisions for housing on the *agregado* plots envisage much self-help.

19. C. K. Meek, in *Land Law and Custom in the Colonies*, London, 1946, comments on the wide difference in the sense of responsibility and interest in the stability of political institutions shown in peasant owner-cultivator areas compared to those where the landlord-tenant system prevails.

20. If the birth control activities of the Puerto Rican Department of Health were expanded, this service would also help to raise the status of women in low-income groups. British West Indian women will profit from the equalization of educational opportunities in their colonies.

21. Individual enterprises need not be large. The small, decentralized textile undertakings in prewar Indonesia demonstrated the advantages of that type of industry for colonial conditions. They used an important percentage of the population surplus (not being highly mechanized), required relatively little capital (thus avoiding the higher expense and po-

tential domination accompanying foreign capitalization), and were more flexible in the face of world depression.

22. F. W. Notestein, "Problems of Policy in Relation to Areas of Heavy Population Pressure," in *Demographic Studies of Selected Areas of Rapid Growth*, Milbank Memorial Fund, 1944, p. 147.

23. *Ibid.*, pp. 150-53 and Simey, *op. cit.*, pp. 150-56.

24. Whenever officially directed migration has been considered in the past it has quickly been discarded as a practical measure partly because no suitable area for resettlement seemed readily available. Both British and American authorities are now reconsidering earlier conclusions, with special attention to the mainland territory of the metropolitan governments.

25. Senior, *op. cit.*, pp. 116-18.

26. Idle capital existed for many years in Puerto Rico despite a great need for investment, because the owners were fearful of risking their money in new enterprise. The state, being more concerned with the ultimate expansion in national productivity than in immediate profits, may be more willing to devote a larger share of the increase in national income to investment than is the case with private enterprise (League of Nations, *op. cit.*; see also K. Mandelbaum, *The Industrialisation of Backward Areas*, Oxford, 1945).

CHAPTER VII

1. For the percentage of the total assistance recommended under the 1929 Colonial Development Act which was devoted to particular kinds of activities, see "Colonial Development Advisory Committee," *Crown Colonist*, October, 1941, p. 468.

2. The Colonial Development and Welfare Act of 1940 provided that certain loans and advances made under the 1929 Development Act be remitted in part or in whole.

3. *Development and Welfare in the West Indies, op. cit.* The British West Indies also received other kinds of subsidies, notably a higher price for their raw sugar than the world market price. In 1947-48 the average subsidy per ton was estimated at £15 7s., and the total was about £5,800,000 (*Crown Colonist*, July, 1947, p. 377).

4. West India Royal Commission, *Report*, pp. 356-58.

5. The Ten-Year Development Plan reported on in Barbados in 1947 illustrates the method of financing. The colony was to provide the bulk of the total expenditure of £3,500,000, and Development and Welfare was to contribute £800,000. From the surplus in the Barbados Treasury was to come £600,000; current revenues would provide £1,000,000, and another £1,000,000 would be raised by loan (*Crown Colonist*, May, 1947, p. 284).

6. For example, because British Guiana has unusual physical obstacles to its economic development, extraordinary expenditures from the Development and Welfare fund were provided this colony for irrigation and

drainage. On the other hand, Trinidad's physical resources have permitted that colony to carry on necessary development financed partly through oil royalties. Therefore, Development and Welfare grants to Trinidad have been limited to projects which have Trinidad as their center but which benefit a number of needier neighboring colonies.

7. Some exception should be made for the preliminary planning involved in the partially implemented Chardón Plan for Puerto Rico and the report of H. D. Brown, chief of the Efficiency Bureau, to Congress in 1930, recommending a rehabilitation program for the Virgin Islands. (See L. H. Evans, *The Virgin Islands: From Naval Base to New Deal*, J. W. Edwards, 1945, p. 282.)

An example of the lack of continuity was the action of the second session of the Eightieth Congress in renewing the Virgin Islands Company's charter for only one year.

8. United States Tariff Commission, *The Economy of Puerto Rico*, Washington, 1946, p. 5. Three direct Federal expenditures alone in 1940 equaled 15 per cent of the Insular net income (Creamer, *op. cit.*, p. 40).

9. As was pointed out by the United States Tariff Commission, these loans meant that island borrowers had access to funds at lower rates than they could have obtained elsewhere. This was especially advantageous at times when they could not obtain funds from other sources or only in restricted amounts at exorbitant rates (U. S. Tariff Commission, *op. cit.*, p. 5).

10. New York *Times*, Sept. 26, 1948.

11. *Tugwell, Public Papers*, pp. 148, 178, 192, 293, and 317.

12. Covering local governmental deficits has also been a British contribution to needy colonies. However, colonial governments have usually avoided such a "grant-in-aid" if at all possible because it was given at the expense of budgetary autonomy and required British treasury control of local expenditures.

13. The instability of this source of revenue may be seen from the variations in the percentage of the total Insular Government receipts represented by the return of United States internal revenue. In 1940-41 this was 22 per cent; in 1943-44, 61 per cent (the high point); and in 1945-46, 40 per cent.

14. Testimony of a former auditor of Puerto Rico, House of Representatives Committee on Insular Affairs, *Investigation of Political, Economic, and Social Conditions in Puerto Rico, Hearings*, 78th Congress, 1st Session, Pt. I, p. 195.

15. An Insular income tax was collected, and the rates were raised in 1943 to conform more closely than previously with the Federal rates. Puerto Rico also had its own inheritance tax.

16. Statement of the Assistant to the Administrator of the Federal Works Agency, *ibid.*, Part II, Appendix, p. 167.

17. Testimony of Governor Harwood, *ibid.*, Pt. III, pp. 318-19.

18. Cited in B. W. and J. W. Diffie, *Porto Rico: A Broken Pledge*, Vanguard, 1931, p. 137. In recent years Muñoz Marín has viewed the tariff from a different angle.

19. U. S. Tariff Commission, *op. cit.*, pp. 5-6.

20. Note, however, that the list of exceptions includes the staple diet items of the poorer classes in Puerto Rico—rice, legumes, and dried fish. It has been suggested that the duties on such articles coming into Puerto Rico could be lowered or eliminated for Puerto Rico without harm to domestic producers (E. S. Garver and E. B. Fincher, *Puerto Rico: Unsolved Problem*, Elgin Press, 1945, p. 44).

21. U. S. Tariff Commission, pp. 6-11. Returns on the property of non-residents amounted to only 1½ per cent of the net income of Puerto Rico in the early 1940's (Creamer, *op. cit.*, p. 28).

22. Since these duties were much lower than those in the United States, all shipments from the islands to the mainland were considered as from a foreign country and subject to full duties unless of Virgin Islands origin or containing materials of foreign origin not exceeding 20 per cent of their value (U. S. Department of the Interior, *The Virgin Islands*, Washington, 1939, p. 22).

23. Another form of indirect subsidy was the British Government's willingness to abandon certain tax resources in the colonies in order to permit the colonial governments to use them.

24. The British West Indies, and the sugar colonies of Mauritius and Fiji, have been the chief beneficiaries of the imperial preference system, while the United Kingdom has lost more than it gained from colonial preferences. Canada merely shared the cost, but its loss was enlarged because of the shipping subsidy connected with the Canadian-West Indian preference arrangements (F. V. Meyer, *Britain's Colonies in World Trade*, London, 1948).

25. *Report by the Hon. E. F. L. Wood, M.P., on his Visit to the West Indies and British Guiana, December 1921-February 1922*, London, 1922 (hereinafter referred to as *Wood Report*).

26. Joint declaration, January 14, 1946, *Report of the Anglo-American Caribbean Commission, 1945*, Appendix C, pp. 29-39.

27. One example was the conflict which arose over the variation between some local practice and the labor standards established by the Americans in building military bases in the British West Indies. Another was the increased racial friction which developed because of the behavior of some Americans operating in the islands during the war.

28. Governor of the Virgin Islands, *Annual Report, 1940*, Washington, p. 53, and testimony of Governor Harwood, House of Representatives, *loc. cit.*, pp. 288 and 317.

29. West India Royal Commission, *Report*, pp. 76-87, and 90.

30. Taxes on companies operating in the colonies but registered in the United Kingdom have usually been divided so that the colonial treasury

received no more than half. There have been some proposals to give the colonies a larger share, especially to avoid the necessity of charging more than the full British rate to secure a larger return (Sir Bernard Bourdillon, "Colonial Development and Welfare," *International Affairs*, July, 1944).

31. *Report of the Economic Policy Committee*, Jamaica, 1945. The committee pointed out that in 1943-44 Great Britain provided over £1,000,000 for expenditure in Jamaica while the total revenue from colonial and local taxation was about £4,500,000.

CHAPTER VIII

1. For his views, see Lord Hailey, *The Future of Colonial Peoples*, Princeton University Press, 1944.

2. "The New Philosophy of Colonial Rule, Address to Royal Empire Society," *Crown Colonist*, January, 1942.

3. A. Creech Jones, "Introduction," *Fabian Colonial Essays.*

4. As a minor phase of the program the Comptroller could grant up to £200 per project for a variety of small schemes where communities had shown a desire to help themselves. This was intended to encourage and stimulate local efforts.

5. This procedure has been criticized as unduly cumbersome and time-consuming, tending somewhat to dilute and distort the general development program. See Simey, *op. cit.*

6. Speech of Colonel Stanley, *Parliamentary Debates, House of Commons*, February 7, 1945, p. 2105.

7. An example was the Colonial Secretary's dispatch on "Certain Aspects of Colonial Policy in War-Time" (1941), which recommended to the colonial governments, *inter alia*, increased local food production, training of local personnel, and preparation of postwar development plans which could be implemented by Development and Welfare funds (*Crown Colonist*, October, 1941).

8. For example, see Harold Stannard, "The British West Indies," in *Fabian Colonial Essays*, p. 208, and Simey, *op. cit.*, pp. 203-09.

9. Evans, *op. cit.* See also J. A. Jarvis, *Brief History of the Virgin Islands*, St. Thomas, V. I., 1939, for an account of local opposition to the improvements sought by the well-intentioned Governor Pearson, first civilian governor of the Virgin Islands.

10. Simey, *op. cit.*

11. The Caribbean Commission might prove to be a most effective medium for realizing the ideal of colonial government, described as the "proper blending of stimulus and direction from outside with disinterested leadership and executive ability from within." Simey, *op. cit.*, p. 181.

12. *Minimum Standards of Social Policy in Dependent Territories*, International Labor Office, Montreal, 1944, pp. 15-16.

13. The planners of "economic intervention" in the Netherlands East Indies were tolerant of the conservatism of the People's Council, accepting explanatory preambles, reassuring titles, and restrictive riders. Thus they allayed misgivings over plans which few colonials dared to support wholeheartedly but none could turn down. In time there was general acceptance of their program as the new policies proved beneficial and were seen to be applied with ability, fairness, and moderation (Hart, *op. cit.*, p. 55).

14. Reply of the Secretary of State to a Member of Parliament during the question period in the House of Commons, April 3, 1946, cited in *Empire*, London, May-June, 1946.

15. A. Creech Jones, *Labour's Colonial Policy*, London, 1947.

16. On the first occasion for using the governor's reserved power under the three-year-old Jamaican constitution, the executive overrode the local legislature's refusal to vote a salary for an imported official because it believed qualified Jamaicans were available for the post (*Crown Colonist*, September, 1947).

The newly appointed Governor of Trinidad in 1947 made a point of directing department heads to fill posts with Trinidadians if at all possible (*ibid.*, October, 1947).

17. An example was the Federal Works Agency. See testimony of Major General Fleming, FWA Administrator, and G. H. Field, Assistant to the Administrator; House of Representatives, Committee on Insular Affairs, *op. cit.*, Part II, October, 1943, pp. 103, 117.

18. New York *Herald Tribune*, Dec. 3, 1945; Tugwell, *Public Papers*, *op. cit.*; and Tugwell and Tugwell, "Puerto Rico's Bootstraps," *loc. cit.* These actions were taken by a governor who in general favored using local personnel, and who often cited their loyalty and competence.

19. The Crown Agents purchase, inspect, ship, and insure stores; design and draw specifications for buildings and other public works; negotiate contracts for public works; negotiate, issue, manage, and arrange repayment of loans for such activities; invest funds, select technical appointees; and conduct other commercial, financial, and similar business in which the colonies may need assistance (*Crown Colonist*, February, 1943).

20. The practice of paying differential salaries to local and metropolitan officials is a constant source of irritation to the people in the dependencies, but this should also diminish with an increased use of local personnel.

21. *Crown Colonist*, April, 1944, p. 288.

22. Sir Drummond Shiels, "Self-Government for Advanced Colonies," in *Fabian Colonial Essays*, p. 116.

23. *Development and Welfare in the West Indies, 1940-1942*, Colonial No. 184, London, 1943; pp. 66-67; *ibid., 1943-44*, Colonial No. 189, London, 1945, pp. 42-43; and *ibid., 1945-46*, Colonial No. 212, London, 1947, pp. 86-87.

24. Testimony of Field, *loc. cit.*

25. Furthermore, the duties set by the American tariff system have greatly restricted this obvious market for most British West Indian products and hindered British West Indian industrialization by penalizing processed materials (see Meyer, *op. cit.*, p. 184).

26. A few of these were the Colonial Products Research Council, the Imperial Forestry Institute, the Colonial Advisory Committee on Education, Advisers in the Colonial Office on Public Health and on Air Transport, and the Colonial Research Committee of the Development and Welfare Fund. See "Colonial Office Advisory System and Its Growth," *Crown Colonist*, July, 1945, for a chart of all boards and advisers in existence at that time.

27. See Bolívar Pagán, *Puerto Rico: The Next State*, 1942.

28. Indeed, a colonial specialist in the Far East, J. S. Furnivall, regarded the customary colonial labor reforms as benefiting labor in the mother country rather than the natives in whose interest such changes were declared to be made. ("Some Problems of Tropical Economy," *Fabian Colonial Essays*, p. 178.)

29. See Emanuel Moresco, *Colonial Questions and Peace*, International Institute of Intellectual Co-operation, Paris, 1939, for common causes of violence arising in the colonies.

30. Yet failure to improve living standards may be even more risky, providing in the unenlightened mass of colonial peoples "ready material for the pernicious agitator who may promise Utopia in exchange for such liberty as they possess" (J. F. Rippy, *The Caribbean Danger Zone*, Putnam, 1940, p. 18).

31. The absence of conflict does not necessarily imply co-operation. Some observers fear that plans for collective activity in Puerto Rico, requiring meticulous co-ordination on a voluntary basis, will fail because the cultural trait of strong individualism has operated against the development of co-operation.

32. Evans, *op. cit.*, pp. 118 and 215.

33. Flogging for praedial larceny, reintroduced in Trinidad during the war, hardly seems a constructive solution to this problem. Conceivably, the reduction in personal distrust might promote a narrow class solidarity and aggravate group conflicts by organized pressure for change, through violence if necessary. A nondiscriminatory policy toward all racial groups would therefore appear doubly necessary in order to foster a public spirit rather than a class spirit.

34. C. C. Rogler, *Comerío*, University of Kansas, 1940, p. 66.

35. Olivier, *op. cit.*, p. 432.

36. Simey, *op. cit.*, pp. 169-71 and 182.

37. Rogler, *op. cit.*, p. 66.

38. Furnivall, *op. cit.*; and *Idem, Colonial Policy and Practice*, Cambridge, 1948.

39. F. M. Keesing, "Applied Anthropology in Colonial Administration," in *Science of Man in the World Crisis,* ed. by Ralph Linton, 1945.

40. Fortes, *op. cit.,* p. 230.

41. *Ibid.,* p. 232.

CHAPTER IX

1. B. M. Malinowski, "Native Education and Culture Contact," *International Review of Missions,* October, 1936, quoted in Margaret Wrong, "Is Literacy Necessary in Africa?", *Fabian Colonial Essays,* p. 156.

2. For a general description of the variations in British colonial government see *Towards Self-Government in the British Colonies,* rev. ed., British Information Services, 1947.

3. Until the passage of the Organic Act of 1936, which created a third over-all legislative body for certain purposes, the entire legislative function was exercised separately by municipal councils for the two municipalities comprising the islands of St. Thomas and St. John, and St. Croix.

A provision of the Virgin Islands Colonial Law dating from the Danish regime required consultation with the local councils before legislation regarding the colony was finally acted on by Congress, but this was ignored in practice. Evans, *op. cit.,* p. 258; a description of the relative powers of the governor and legislative bodies prior to 1936 may be found in pages 71-88 of the same volume.

4. Other administrative appointments (to offices where the salaries were to be paid locally) have been made by the governor with the advice and consent of the appropriate municipal council.

The governor's veto powers included the item veto in money bills. If two-thirds of the appropriate legislative body repassed a vetoed bill it could be transmitted to the President, whose approval or disapproval was final.

5. Besides making the governorship an elective office, the 1947 Congressional amendment to the Organic Act provided that the Attorney General and Commissioner of Education be appointed by the governor with the advice and consent of the Puerto Rican Senate. It also established a Coordinator of Federal Agencies. Presidential and Congressional powers over Puerto Rican affairs remained otherwise unchanged, except that under certain circumstances the President could declare particular Federal laws inapplicable to Puerto Rico.

6. The American dependencies have a special problem not shared by the British colonies, which are under the complete jurisdiction of the Colonial Office. Despite nominal supervision by the Division of Territories and Island Possessions, responsibility for Puerto Rico and the Virgin Islands is divided among so many Federal agencies that confusion in policy is chronic.

7. Trumbull White, *Puerto Rico and Its People*, Stokes, 1938, p. 152. For a description of the administrative impotence of an American governor in Puerto Rico see R. G. Tugwell, *The Stricken Land*, Doubleday, 1947, pp. 12-13, 380-81.

8. Lord Hailey, "Great Britain and Her Dependencies," *Problems of the Post-War Settlement in the Far East*, Royal Institute of International Affairs, for Institute of Pacific Relations Conference, 1942 (mimeo.), London, n.d.

9. *Wood Report*, p. 7; see Leopold Schwarzschild, *Primer of the Coming World*, Knopf, 1944, p. 176, for a recent example of the same reasoning.

10. For example, see Hailey, "Great Britain and Her Dependencies," p. 25; West India Royal Commission, *Report*, p. 449; *Jamaica Constitution: Despatch from the Secretary of State for the Colonies to the Governor of Jamaica*, London, 1943.

11. The traditional autonomy of Bermuda has been a barrier to social progress and suggests why some fear that a too-rapid grant of autonomy in other areas might impede social and economic development. The Bermuda House of Assembly as late as 1946 rejected the introduction of an income tax into the colony even in the face of a deficit of £60,000. In British Honduras, on the other hand, a majority of the Legislative Council —similarly dominated by the local elite but lacking the extensive powers of the Bermuda Legislature—opposed an increase in the income tax, only to have the governor use his overriding powers to make the bill a law. *Crown Colonist*, August, 1946, pp. 617-18.

12. For example, see Concurrent Resolution No. 1 Approved Unanimously by the Insular Legislature—February 20, 1945, quoted in *Puerto Rico's Future Political Status?*, Office of Information for Puerto Rico, n.d. (probably 1946), p. 5.

13. Theodore Roosevelt, *Colonial Policies of the United States*, Doubleday, 1937, pp. 105-06.

14. Jarvis, *op. cit.*, pp. 161-62.

15. Olivier, *op. cit.*, pp. 415 and 421. For other complaints along these lines see the West India Royal Commission's *Report*, pp. 58 and 451, on irresponsible criticism and governmental deadlocks; Shiels, *op. cit.*, p. 104, also mentions the tendency toward personal attacks to which officials cannot reply; A. Creech Jones in Rita Hinden *et al.*, *Freedom for Colonial Peoples*, London, 1942, on the ineffectiveness of a Legislative Council which can merely block and criticize; Arthur Calder-Marshall, in *Glory Dead*, London, 1939, on Trinidad's legislative "farce," and "elaborate game in which the opposition is allowed from time to time to win a point or two so that they may not feel too sore"; C. L. R. James, *The Case for West-Indian Self-Government*, London, 1933, on the irresponsibility of a governor occupying a triple position in a crown colony; W. M. Macmillan, *Warning from the West Indies*, Harmondsworth (England), 1938, on

paralyzing the executive and the insufficient exercise of responsibility permitted West Indians in teaching them the difference between talking and doing; and Esther Chapman, "The Truth about Jamaica," *West Indian Review*, July, 1938, on the low quality of personnel willing to seek election for the Legislative Council because of its farcical operations.

16. Lord Olivier, "The Truth About the West Indies," *The Nineteenth Century*, July, 1938.

17. Devolution, in which full power over particular subjects might be given the local legislature while the governor's veto remained in the background for other subjects, has sometimes been advoated as an alternative method of expanding self-government. The main objection to applying this method in the Caribbean is the small scale of government operations, even when all fields of legislation are combined.

18. The outlines of the constitutions of the various British West Indies may be found in *Closer Association of the British West Indian Colonies*, London, 1947, and autonomy developments in *Towards Self-Government in the British Colonies*.

In 1949 the Secretary of State for the Colonies offered Trinidad a new constitution along the lines approved by a majority of a special committee of the Legislative Council; but the manner in which this majority was constituted and the strong opposition of the minority cast doubt on its acceptability. In any case it stopped short of a fully elected Legislative Council. Furthermore the practical effect of the changes in the Executive Council will hardly broaden popular participation in the government despite a surface appearance of liberality (see David Pitt, "Trinidad's New Constitution," *Venture*, London, March, 1949, pp. 5-6 and 9).

19. Following the first election under universal suffrage the governor's appointments to the Executive Council gave the elected members the largest single bloc, while the unofficial members held a majority in the council and also in its Estimates Committee and Finance Committee. This arrangement expressed the governor's desire to make the people "feel this was their government" (*Crown Colonist*, September, 1946).

20. West India Royal Commission, *Report*, pp. 450-53.

21. *Ibid.*, p. 449.

22. *Towards Self-Government in the British Colonies*, p. 22; *Crown Colonist*, January, 1947.

23. Quoted in Diffie and Diffie, *op. cit.*, p. 194.

24. U. S. Tariff Commission, *op. cit.*, pp. 17-24, and *Puerto Rico's Future Political Status?*, p. 27. See Tugwell, *The Stricken Land*, pp. 492, 496, 540-41, 543-61, 564, 594-95, 598-603, and 625, for some of the struggles over changing the status of Puerto Rico.

25. In July, 1946, President Truman had already appointed as successor to Governor Tugwell Jesús T. Piñero, who had been elected by Puerto Rico at large as Resident Commissioner in Congress.

26. San Juan, *El Mundo*, July 5, 1948.

27. Tugwell, *The Stricken Land*, p. 78. Similarly, Virgin Islands legislators regularly appointed themselves to administrative posts they had created, until the practice was declared illegal by the Federal District Court in the Virgin Islands in 1948.

28. James, *op. cit.*, p. 30; and Sir R. St. Johnston, *Strange Places and Strange Peoples*, London, 1936.

29. Calder-Marshall, *op. cit.*, p. 172.

30. *Ibid.*, p. 279.

31. West India Royal Commission, *Report*, p. 379. This report gives detailed property, tax, and salary or income qualifications for the electorates of the various colonies current in 1939, pp. 378-79.

32. In 1947 Legislative Council members were still unremunerated in Barbados, British Guiana, and British Honduras, although the first two were considering payment. Thus, only the well-to-do could afford to serve.

33. See table in West India Royal Commission's *Report*, p. 381, for detailed requirements in force in 1939.

34. Franchise and officeholding qualifications as of 1947 are listed in *Closer Association of the British West Indian Colonies*, pp. 26-29.

35. Shiels, *op. cit.*, pp. 112-13.

36. Raymond Kennedy, "The Colonial Crisis and the Future," in Linton, *op. cit.*, p. 326.

37. By contrast, in Puerto Rico, where there is universal suffrage and a high degree of legislative autonomy, the percentage of registered voters actually voting has been higher than in the United States.

38. West India Royal Commission, *Report*, pp. 90, 383, and 398-99; Calder-Marshall, *op. cit.*, pp. 281-82; *Crown Colonist*, May, 1941; *ibid.*, June, 1943; Evans, *op. cit.*, pp. 91-92.

39. Government of Jamaica, *Report on the Reform of Local Government in Jamaica*, Kingston, 1943.

40. See Simey, *op. cit.*, pp. 209-214, on the problem of fitting in community-based welfare activities with an inadequately functioning local government system.

41. Without some kind of union to supply a larger domestic market than is available in the individual islands, industrialization would not be profitable in the West Indies (League of Nations, *op. cit.*, pp. 40-42).

42. *Closer Association of the British West Indian Colonies*, contains the dispatch and memorandum on the problem and possible ways to meet it; see also *Empire*, November, 1947, and H. V. Wiseman, *The West Indies: Towards a New Dominion?*, London, 1948.

43. Moresco, *op. cit.*, p. 262. See also, *Empire*, May-June, 1946: "Every thinking West Indian knows that there is no future for his country as long as it remains a separate little island remote in political and economic arrangements from its neighbours."

44. Hailey, "Great Britain and Her Dependencies," p. 28.

45. P. H. Hiss, *Netherlands America*, Duell, Sloan and Pearce, 1943, p. 178.

46. Eric Williams, "Crossways of the Caribbean," *Survey Graphic*, November, 1942.

47. Everett Stonequist, *The Marginal Man; A Study in Personality and Cultural Conflict*, Scribners, 1937, pp. 27-31.

48. *Ibid.*, p. 31.

49. *Ibid.*, p. 30.

50. See also Williams, *op. cit.*, p. 514; *idem, The Negro in the Caribbean*, Associates in Negro Folk Education, 1942, pp. 60-66; James, *op. cit.*, pp. 8-10, 19-21; and Frederick Pilkington, "Rising Race of Coloured People," *Crown Colonist*, November, 1940. Albert Campbell drew a similar class portrait for the Virgin Islands in *St. Thomas Negroes—A Study of Personality and Culture*, pp. 22-35 and 57-58.

51. These leaders were often middle-class members rebelling against their situation. The colored intellectual group is now split between the traditional conformists and the racial revolutionaries, a phenomenon observable in many other parts of the world (Blanshard, *op. cit.*, pp. 57-58).

52. *Crown Colonist;* September, 1943, October, 1943, and January, 1944.

53. Evans, *op. cit.*, pp. 29 and 89.

54. J. A. Jarvis, *The Virgin Islands and Their People*, Dorrance, 1944, pp. 154-55.

55. R. G. Tugwell, *Changing the Colonial Climate*, Government of Puerto Rico, 1942, p. 57, and *idem, The Stricken Land*, p. 38.

56. Rogler, *op. cit.*, p. 106.

57. For a description of Muñoz Marín's political techniques, see "Puerto Rico," *Fortune*, February, 1941. Of course, the older vote-getting techniques could still be effective.

58. Rogler, *op. cit.*, p. 39. He explains that since race changes its meaning with different social situations, the rules of admission are in one sense flexible. However, members or would-be members of the elite must have some nonracial attribute prized by society. Therefore the ability to lessen social and racial distance has been slight, because such attributes are limited by many complex social and economic conditions.

59. Eric Williams, "Race Relations in Puerto Rico and the Virgin Islands," *Foreign Affairs*, January, 1945.

60. Tugwell, *The Stricken Land*, pp. 252-53, 370-71.

61. For example, an earlier attempt at a major constitutional modification was opposed because there was no demand for change from the "substantial element" in the colonies (*Wood Report*, pp. 13, 18, 19, 21, 23, 24).

62. Stonequist, *op. cit.*, p. 160.

63. A notable exception was Sir Gordon Lethem, Governor of British Guiana, who in his Annual Address of May 15, 1946, urged the colony to work toward self-government. "It is no use hesitating and doubting.

There will be difficulties and controversies between sections, arising from the fear of majority rule and the problems of minorities, of course." These were inevitable, but he could see no other lasting remedy for a colony like British Guiana (*Crown Colonist*, July, 1946).

64. For instances see *Crown Colonist:* December, 1938, October, 1940, December, 1940, October, 1941, April, 1942, and January, 1943.

65. Williams, *The Negro in the Caribbean,* p. 61.

66. *Jamaica Constitution: Despatch from the Secretary of State for the Colonies,* p. 3.

67. *Crown Colonist:* October, 1944, December, 1944, and July, 1945.

68. *Crown Colonist,* November, 1945, and January, 1942.

69. See Creech Jones, *Labour's Colonial Policy.*

70. *Empire,* May-June, 1946, and May, 1947.

71. The Bahamas did not participate, already having expressed their view as worded by a Bahama newspaper: "Even the thought . . . is repellent to our people" (*Crown Colonist*, October, 1945).

72. Tugwell, *The Stricken Land,* pp. 568-69; Martin Ebon, *World Communism Today,* McGraw-Hill, 1948, pp. 306-07.

73. Governor Tugwell claimed that the behavior of the Bell Committee of the House which investigated Puerto Rican conditions in 1943 was so antagonistic to the ruling party that it revived the extreme *independentista* movement which Muñoz Marín had sought to curb as suicidal (*The Stricken Land,* p. 536).

74. For references on the status issue in Puerto Rico, see Theodore Roosevelt, *op. cit.,* pp. 100, 115-117; Diffie and Diffie, *op cit.,* p. 194; White, *op. cit.,* pp. 298, 306, 316, 364; Daisy Reck, *Puerto Rico and the Virgin Islands,* Farrar and Rhinehart, 1939, p. 69; Tugwell, *Changing the Colonial Climate,* p. 176, and *idem, The Stricken Land,* pp. 492, 496, 540, 549, 558-60, 598-600, 686; Wenzell Brown, *Dynamite on Our Doorstep,* Greenberg, 1945, pp. 192, 193, 195, 215, 251, 252; Bolívar Pagán, *op. cit.;* Garver and Fincher, *op. cit.,* p. 72; Petrullo, *op. cit.,* p. 108; Clarence Senior, *Self-Determination for Puerto Rico,* Post-War World Council, New York, 1946; Olive Holmes, "Puerto Rico: An American Responsibility," *Foreign Policy Reports,* March 1, 1947; Blanshard, *op. cit.,* pp. 223-25; Office of Information for Puerto Rico, "Puerto Rico's Future Political Status?", and *idem, Puerto Rico Handbook,* 1946, p. 22.

75. Governor of the Virgin Islands, *Annual Report,* 1940, pp. 48-49.

76. *Ibid.,* pp. 49-50; Jarvis, *Brief History of the Virgin Islands,* pp. 232-34, 237; *idem, The Virgin Islands and Their People,* p. 155; and Wenzell Brown, *Angry Men, Laughing Men: The Caribbean Cauldron,* Greenberg, 1947, pp. 213-17.

77. Bustamante's Jamaica Labor Party won twenty-three seats, the People's National Party, four, and the "independents," five; while the recently organized conservative Democratic Party obtained none. The Labor Party thus held the embryo ministerial posts.

78. The following are samples of his language on several occasions: "If my Party, my Union, or myself feel that dictatorship is the best means to obtain these improvements, I, Bustamente, will adopt it." "This is to instruct sugar workers through the country that when the time comes for this year's crop to be taken off, I will give the order." "I am going to destroy the *Gleaner*" (chief newspaper in Jamaica, which had criticized him). "I am going to start a war of race hatred. If I have got to be a dictator or a Hitler in Jamaica, I am going to crush every Jew in Jamaica or compel them to leave the island" (*Empire*, May-June, 1945).

79. The sequel indicated that employing interests were not above taking advantage of labor schisms, while the rival labor groups could occasionally overcome their differences. A waterfront "sympathy strike" of a Busta-mente union following the trial was shortly ended on Bustamente's request. Ignoring the promise to return to work, the United Fruit Company hired workers from a rival union. A delegation from the House of Representatives prevailed on the government to intervene, and a settlement long advocated by the Labor Adviser was the outcome, the members of both unions finally working together (*Crown Colonist*, September, 1946, p. 692).

80. For references on the Jamaica constitution and the first elections and their aftermath, see *Crown Colonist:* May, 1943, September, 1943, October, 1943, November, 1944, February, 1945, March, 1945, May, 1945, September, 1945; also *Empire:* March-April, 1945, May-June, 1945, May-June, 1946; also Brown, *Angry Men, Laughing Men*, pp. 68-75; and Blanshard, *op. cit.*, pp. 94-98.

CHAPTER X

1. When the British Government began to take an intensive interest in colonial labor relations, the International Labor Organization draft conventions which it had signed were in many cases not locally accepted. Child labor regulation was a noteworthy example. *Labour Supervision in the Colonial Empire, 1937-1943*, London, 1943, recounts the British Government's accomplishments in reforming colonial labor regulation.

2. For example, in the late thirties, the official policy in Trinidad was on the one hand to encourage the development of trade unions. On the other, the colonial government ordered police to attend all private meetings of trade unions, and otherwise harried union organizers and their followers.

3. There was some local resentment at the West India Royal Commission testimony for allegedly stirring up unrest. However, this attitude had something in common with that of the British Government, which refused to publish the report until some years after its evidence could have created any sensation.

4. *Trade Union Organisation and Industrial Relations in Trinidad*, pp. 4-7, 31-34, and 36. These advances were noted, even though attention was

directed to many specific social problems still unsolved and to the crying need for more extensive economic development.

Further comparison can be made between the attitude of the elected members of the Trinidad Legislative Council in 1938 and 1946. In the earlier case they refused to vote for a salary and allowances for an Industrial (relations) Adviser, which had to be carried by the official majority. Eight years later they approved a comprehensive program of social welfare drawn up by the Social Welfare Office of Development and Welfare, which involved quadrupling the financial provision for a social welfare staff.

5. *Crown Colonist*, April, 1939, and May, 1939.

6. Bustamente showed little interest in nationalization as a general policy, although he favored government ownership of the docks after a rival union became established among dock workers over whom he had formerly had complete control.

7. For example, upon being questioned in Parliament, the Secretary of State declared that the complaint regarding unsatisfactory local administration of Jamaican medical services was now a concern of the Jamaican Government, and that he would not institute an inquiry (February 28, 1945, cited in *Empire*, May-June, 1945).

8. "Lines of Progress in the British West Indies," *Crown Colonist*, July, 1945, pp. 453-54.

9. For example, Puerto Rican parents of the poorer classes are reported to be pathetically eager to have their children educated, making great sacrifices so that their children might thus improve their social status (Rogler, *op. cit.*, pp. 123-24).

10. The first election under universal suffrage in Trinidad resulted in leftist parties winning eight of the nine seats in the Legislative Council, while the ninth was won by an independent left candidate (*Empire*, August, 1946, p. 9).

11. *Empire*, May, 1944, and September, 1946.

12. Within a few years following 1940 the following were established: a Land Authority to carry out land reforms; a Water Resources Authority to promote greater use of the water supply for power and irrigation; a Development Company to initiate and manage industries and assist private enterprises in establishing or expanding business and industry; a Development Bank to make government funds available for encouragement of industry and to be a central financial agency for the municipal and Insular governments; an Agricultural Development Company to stimulate commercial development of agricultural resources; Transportation and Communications authorities to improve and augment these facilities under government auspices; an Aqueduct and Sewer Service; a Minimum Wage Board; and a Planning, Urbanizing, and Zoning Board. Also, the sugar industry was made a public utility.

13. Theodore Roosevelt, *Colonial Policies of the United States*, p. 120.

14. More recently the Association of Sugar Producers, representing thirty-two of the thirty-six existing mills, has been reported to favor the government's industrialization program because it would permit the sugar companies to mechanize the sugar industry, a process which they believe depended on the opportunities for displaced agricultural workers to become employed elsewhere (New York *Times*, March 27, 1948).

15. U. S. Tariff Commission, *op. cit.*, pp. 29-30.

16. See W. M. MacMillan's comment in *Democratise the Empire!*, London, 1944, that British neglect of colonial economic development was responsible for the fact that government service was desired as the most promising career for colonial talent. He declared that Legislative Council discussions often gave precedence to questions about preferential employment of local personnel and rates of pay rather than to welfare questions. Suitable opportunities in private employment were needed for the small progressive class of educated individuals in the colonies. Then they might view the public service with greater objectivity, and cease their intense competition for governmental favor.

17. Returning in 1947 from the preparatory conference at Geneva of the United Nations Conference on Trade and Employment, the Puerto Rican representative on the American delegation advised Puerto Rico to prepare itself to compete in American and other markets with less protection from quotas, subsidies, and similar support. The British West Indian delegate concluded that the colonies he represented needed a greater degree of autonomy, so that their interests would receive greater attention.

18. "Puerto Rico," *Fortune*, February, 1941. There has been some improvement in rate-making in recent years. Actually the freight rates to the Virgin Islands, not under the coastwise shipping restrictions, have been higher than those to Puerto Rico.

19. Today's colonial areas are in striking contrast to the largely white dependencies which won their freedom by the opening of the twentieth century partly because of their ability to bear the expense of their own government and defense (Knorr, *op. cit.*, p. 353).

20. Rita Hinden, "Imperialism Today," *Fabian Quarterly*, April, 1945. Wilfrid Benson, in "A People's Peace in the Colonies," *International Labour Review*, February, 1943, also argued that there were strong economic forces favorable to continuing and expanding development policies in the colonies.

21. Sec. 14 of the Tydings Bill, S. 227, and Sec. 213-14, 410 (d) of the Tydings-Piñero Bill, S. 1002, 79th Congress, 1st Session.

An example is the long period during which the five-hundred-acre restriction in the Puerto Rican Organic Act remained unenforced. Similarly, the provision in the law granting Southern Rhodesia semi-dominion status which made the Dominion Office responsible for guaranteeing natives against discriminatory local legislation has long been inoperative (*Empire*, March-April, 1946).

22. U. S. Department of State, *Analysis of General Agreement on Tariffs and Trade*, Government Printing Office, 1947, pp. 1, 128, 154.

23. In 1946, however, Development and Welfare conducted an extensive consolidated census in the West Indies, except for Jamaica, which took one in 1943 as the basis for introducing universal suffrage.

24. S. 1002, 79th Congress, 1st Session.

25. For the war contribution of the British West Indies see *The Colonial Empire, 1939-1947*, London, 1947. For Puerto Rico, see Office of Information for Puerto Rico, *Puerto Rico in the War*, n.d.

26. There is growing pressure for the inclusion of colonial trade-union representatives in the delegations. Counterbalancing this, the West India Committee (a metropolitan organization of West Indian employing interests) has also sought a stronger voice in the International Labor Organization conferences as colonial labor standards receive greater attention (*Empire*, January-February, 1946, p. 7). In 1947 the Puerto Rican chairman of the Insular Public Welfare Board was appointed as one of the two United States members of the Permanent Committee on Social Policy for Dependent Areas.

27. There are instances (notably the Geneva International Trade Conference of 1947) where officials from the Caribbean dependencies have been on the staffs of British and American delegations to international conferences. Significantly, the Department of Trusteeship and Information from Non-Self-Governing Territories of the United Nations Secretariat has been partly staffed with people from the dependent areas.

28. Royal Institute of International Affairs, *op. cit.*, p. 275.

29. Hiss, *op. cit.*, p. 128.

30. *Crown Colonist*, May, 1943.

31. See Lord Olivier, *Jamaica, The Blessed Island*, for the long history of foreign banana trade monopolies in Jamaica, and the almost successful resistance of the co-operative Jamaican Banana Producers' Association, which later succumbed to economic pressure and fell into line with the United Fruit Company's policies.

32. These were the conclusions of three economists, Gayer, Homan, and James, regarding the drain of profits, *op. cit.*, pp. 289-91.

33. However, he did criticize the foreign companies for not making more use of their funds in advancing the industrial or agricultural interests of the island (*Changing the Colonial Climate*, p. 138).

34. *Ibid.*, p. 50.

35. This would also hold true of the influence exercised by metropolitan capitalists whose interests compete with those in the colonies. The beet sugar growers are an outstanding example. Fear of Senatorial displeasure has held up the undertaking of rice milling in Puerto Rico, although this activity is economically and socially desirable. It has been pointed out that

congressmen responsive to their constituents' pressure could prevent industrialization in Puerto Rico as long as Congressional committees are the final determiners of Puerto Rican policy (Petrullo, *op. cit.*, p. 165).

36. Nevertheless, the shift in the center of business gravity to the Netherlands East Indies from the mother country, although very slow, was stimulated somewhat by the growth in local government authority (Hart, *op. cit.*, p. 47).

37. W. A. Lewis, in Hinden, *Freedom for Colonial Peoples*, p. 18.

38. Holmes, *op. cit.*, p. 283; Simey, *op. cit.*, p. 6.

39. Reck, *op. cit.*, pp. 95-96.

CHAPTER XI

1. Tariff preferences existing between independent countries do not carry the same danger of political dependence. They are negotiated rather than unilaterally determined; even when the parties are not equal the bargaining power of the weaker is likely to be much greater than in the case of dependencies.

2. Rogler, *op. cit.*, pp. 65, 94; Senior, *op. cit.*, pp. 113-122; Notestein, *op. cit.*, pp. 150, 152-54.

3. The strong political resistances to large-scale emigration of colored peoples are a substantial hurdle which must be overcome if population pressure in the Caribbean is to be relieved by this method.

4. Furthermore, as remarked by H. D. Lasswell, to defer to self-respect by enabling local interests to participate in stimulating the flow of trade and investment is a good offset to communist propaganda in backward areas (*World Politics Faces Economics*, McGraw-Hill, 1945, p. 69).

5. Rita Hinden, "The Challenge of African Poverty," *Fabian Colonial Essays*, pp. 51-66.

Increasing the means of political expression may appear in some cases to increase social conflict, but the conflict is likely to have existed already and to become more serious if covered up through lack of expression.

6. Metropolitan financial aid may even need to be greater than before, at least temporarily, if the sources of private capital continue to diminish.

7. *Crown Colonist*, March, 1945, p. 150, citing article in the London *Times*.

8. Benson, *op. cit.*, p. 151.

9. *Development and Welfare in the West Indies*, 1940-42, pp. 66-67; see also *ibid.*, 1943-44, p. 42; and *ibid.*, 1945-46, pp. 86-88.

10. *Ibid.*

11. Fortes, *op. cit.*, p. 227.

12. *Ibid.*, p. 231.

13. Tugwell, *Changing the Colonial Climate*, p. 192.

14. *Empire*, November-December, 1945.

15. Ever since Puerto Rico was taken over in 1898 its people have been led to believe that they would eventually be self-governing. The Wood Report on the British West Indies made in 1922 explained at length why greater autonomy was inevitable and then proceeded to recommend such halting steps in this direction that its claim to a "modest constitutional advance" was an overstatement.

16. The solution to the Netherlands East Indies problem which the Dutch and Indonesian republican leaders agreed upon at Linggadjati was not unlike the French blueprint regarding Indo-China: a federation of more or less autonomous native states within the Dutch empire, united with the metropolitan government for certain joint purposes, including the conduct of foreign relations and, "as far as necessary," finance (Charles Wolf, Jr., *The Indonesian Story*, John Day, 1948, pp. 175-78).

17. Hinden, "Imperialism Today," pp. 5-12.

18. See R. H. S. Crossman, M.P., speaking on "British Colonial Policy," at the Fifteenth Annual New York *Herald-Tribune* Forum on Current Problems, Oct. 28, 1946, reprinted in the New York *Herald Tribune*, Nov. 3, 1946.

19. The United Nations Charter proceeds further in the direction of international responsibility in the chapters dealing with trusteeships, which were primarily intended to apply to ex-enemy dependencies and the former League of Nations mandates. However, growing fear of Russian hegemony which makes use of these sections of the Charter has made the colonial powers timid about implementing the trusteeship provisions except for the mandates. In any case they would not apply in the Caribbean. Article 77 does, however, provide that the trusteeship system can apply to "territories voluntarily placed under the system by states responsible for their administration."

20. On the value of the United Nations to the colonies see Wilfrid Benson, "International Organization and Non-Self-Governing Territories," *The Journal of Negro Education*, Summer, 1946, pp. 300-10.

21. For example, see W. R. Espy, "Dams for the Floods of War," New York *Times* Magazine, Oct. 27, 1946, pp. 12-13, 56-58. Concerning the management corporation as a means of spreading modern technology, H. D. Lasswell has said, "Not permanent tutelage but an opportunity to aid some backward country to join the modern world economy is the dream of many gifted engineers who have played a conspicuous part in conquering the globe for modern methods. These engineers and managers conquer as teachers, not as dictators—a special form of civilized advance" (*op. cit.*, pp. 70-71).

22. For example, see J. M. Jones, "Caribbean Laboratory," *Fortune*, February, 1944.

23. R. J. Bunche, "The Anglo-American Caribbean Commission: An Experiment in Regional Cooperation," *American Council Paper No. 7*, prepared for the Ninth Conference of the Institute of Pacific Relations, Hot

Springs, Virginia, January, 1945, American Council, Institute of Pacific Relations, 1945.

24. One problem encountered by the British in providing for colonial participation was the inability of the local governments to agree on nominations of the two British colonial members on the commission. Earlier the fear of colonial rivalry regarding representation had been given as a reason for no local representation. When the policy was changed the British Government proposed that the British unofficial delegates to the second session of the West Indian Conference decide on the selection, and that the office be rotating. It was also agreed that the British unofficial delegates to future conferences be elected by vote of the unofficial members of the legislative councils in the colonies. One of the two West Indian Commissioners finally had to be nominated by the Secretary of State because of the inability of the unofficial delegates to the Second West Indian Conference to agree (*Crown Colonist*, August, 1945, September, 1946). The Colonial Office decided on a new procedure in 1948, whereby the unofficial West Indian conference delegates would elect the members by majority vote from a panel nominated by the popular legislative bodies in the colonies. Where no candidate or only one received a clear majority, the selection would be completed by the Colonial Secretary (*ibid.*, April, 1948).

25. C. W. Taussig, "A Four-Power Program in the Caribbean," *Foreign Affairs*, July, 1946.

26. See Elizabeth Armstrong, "The West Indian Conference: Third Session," *Department of State Bulletin*, February 20, 1949, pp. 221-26.

27. "The International Interest in Colonies," *Round Table*, December, 1944.

Index

Absentee ownership, *see* Exploitation

Administration,
  appointments, 149-50, 152
  personnel, 121, 143, 169 *ff.*, 189
  reforms, 189
  responsibility for, 121 *ff.*, 194
  supervision, 110, 123 *ff.*, 143 *ff.*, 194
  unification of services, 152

Adult education, *see* Education

Agregados, 61

Agriculture, 6
  crop-diversification, 32, 40, 48, 76
  rehabilitation of, 48, 76, 82 *ff.*, 188, 240

Agricultural Adjustment Administration, 39, 62 *n.*, 78, 126

Airways, *see* Transportation

Aid, *see under* Financial, Metropolitan, or Technical aid

American citizenship, *see* Citizenship

Armstrong, Elizabeth, 264

Atlantic Charter, 147

Attitudes, *see* Social attitudes

Autonomy, *see* Self-government

Backwardness, 5 *ff.*

Bahamas, 120, 144, 171, 182

Barbados, 31, 144, 153, 158, 172 *ff.*

Bartlett, F. D., 240

Bauxite, 37, 208

Beet sugar, 40, 193

Beneficiaries of social and economic development, *see under* Social development and Economic development

Benham Committee, 169, 240

Benson, Wilfrid, 206, 260, 263

Bermuda, 120, 144, 182

Birth rates, birth control, *see* Overpopulation

Black Negroes, *see* Class structure

Blanshard, Paul, 243, 256

Blauch, L. E., 241

Bonn, M. J., 236

Bourdillon, Sir Bernard, 249

British Crown Agents, 250

British Guiana, 37, 108, 125, 151, 158, 171-72

British West Indies,
  diminishing conservatism in, 181 *ff.*
  economic development in, 47 *ff.*
  social development in, 63 *ff.*

Brown, A. J., 244

Brown, Herbert, 240

Brown, Wenzell, 257

Bulk purchase, *see* Price support

Bunche, R. J., 263

Bustamente, Alexander, 170, 177 *ff.*, 185, 258

Butler, Tubal Uriah Buzz, 68-70

Calder-Marshall, Arthur, 253

Calypso, 23, 156-57

Campbell, A. A., 236

Canada, 248

Capital, need for, 75, 243

Trinidad, 31, 37, 71, 108, 116,
151, 158, 171-72, 209
Tropical agriculture, 28, 242
Truman, President, 33, 155, 175,
243, 254
Trusteeship, 114, 237
Tugwell, Rexford G., 32, 61 *n.*,
110, 134 *n.*, 160, 179, 224,
240, 256
Tydings, Millard E., 154-55, 175
Tydings-Piñero bill, 200

Underdeveloped, *see* Backward
Unemployment, 6, 49, 58, 79, 82,
87 *ff.*
Unification of services, *see* Admin-
istration
Unions, *see* Labor
United Fruit Company, 70, 204, 208
United Nations, 20, 227 *ff.*
United Nations Charter, 23, 228
U. S. interest in colonies, 29
U. S. policy, 24-25
toward republics, 35
changeability of, 197
U. S. Tariff Commission, 99, 100,
189 *n.*, 247
Universal suffrage, *see* Franchise
University of Puerto Rico, 58, 122
Unrest, *see* Violence

Vandenbosch, Amry, 241
Veterans, 58 *n.*, 137

Veto, 156
See also "Reserved powers"
Violence, 30, 31, 81, 183
reduction of, 135 *ff.*, 190, 210
Virgin Islands,
cattle-raising, 45 *ff.*
economic development in, 45 *ff.*
social development in, 62-63
Virgin Islands Company, 33, 45-46
Vocational training, 58-59, 138

Walker, E. A., 236
West India Royal Commission, 31,
47 *ff.*, 94 *ff.*, 124, 130, 151 *ff.*,
158, 238
West Indian Conferences, 52, 118-
19, 203, 231, 243
West Indian University, 65, 128,
163
White, Trumbull, 253
White collar workers, 87, 128
"White man's burden," 19
Williams, Eric, 242, 256
Wiseman, H. V., 255
Woman suffrage, 158
Women's status, 69, 86
Wood Commission, 164
Wood, Hon. E. F. L. (Lord Hali-
fax), 146, 248
Work relief, 57, 126

Youth activities, 70, 119